VICTORIAN
POTTERY AND PORCELAIN

BY THE SAME AUTHOR

Collecting Antiques
More About Collecting Antiques
Horse Brasses and Other Small Items for the Collector
English Painted Enamels (with Therle Hughes)

SOME 19TH-CENTURY PIECES FROM MR BERNARD HUGHES'S COLLECTION

Upper row (left) Cake plate from a bone china tea service with lithographed flower decoration, mazarine blue painted rim enriched with transferred gilding: impressed H & CO crowned, the mark of R. Hammersley and Son, Burslem. Late 1890s; (right) Cabinet plate, one of a set of six, with hand-painted flowers in gilded reserves and ground colour in mazarine blue. Late 1830s.

Lower row (left to right) Parian ware jug by W. T. Copeland and Sons; the design was registered at the Patent Office on 24th January, 1868. Greyhound in black-glazed red earthenware touched with gilding; Staffordshire. 1830s. Biscuit barrel with metal lid and handle; decorated with brilliant enamels and burnished gilding. Marked Davenport, Longport, in script. 1870s. Fox head stirrup cup in Staffordshire bone china. 1830s. Cup and saucer from a forty-piece tea service in bone china, painted with various species of heather; gilded rims. Mid-Victorian and unmarked. Vase with crackle finish painted in transparent enamels with Oriental motifs; made in Derbyshire. 1880s.

VICTORIAN POTTERY AND PORCELAIN

G. BERNARD HUGHES

SPRING BOOKS·LONDON

Originally published in 1959
by Country Life Limited
© Copyright G. Bernard Hughes 1959
This edition published 1967 by Spring Books
Drury House · Russell Street · London W.C.2

Printed in Czechoslovakia by Tisk Brno,
T 1868

Contents

Illustrations

Acknowledgments

The author wishes to express his grateful thanks to the following for allowing photographs of pieces in their possession to be used for his book:

By Gracious Permission of Her Majesty the Queen (Plates 2, 3, 4, 65, 88)

Belfast Museum and Art Gallery (Plate 89)

Brighton Art Gallery and Museum (Plates 28, 67, 68)

Chicago Art Institute (Plates 53, 54, 55, 56, 58)

Mr Clifford Chubb (Plate 66)

Messrs Christie, Manson & Woods (Plates 26, 35, 60, 61, 62)

Mr Gresham Copeland (Plates 30, 87)

Messrs Delomosne & Co. Ltd (Plates 41, 57, 59, 82)

Messrs Doulton & Co. Ltd (Plates 5, 6, 7, 8)

Mr K. Glover's Collection (Plates 76, 77)

Messrs Greenwood & Clark (Plates 24, 45)

Hanley Museum and Art Gallery (Plate 81)

Leeds City Art Gallery (Plates 14, 20, 21, 36, 39)

Number Three, Ltd (Plate 44)

The Pottery Gazette (Plates 17, 18)

Preston Art Gallery and Museum (Plate 25)

Royal Doulton Museum (Plates 46, 47)

Royal Worcester Porcelain Company Museum (Plate 83—left)

Spode-Copeland Museum (Plates 13, 15, 23, 31, 32, 34, 69, 72, 73)

Mrs Mary Stephens (Plates 10, 11)

Sunderland Museum (Plates 1, 27)

Mrs Kenneth Symes (Plates 42, 43)

Victoria and Albert Museum (Plates 22, 29, 40, 48, 49, 50, 51, 52, 63, 64, 70, 71, 74, 75, 78, 79, 80, 83, 84, 85, 86)

Wedgwood Museum (Plates 9, 12, 16)

Introduction

THE 19TH CENTURY witnessed revolution to the entire craft of the potter. The result was an industry that permitted Britain to dominate world markets for a century. More than this, it meant that fine china could be used freely as well as admired, and in everyday homes as well as mansions. It is small wonder, then, that the old attitude of aesthetic contempt for 19th-century English ceramics has been replaced by a delight that has sent their value soaring. Today any piece of 19th-century ware is worth a second glance: it is the purpose of this book to make that inspection of value in establishing the period and often even the maker of the piece from among the enormous number of potters and processes that contributed to the richness and fascination of this exciting era.

It is not always sufficiently emphasised that the technical advances were really startling, achieving, step by step, table ware that was whiter and more richly coloured, capable of far more enduring service than had ever been possible before, yet within purse reach of the general public. For instance, the muffle kiln designed in 1812 by Samuel Walker while he was employed by Barr, Flight and Barr at Worcester resulted in a brilliance of enamel decoration never possible before on an industrial scale (see p. 70). This is but a single instance of the hundreds of technical improvements which enable collectors to attribute correct periods to their 19th-century specimens.

By the time of the accession of Queen Victoria the capacious china closets of the gentry and middle classes were shelved to the ceiling and packed with useful ware painted in rich, lustrous enamels and sold at prices permitting everyday use. Such a display in the 18th century could have been afforded only by the very rich. A china closet recently opened astonished its inheritor by displaying services of bone china by Spode, Coalport and Derby and a magnificent dinner service in stone china marked COPELAND / & GARRETT; there were extensive toilet services in semi-china; dessert services, and a host of miscellaneous pieces.

Ceramics of this type are being sold now in England and the United States of America at prices climbing higher and higher almost by the month. A Spode dinner service, for instance, consisting of one hundred and thirty pieces of felspar porcelain enamelled with the celebrated peacock and peahen pattern and marked in red No. 2118, sold at Christies for £280, after standing undisturbed in a cupboard for more than a century.

The development of a collector of 19th-century pottery and porcelain is usually gradual, perhaps beginning with a few pieces of resist lustre; a Copeland vase with a *bleu de roi* ground, lavishly gilded and meticulously painted with Watteau scenes; or an example of Minton majolica of the 1860s. Perhaps the idea comes to complete a set from a single

piece, no matter how long this may take. Queen Mary was more than thirty years com-
pleting a cabaret set of Sèvres porcelain, glimpsing the final cup and saucer in an antique
shop window when the traffic caused her car to slow down outside. A collector of Staffordshire blue has spent twenty years searching for pieces decorated with Dr Syntax scenes.
Although eighty-two different pictures have been found produced by five potters, the
envisaged dinner service is still far from complete. None of these pieces cost as much as ten
shillings.

So far as space permits, this book gives facts by which the collector looking into the
windows of dealers' shops will be able to recognise worthwhile pieces of the 19th century,
ranging from bone china of 1800 to the so-called art productions of the 1890s.

Some collectors prefer to concentrate upon one unusual aspect of 19th-century ceramics, such as lithophanes, parian statuary or puzzle jugs in Chesterfield brown ware.
Already, for instance, the mocha ware referred to on page 67 is almost unobtainable; yet
throughout the 19th century it was an extremely common domestic earthenware. There
are some who specialise in collecting chronological sequences of teapots. There are even
a few collectors attracted by the food warmers which performed the duties of a bedroom
night light shelter before matches came into use and at the same time ensured a warm drink
for the fitful sleeper: even among these a collection may run into fifty different patterns.

G. BERNARD HUGHES

1

Basaltes and Egyptian Black

ETRURIA, PERHAPS the most widely known pottery in England, was first spoken of merely as the Black Works. The estate was bought and the pottery erected for the specific purpose of developing a new range of stonewares that could be shaped into Etruscan vases, Roman busts and similar neo-classical delights. It is surprising, therefore, to find how little is generally known about these long-favoured wares made in a wide range of ornaments and useful pieces by Josiah Wedgwood, his rivals, and his successors throughout the 19th century.

Josiah Wedgwood first developed a black vitreous stoneware characterised by its fine grain and dense, uniform texture, with a surface richer and smoother than that of any ceramic formerly known. When fired at a high temperature its body was so hard that it was practically impervious to water and required no glaze. There was no unevenness of surface, and being unglazed it was devoid of crazing.

Formerly black stonewares had been coloured with oxide of iron. Wedgwood's new black ware consisted of Staffordshire ball clay, calcined ochre, ground glassy slag from ironstone, and ten per cent of manganese dioxide. A surface polish was secured by coating the black biscuit with varnish and re-firing at red heat. After removal from the kiln, while slightly warm, it was rubbed with a soft rag dipped in skim milk. This produced a permanent, slightly glossy appearance.

Immediately perfection was realised, Wedgwood bought the Ridge House estate, Shelton, and began building what was at first known as 'the Black Works' and later developed into the world-famous Etruria. These premises were devoted entirely to the production of the new black stoneware which Wedgwood named basaltes, after the natural volcanic rock of such well-known phenomena as the Giant's Causeway in Northern Ireland and Fingal's Cave in the Hebrides. The success of fine basaltes for thrown and turned work was such that he took Thomas Bentley into partnership as sales executive.

It was soon discovered that basaltes constituted an excellent body for intricate, sharply defined ornament, produced by hand-pressing bats of clay into moulds: hollow-ware pressing and flat-ware pressing were skilled branches of the potter's craft. From about

1775 bas-reliefs of classic figures and groups were pressed and then sprigged—applied—to the surface of thrown ware.

In their London catalogue of 1779 Wedgwood and Bentley described their black stoneware as 'a fine Black Porcelain having the same property as Basaltes, resisting the Attacks of Acids; being a Touchstone to Copper, Silver and Gold... admitting a good polish and equal in hardness to Agate and Porphyry. The Black is Sterling and will Last for Ever'. Among the basaltes listed in the catalogue were: 'Antique vases of black porcelaine or artificial basaltes, highly polished with bas-reliefs; lamps and candelabra; busts and small statues, boys and girls; heads of illustrious Romans and moderns; flower pots and root pots; vases and tripods; inkstands; tea and coffee services, including chocolate pots, sugar dishes, cream ewers, cabinet cups and saucers, plain and enriched.'

Vases were sometimes of an immense size, such as the replicas of a Greek vase in the British Museum, thirty-three inches high and eighteen inches in diameter. Busts for ornamenting libraries measured as much as twenty inches in height, and the subjects included Shakespeare, Bacon, Ben Jonson, Cicero, Cato, Seneca, Grotius and Plato.

Antique gems in cameo and intaglio were copied in basaltes. Sulphur casts were taken from originals by James Tassie, whose first account, dated 1769, was for seventy impressions at twopence each. Many basaltes cameos were given a brilliant reflecting surface by polishing on the lapidary's wheel: the bevelled rims of portrait medallions might be finished in the same way.

Tea-table basaltes might be ornamented with sprigged work in relief, all-over embossed work, engine-turning or painting in encaustic colours. Wedgwood is often credited with the invention of the engine-turning lathe in the early 1760s: it has also been attributed to William Baddeley of Eastwood. Such a lathe, however, was used in the 17th century, being fully described and illustrated in *L'Art de Tourner*, by Charles Plumier, 1701. The ornament appeared on silver bearing hall-marks earlier than 1760.

No doubt either Wedgwood or Baddeley introduced engine-turning to the Staffordshire pottery trade. Simeon Shaw records that Josiah Wedgwood offered to buy lathes from Baddeley at 'eighty guineas each for six provided Mr. B. would not sell under the price to other persons'. Wedgwood, however, made his own machines, and Baddeley, in addition to his pottery and flint-grinding yards, established a lathe-making business. The engine-turning lathe rotated the article to be decorated with an eccentric oscillating motion while the cutting tool remained still. It could be adjusted so as to provide a wide range of complicated geometric, diced and fluted designs on dried unfired basaltes of leather hardness. This did not pull against the tool, which left clear-cut lines. The machine was in continual use throughout the Victorian period.

Wedgwood's black basaltes proved to be a perfect ground for colourful ornament. Ordinary enamels with a basis of glass were unsuited to its extremely smooth surface, however, and quickly flaked off. Wedgwood therefore evolved a type of encaustic or burnt-in paint for which he was granted a patent (No. 939, November 16th, 1769). This was described in the specification as 'a peculiar species of encaustic painting in various colours in imitation of the ancient Etruscan and Roman Earthenware... for the purpose of ornamenting earthen and porcelaine ware'. By mixing ten ingredients in different proportions seven colours were possible—red, white, orange, green, blue, yellow, dryblack. These were mixed with wax and painted on the basaltes, to which they were fused by firing.

Wedgwood's style of applying the colours was the reverse of the ancient process. He used a black body and enriched it with painted designs, chiefly in red: Roman originals which he copied, in the British Museum, were in red terra-cotta with grounds of black glaze, the patterns silhouetted in unglazed red. Wedgwood also made a red stoneware which he named rosso antico, and this he painted with backgrounds in shining black, also protected by his patent.

An encaustic gold bronze, too, was covered by the patent. This was painted over basaltes moulded and tooled into forms resembling the finest efforts of bronze workers and produced at a fraction of the cost. The prepared bronze powder was ground in oil of turpentine and smoothly applied by sponge or pencil brush to the basaltes when shaped and ready for firing, but not quite dry. After firing in the kiln the coating of bronze was hand-burnished to a mirror-bright polish. Bronzed basaltes for many years were to be found in the great homes of Britain and the Continent. Encaustic bronze would not withstand intensive cleaning, for crevices in apparently black basaltes have been noted containing traces of bronze. Wedgwood's principal bronze worker from 1784 to 1845 was Aaron Steele, thus proving the long period over which the decoration was made. Silvering has also been recorded and coppering noted. Professor Church describes encaustic painting as 'mechanically perfect but artistically defective'.

Josiah Wedgwood died in 1795, when war-time hardship resulted in negligible demands for costly basaltes. Selling prices were greatly reduced by casting basaltes in moulds instead of hand-throwing or pressing, and by omitting the special varnish firing. Cast basaltes had long been made by other potters and marketed as Egyptian black. Cast hollow-ware needed to be finished in the lathe, thus giving it a dull, dead-black unfired appearance. The Wedgwood firm, however, continued making basaltes by their original methods throughout the 19th century.

Wedgwood basaltes exhibited at the Great Exhibition of 1851 included: 'Black vase, 8 inches (with pedestal 9 inches) "Apotheosis of a Poet"; two vases 16 inches each, "Water and Wine"; various other vases, plain, of different sizes; lamp and candlestick; copy of Portland or Barberini vase, 10 inches high with white jasper bas-reliefs [this was also exhibited in dark blue jasper]; black vase with red Etruscan figures; vases, various and with inscriptions.'

Wedgwood basaltes made before 1769 were unmarked: since then the ware has always been impressed with a trade-mark. Since 1780 this mark has always consisted of the name WEDGWOOD, and ENGLAND might be added to specimens made from 1891 onwards.

Black stoneware was widely made in imitation of Wedgwood's basaltes. William Baddeley of Eastwood made excellent ware which he tried to pass off as Wedgwood's basaltes by impressing his trade-mark EASTWOOD with EAST indistinct and WOOD showing clearly. China sellers might then persuade the unwary that they were buying the more costly basaltes. In Holden's *Directory*, 1805, the firm is entered as 'Egyptian black mfg, Shelton'.

Humphrey Palmer of Hanley was a copyist of all Wedgwood's ornamental stonewares, first copying his basaltes, pirating his designs immediately they appeared on the market, and using a circular trade-mark which at a casual glance on a black surface might be mistaken for Wedgwood and Bentley's stamp. The quality of Palmer's work, as Wedgwood acknowledged, was excellent. That Palmer was fully experienced as a potter in black stoneware is proved by the existence of a vase in the British Museum, bearing reliefs representing 'Venus and Cupid in Vulcan's Smithy'. This is impressed with Palmer's name and the date 1769, and is inscribed 'Voyez Sculp'.

Palmer's pottery operated until 1817, although he failed in 1778, when James Neale acquired the business, continuing as a Wedgwood imitator using fine-quality bodies, first-class craftsmanship and a similar range of productions, but of smaller proportions. Robert Wilson joined him in 1786 and directed the firm's energies to cream-coloured earthenware and tea and coffee services in poor-quality Egyptian black impressed NEALE & WILSON in a single line. Wilson died in 1801 and was succeeded by his brother David, who traded as David Wilson and Sons until his death in 1816. His Egyptian black was impressed WILSON with a crowned C above.

The styles of Egyptian black stoneware teapots made in the early 19th century are outlined in an invoice made in 1797 by John Twemlow of Shelton, formerly in the possession of Jewitt: 'E Black Teapots, Capt., fest^d., and fig^d. [Egyptian black teapots, capped, festooned and figured]; ditto upright, fest^d. and fig^d.; Oval E Black Teapots; ditto prest leaf; scollop top fest^d., fig^d. and banded; ditto prest leaf and fest^d. and figured and banded a' tip; ditto creams to match; ditto fluted; ditto coffee pots; octagon pots with scollop top and creams to match; oval plain teapots.'

The tradition that Egyptian black stoneware was bought exclusively for mourning occasions hardly bears examination, although this was no doubt a mid-Victorian fashion. The amount made during the 19th century was prodigious, huge quantities being exported to Holland, the Baltic countries, and America. Even as late as 1860 Harry Venables of Hanley found it profitable to establish a pottery specialising in Egyptian black, and in 1880 H. Aynsley and Co. of Longton were making it from the moulds of Robinson and Chetham, who had operated the works from about 1820 to 1870. This was the only inexpensive fine tea ware of thin section capable of withstanding continual usage with boiling water: tea from the bubbling urn could be poured direct into teapots and cups.

Much 19th-century Egyptian black was impressed with the potter's name: some was anonymous. Of about one hundred potters known to have made Egyptian black, the following are typical:

Elijah Mayer, Hanley, established in the mid-1770s, was an early maker of ornamental ware in Egyptian black, and his table ware was notable for its sharp, well-defined engine-turning. Vases and tea-ware painted in encaustic colours have been recorded impressed with his name, thus dating them between 1783 and 1805, when he was joined by his son Joseph, a prolific maker of fine-quality Egyptian black until 1840, when the works were closed. When Joseph Mayer died in 1860 worth £200,000, a great quantity of costly Egyptian black was discovered stored in the outhouses of his home. The marks were E MAYER until 1805, then E MAYER & SON.

The Keeling family specialised in Egyptian black for nearly half a century, much of it impressed with names that make it possible to determine its period. Anthony Keeling (mark A K or A KEELING) established a pottery at Hanley primarily to supply the Dutch market. By 1802 Antony and Edward Keeling (mark A & E KEELING) were operating two potteries at Burslem, and from 1787 to 1804 Joseph and Edward Keeling potted at Keeling's Lane, Hanley (mark J & E K HANLEY). Financial vicissitudes caused by war-time losses on the Continent appear to have beset the Keelings at this period. When the premises were advertised for sale in 1804 they were described as suitable for the manufacture of Egyptian black. In 1806 Keeling, Toft and Co. acquired the pottery of William Mellor (mark MELLOR) established in 1795. They worked it until 1824, when the firm became Toft and May, closing in 1830.

Hartley, Greens and Co., Leeds Pottery, issued Egyptian black for at least twenty years. The Leeds Public Library possesses the original drawing-book entitled *Blackware Drawing Book* dated 1800. Production continued until 1820. No portrait medallions are illustrated and it is probable that the marked examples known to collectors date from 1888. Tea and coffee services, domestic hollow-ware and the rims of plates and other flat-ware were engine-turned. On a teapot or coffee-pot the handle and spout might be cast in relief ornament. The impressed mark was usually LEEDS＊POTTERY or HARTLEY GREENS & Co LEEDS＊POTTERY.

Another Yorkshire pottery producing Egyptian black in the early 19th century had been established by David Dunderdale at Whitmore Mere, Castleford. From 1793 to 1820 he traded as David Dunderdale and Co., issuing tea-sets and other domestic ware in a deeper brighter black than Leeds. For English taste this appeared overloaded with relief ornament, but huge consignments went to the Baltic countries and to Spain. The marks were variations of DD & Co CASTLEFORD POTTERY.

John Walton, Burslem, about 1805—1835, made tea and coffee wares and poorly modelled figures impressed WALTON.

Shorthose and Co., Hanley, 1783—1823. Impressed marks known are ascribed conjecturally to this firm.

Richard Newbold, Green Dock, Lane End, about 1820—1836.

Edmund John Birch, Shelton, 1802—1814. His work was impressed BIRCH in upper- or lower-case letters.

John Lockett, King Street and Market Street, Longton, about 1825—1875. Impressed LOCKETT.

William Adams, Greenfield. Established 1834. Impressed ADAMS.

Charles Meigh and Sons, Hanley, established late in the 18th century, made Egyptian black until 1861. Jewitt records that their productions included table tea kettles, spill cases and vases decorated with matt and burnished gold and enamels.

2

Terra-Cotta

HANDSOME TERRA-COTTA ornaments, often resplendent with colour, enriched the Victorian scene until the 1870s, warmly red in hues that ranged from lobster brilliance to the matt opacity of brick dust. Sharpness of modelled detail distinguishes the hard Victorian terra-cotta from earlier, softer qualities. It became a fashionable earthenware for ornamental and useful accessories in the home. A pair of giant vases decorated in the Etruscan manner might dominate a vestibule; figure groups gave colourful elegance to the drawing room; Stilton cheese stands and trays served on the dining-room sideboard— these are a few of the pieces now attracting the attention of collectors. This hard terra- cotta also made elegant garden fountains and balustrades, hanging baskets and conserva- tory equipment. Some of the larger works, notably plaques depicting contemporary scenes and measuring two to three feet in length, were set in building façades.

Terra-cotta, meaning baked clay, is defined in the *Oxford English Dictionary* as 'a hard unglazed pottery of fine quality, of which... statuary, vases and the like are made'. Originally terra-cotta was no more than purified clay, hand shaped and hardened by baking in the sun. Two thousand years ago the clay was fired in primitive kilns, yet the potters produced such wonderful terra-cottas as the Greek vases now in the British Museum. Decoration was carried out in a dark pigment blended with quick-drying oils, made per- manent by firing. Black silhouette against the red ground of the terra-cotta was the earliest ornament: later the grounds were coloured black, leaving the silhouette forms in red.

The manufacture of English terra-cotta was a skilled branch of the potter's craft. Coarse particles were removed from the clay, usually a local deposit and often adjoining a coal seam, and all the ingredients ground to flour fineness. This produced a finely textured paste, thus ensuring a smooth, unflawed surface or skin after firing. Contraction in the kiln was greater than with ordinary earthenware, a defect tending to cause fire- cracks and distortion and thus an unduly high proportion of wasters. Its hard, compact texture ensured a smooth, impervious surface, faintly glossy yet capable of holding decoration without glazing: the interior of hollow-ware, however, was moderately porous. Variations in colour on a single piece were possible, but this feature was rarely exploited. A rich red colour was secured by spraying the ware with ferric chloride solution before firing. Terra-cotta emits a clear ringing note when struck.

The Jury of the Great Exhibition, 1851, considered that 'the art of producing ornamental works in terra-cotta was lost for centuries until Josiah Wedgwood discovered methods of duplicating the finest works. By employing Flaxman and other artists, he left specimens of art now eagerly sought after in the present day.' In the late 1760s Wedgwood had produced a terra-cotta harder than any hitherto known, by adding to iron-free potter's clay a proportion of calcined flints and pulverised potsherds. The air-dried greenware was fired in high-temperature kilns, which formed terra-cotta approaching the texture of stoneware although the materials did not fuse together. Wedgwood decorated this with a shining black pigment, for which he was granted a patent in November, 1769. His products included vases and a range of tea ware, decorated with engine-turning, applied festoons and other relief work, and dipped and scraped ornament.

Terra-cotta does not appear to have been made in England by any other potter until about 1835, when Sir Frederick Fowke, Bart., established a terra-cotta pottery at Lowesby, Leicestershire, using deposits of local red-burning clay. Richly red in colour, this was thrown into vases of antique shape, decorated black in the Etruscan style, but also enriched with coloured enamels and burnished gilding carried out by his London agent William Purden at his showrooms in King William Street. A wide range of domestic goods was also made. The venture, however, proved unprofitable, and no terra-cotta was made by him after 1840. Downman and Gunn record that tortoiseshell ware in the Whieldon manner was made, and Egyptian black such as the marked example in the British Museum enamelled with naturalistic butterflies and flowers. The mark was an impressed fleur-de-lys below the name LOWESBY.

A much finer terra-cotta, uniform of tint, requiring no artificial colouring, wash, paint or stopping, was evolved by H. H. Blanchard, who established a pottery at King Edward Street, Blackfriars, London, in 1839. This incorporated best white pipe clay, crushed pottery, powdered calcined flints, flour glass and white sand. Blanchard's early vases and urns were bought by Thomas Battam, 2 and 3, Johnson's Court, Fleet Street, London, who decorated them in the Etruscan style from the mid-1840s. His display at the Great Exhibition was in the form of an Etruscan tomb, and caused much comment. Several niches contained urns, and sacrificial vessels stood on the floor, twenty-seven pieces in all. Battam's vases and urns were obviously costly, and in some instances measured as much as four feet in height. They were designed to be sold in pairs.

A typical pair would be encircled with scenes such as 'Telemachus in Search of his Father', its companion being 'The Rape of Orithyia', or 'Chorus in Honour of Bacchus' and 'The Toilet of Aphrodite'. A classical scene might be painted on each face of a vase, such as 'A Princess and Priest of Bacchus', with 'Minerva and Hercules' on the reverse.

None has been noted impressed with the name of Battam, although examples with his painted signature have been recorded.

A highly vitreous terra-cotta, richly red and an ideal ground for classical scenes in brilliant polychrome enamels, was made by F. and R. Pratt, Fenton, from the early 1840s. Many of the designs were adapted from Flaxman's *Iliad*. The firm was awarded a silver medal by the Society of Arts in 1848 for the largest pair of vases so far potted in the Etruscan style: these measured nearly five feet in height and were bought by Prince Albert. Clock cases for drawing-room mantelshelves were a feature of the Pratt Brothers' terra-cotta, painted with all-over mosaic patterns in vivid colours. The impressed mark was F & R PRATT FENTON.

William Baddeley, Hanley, added terra-cotta potting to his other manufactures in the late 1840s, decorating much of this with coloured japans, fired at a lower temperature than enamels. These were impressed W BADDELEY. For three or four years Baddeley made terra-cotta handles for the Sheffield cutlers in imitation of bone and the horn of stag, buck and buffalo. Eventually the Sheffield handle-makers realised that their trade was adversely affected and refused to work them up. Threats were made to several master cutlers that their works would be blown up if terra-cotta handles were not discontinued. Their use was then abandoned. Baddeley's son William founded a specialist terra-cotta pottery at Longton in the late 1860s, using the same mark as his father. For the home he made vases, globe stands, mignonette boxes, inkstands and wine coolers, but his principal productions were vessels for the conservatory, characteristic ornament in high relief consisting of exceptionally finely modelled trees and plants.

Herbert Minton made some outstanding terra-cotta designed by well-known industrial artists. A large rectangular plant vase designed in 1850 by Baron Marochetti, the sculptor, was protected by registration. This was decorated in bas-relief, one side with figures representing 'Neptune and Amphitrite', and the reverse with 'Sirens Restraining Boreas'. These were impressed with a rectangle enclosing BARON/MAROCHETTI, the diamond-shaped registration mark (see Chapter 26), and Minton's three-piece arrow-head symbol. Ornamental mignonette boxes for drawing room and vestibule were made by many terra-cotta potters, the flowering plants providing an attractive perfume in days of perfunctory ventilation and sanitation. Minton's contributions were in a deep red, each panel containing a bas-relief in white parian. One of these was copied from Thorwaldsen's 'Four Seasons'.

The Jury of the Great Exhibition praised the terra-cotta displays and added that they would like to see 'greater attention paid to this branch of the manufacturing art for which there is ample room'. This advice was accepted by the pottery industry, for during the next ten years terra-cotta departments were operating in many established potteries and specialist newcomers entered the field to meet the demand for drawing-room and domestic terra-cotta.

Two-colour terra-cotta, mainly combinations of deep reds and delicate tints, was introduced in about 1860 by W. and T. Wills, Euston Road, London. The firm, long established as sculptors in marble and stone, issued many exceptionally successful figures, groups and busts all hand finished by professional sculptors and impressed W & T WILLS. From here came the tall, long-necked vases with globular bodies, hand carved all over with Oriental designs. These are in a rich, almost scarlet, hue intended to imitate the carved red lacquer vases of China and, like them, may have gilded mounts fitted to their rims. Staffordshire potters made similar vases but failed to achieve comparable carving or colour.

William Kirkham, exploiting a red clay deposit at Stoke-upon-Trent, in 1862 evolved a hard, dense terra-cotta ideal for turned hollow-ware. Borders in deep relief work are characteristic in association with enamelled ornament enriched with matt and burnished gilding. Kirkham's transfer figure and flower groupings were among the best of their kind on vases, flower holders, table jugs, spill cases and tobacco jars. The mark was W KIRKHAM impressed.

Some of the most skilfully painted terra-cotta was decorated by Pinder, Bourne and Co., Burslem, from the early 1860s until 1877. Flower vases, water bottles, jardinières, jugs were decorated with colourful birds, flowers and butterflies against grounds of gilded arabesques. Hand-painted woodland scenes in deep orange against an almost ruby-red terra-cotta have been recorded bearing the signature W. Gedge, a name otherwise unknown as a decorator, but associated with a patent granted in 1874 for 'imitation faience Parisienne'. This firm's productions bear printed marks, usually in black, but dark blue has been noted. Marks included a garter containing the pattern name and P B & Co. surmounted by a crown, the whole within a laurel wreath; and a triangle enclosing PINDER BOURNE & Co / NILE ST / BURSLEM with an arrow.

A magnificent array of claret-red terra-cotta figures was shown at the Philadelphia Exhibition, 1876, by Bates, Walker and Co., Burslem. These were fired in a biscuit oven, thus making them hard and vitreous with a marble-smooth surface. The catalogue includes 'Time Unveiling Truth' by Crispie; 'The Fighting Gladiator' and 'The Young Apollo', a pair by William Beattie; and John Flaxman's wine and water vases after Wedgwood. These and other figures were impressed BATES WALKER & Co or B W & Co.

Collectors of late Georgian jasper ware may be surprised to learn that Bates, Walker and Co. reproduced John Turner's jasper from the original 18th-century moulds which came into their possession during the early 1860s. These have a hard terra-cotta body covered with appropriately coloured slips in green, blue, chocolate, buff and so on. They were listed as 'Turner's Jasper Ware', but no example has been noted so marked.

Watcombe Terra-Cotta Clay Co., Torquay, established in 1869 with Charles Brock of Hanley as technical director, became an important terra-cotta pottery. The local clay was exceptionally pure and, when fired at a low temperature, produced a richly warm red terra-cotta possessing an attractive surface bloom and, when turned in the lathe for hollow-

1 to 4. (Above) Sunderland pottery: ewer and basin decorated with mottled pink lustre and transfer-prints of Sunderland Bridge, east and west views, the sailing ship *Northumberland*, and verses. Impressed with the mark DIXON & Co, used between 1813 and 1819. (Right and below) A set of three Staffordshire earthenware chimney ornaments displaying the royal arms enamelled in full colour and gold. These were issued as souvenirs of George IV's coronation in 1821.

5 and 6. Salt-glazed stoneware made by Henry Doulton at Lambeth in the second quarter of the 19th century: (Above) Spirit flasks issued at the time of the Reform agitation, two representing Daniel O'Connell with Lord Grey on the right. (Below) A group of stoneware including a Mr and Mrs Caudle flask, William IV reform flask, Silenus jug and Napoleon mug.

ware, an almost velvety smoothness. Watcombe terra-cotta was much softer than its Staffordshire counterpart, and could be modelled and pressed into relief work suggesting the sharpness of jasper ware.

Figures and groups made throughout the 1870s were unusual in that they were often modelled from terra-cottas in three tints, figures, draperies and accessories in different shades of red. Vases and urns might be festooned with applied hand-modelled flowers. Candlesticks modelled in florid rococo designs and parcel gilt were in great demand, but because of fragility few have survived intact. Teapot and cream jug interiors of tea and *déjeuné* services were glazed and the teacups lined with sky blue. Enamels, gilding and transfer printing ornamented a wide range of goods. All productions were marked WAT-COMBE POTTERY or WATCOMBE impressed or printed in black. The printed mark from 1876 was a woodpecker perched on a branch against a distant landscape and a ship on the sea, encircled by a garter inscribed WATCOMBE POTTERY.

The Derbyshire potters preferred to work a buff-tinted terra-cotta. The Denby Pottery from 1847 used Bourne's patent three-chamber kiln (see p. 146), the top compartment being reserved for terra-cotta. It was exceptionally light in weight, and productions included Indian scent jars, mignonette boxes, flower vases, ewers with snake handles, wine coolers, Stilton cheese stands and trays. The several Denby marks, all impressed, contain the name BOURNE & SON.

The Wilnecote Works, established near Tamworth by George Skey in 1862, became important potters of terra-cotta, about six hundred persons being employed in this and other branches of the clay industry. Yet the name is virtually unknown to collectors of Victorian terra-cotta. The firm became well known for its game-pie dishes in a light cream-coloured terra-cotta with very sharply defined relief ornament. Although no more than superficially resembling Josiah Wedgwood's game-pie dishes in fine stoneware, they have been mistaken for the earlier ware when the impressed mark has been ground away. Some large articles for the conservatory were made in this terra-cotta, glazed in a brown enlivened with a tinge of green. This was catalogued as 'rustic ware' and was sometimes so marked. Cylindrical space-heating gas stoves were made by Wilnecote, enriched with a combination of perforations and elaborate designs in high relief: examples noted have been in dark red. The impressed mark was GEORGE SKEY / WILNECOTE WORKS / N^R TAMWORTH in an oval.

A terra-cotta works had been established already at Tamworth by Charles Canning in 1847, a name that became celebrated for architectural terra-cotta. Flower vases, jardinières, wine-coolers, mignonette boxes and a range of useful articles were made, enamelled in a combination of brilliant and matt colours, the fashionable convolvulus being introduced in many of the patterns. This ware was impressed DELLA ROBBIA, to which it bore little resemblance, but was intended to compete in a less expensive market with Minton's Della Robbia introduced in 1850.

Victorian terra-cotta of fine quality was made by many other potters, but few appear to have marked their productions. Outstanding were the 'wicker-baskets' made by John Matthews, Weston-super-Mare. These were massed with garden flowers in the style of Coalport flower-encrusted baskets in bone china but were, of course, less fragile. Each individual leaf and petal was hand modelled and vases were encrusted with similar ornament. The flowers were naturalistically coloured. The mark was printed: the royal coat of arms above the inscription JOHN MATTHEWS / LATE PHILLIPS / ROYAL POTTERY / WESTON-SUPER-MARE. Charles Phillips, the former proprietor, had held the royal warrant as terra-cotta maker to Queen Victoria from 1845 until his death in 1870. He specialised in garden and conservatory terra-cotta.

A magenta tint distinguishes the terra-cotta made by W. H. Goss, who founded his celebrated pottery at Stoke-upon-Trent in 1858. The usual range of goods was marketed, and fern leaves in relief are a characteristic motif. The mark was W H GOSS impressed.

Gothic vases in pale red terra-cotta with granulated pedestals were made by James Pulham, Waltham Cross, in the middle years of the 19th century. One of each pair was impressed J P.

A highly glazed deep red terra-cotta decorated with unusually bright enamels and burnished gilding was made by the Brownhills Pottery, founded at Burslem in 1871. Their manufactures included toilet services. The mark was printed: B P C in a ribbon with the pattern name below.

The unmarked terra-cotta of Edward Banks, established at Hanley in 1875, was regarded by Jewitt as outstanding in colour, potting and decoration. Banks issued three kinds of terra-cotta: clear red, white with a purplish tinge, and buff. Borders, wreaths, swags, groups of flowers and foliage, fern and Japanese figure subjects were his favourite decorative motifs, and might be enamelled, printed or gilded. Production included the usual goods and water bottles with stands and stoppers, water goblets, Malagar jars, alcorazzas, tobacco jars and vases.

Terra-cotta inlaid with mosaic designs in coloured clays appears to date no earlier than 1861 when H. H. Blanchard, Blackfriars, London, was granted a patent (No. 820) for carrying out such decoration. The plastic terra-cotta shaped into its final form was impressed with the design by removing some of the plastic material by means of hand tools or, in the case of cast articles, by indenting the mould. The terra-cotta was then fired in a biscuit kiln, the depressions afterwards being filled with coloured clays arranged in mosaic patterns. The surface was then either turned or scraped level, to reveal a colourful pattern inlaid in the red terra-cotta. This patent also protected another style of decoration —'a device or pattern may be printed on the surface of the terra-cotta, then burnt in, and the design then enamelled'.

3

Pearl Ware

PEARL WARE was an important and attractive useful ware of the early 19th century. But to understand its development one must turn back to the 18th century and the outstanding pioneer work of England's greatest potter, Josiah Wedgwood. Not the least interesting among the stories of his achievements is his gradual development of coarse earthenware into this hard, white, durable ware. This was fourteen years in the making, and more before it became an important item in the English potters' catalogues, but it is doubtful whether it would ever have appeared at all if Josiah Wedgwood had been a less powerful and determined individual.

Wedgwood first transformed deep-tinted cream-coloured earthenware into a lead-glazed ceramic of considerable strength, capable of accepting more skilful manipulation. In 1765 he named his improved earthenware 'Queen's Ware', because Queen Charlotte accepted from him the gift of a tea-set. It is significant that this was probably one of the first to be made in earthenware, which formerly had been too coarse and thick for the tea equipage.

Not until the end of 1775 could Wedgwood make the final improvement to his queen's ware by incorporating Cornish china-clay and china-stone into his formula, for until then their use in ceramics was a monopoly protected by patent No. 898 granted to William Cookworthy of Plymouth on March 17th, 1768, in connection with his hard porcelain enterprise. The only known method of purifying these minerals was covered by this patent (see Chapter 5). Months of costly wrangling in the Commons and finally in the Lords resulted in a compromise in September, 1775, when the Cornish ingredients were made available to makers of opaque pottery.

In the 'Case of the Manufacturers of Earthenware in Staffordshire' submitted to Parliament early in 1775, Wedgwood had stated that 'Queen's Ware has already several of the properties of porcelain, but is yet capable of receiving many essential improvements. The public have for some time required and expected them.... One person is petitioning the legislature, in effect, to stop all improvements in earthenware and porcelain in this kingdom but his own'. Earlier Wedgwood had placed on record that he had 'discovered the art or making Queen's Ware, which employs ten times more people than all the china [porcelain] works in the kingdom. A patent would greatly have limited its public utility. Instead of *one hundred manufactories* [Wedgwood's italics] of Queen's Ware there would have been *one*'.

With unlimited supplies of Cornish china-clay and china-stone at his disposal, Wedgwood marketed an improved queen's ware from late in 1775. And from this in 1779 he evolved the much whiter earthenware, of greater hardness and durability, which he named pearl ware. The Wedgwood firm defines pearl ware as 'a white earthenware body containing a greater percentage of flint and white clay than cream-coloured earthenware. A small amount of cobalt was added to the glaze for a still further whitening effect.' Josiah Wedgwood used his pearl ware mainly in the production of a nautilus shell dessert service decorated with flat washes of delicately tinted enamels, reproducing as far as possible the pearly colours of natural shells. This, no doubt, suggested the name for his new earthenware.

The blue-tinted glaze of early Wedgwood pearl ware had a faintly greenish hue: it was thinly and evenly applied, the effect being the nearest then possible to a pearly glaze. In the hands of other potters pearl ware had a considerable appeal, but they appear to have disregarded any pearly effect in the glaze. It is reasonable to suspect that in some instances the glaze's primary purpose was to conceal the tiny specks and flaws liable to mar the surface of the white earthenware, or to disguise a sometimes grey-looking body.

Pearl ware proved to be an ideal base for underglaze blue transfer printing, the heavy cobalt blue harmonising perfectly with the blue-tinged glaze. Josiah Spode evolved an even whiter pearl-ware body capable of providing the absolutely smooth surface essential for perfect transfer-printing in underglaze blue. This was marketed from 1783 and is notable for its light weight and a glaze silky to the touch, entirely smooth and without bubbles, an outstanding achievement at the time. Examples have been noted marked with the name SPODE impressed. W. B. Honey states that Spode counteracted the remaining yellow tone of the earthenware by incorporating a touch of cobalt blue into the ingredients. The resulting body might not display such a pleasant hue as the off-white ware, but for blue transfer work coated with purely transparent glaze it was excellent. Production costs for this work were greater than for blue printing on cream-coloured earthenware.

The Leeds Pottery evolved a pearl ware, its body less white than Spode's. This was in production by the late 1780s. Here the glaze was coloured with well-purified zaffre, producing a deep soft blue tint. Donald Towner points out that 'although it was usual in Pearl ware to use only just sufficient blue to counteract the cream colour, the Leeds blue was so deep in colour as to give the ware a decidedly bluish cast'.

The Staffordshire earthenware potters preferred the blue-tinted glaze of their pearl ware to display the faintly greenish hue advocated by Wedgwood. The ware was used mainly for table services, and many examples are to be discovered impressed PEARL or PEARL WARE without any maker's name or trade-mark. Painted decoration included

24

feathered borders in a small range of colours—green, blue, red, yellow and brown—and patterned with birds, flowers or views, sometimes with sprayed foliage. Marbling is also found. Swansea made pearl ware with a faintly grey body in the early years of the 19th century. Between 1803 and 1806 it was painted with butterflies, shells, flowers and birds by William Weston Young, who sometimes wrote the Latin name of his subject on the base. Meticulous floral painting was also carried out by other artists. The glaze on these is now finely crazed.

Pearl ware, perhaps with some slight modification of the constituents to make it more porcellaneous in appearance, was also used for figures. These stand upon square shallow plinths, all surfaces smooth, sometimes lined with gilding. The figures themselves display a high standard of modelling, closely resembling that of porcelain, and are always carefully enamelled with good-quality pigment. The small figures date from the 1790s, large figures from early in the 19th century. Neale and Co. of Hanley made some outstanding pearl-ware figures with a cobalt-hued glaze. After the firm was acquired by David Wilson and Sons, pearl-ware figures continued to be made, the glaze so deeply tinted that the body appeared bluish in hue.

Another type of earthenware was named 'pearl pottery'. The *Operating Mechanic*, 1825, reported this to be 'a superb kind of elegant and tasteful ornaments and is so much valued that the workmen are usually locked up and employed only on choice articles'. The ingredients were described as 'blue, [cobalt] and porcelain clay, Cornish stone, a little flint-glass and red lead'. The lack of flint is notable. The result was a dry earthenware body with a finely textured unglazed surface, and it was used like jasper but only for figures and busts.

The fine, hard body of pearl ware, suitably glazed, was discovered to be an excellent base for decoration with gold, silver and purplish pink lustre, sometimes in combination with moulded ornament. The finest quality, burned until almost pure white, gave a unique brilliance to the metallic coating. Pearl ware, as a white earthenware with a blue-tinted lead glaze, continued in production throughout the first half of the 19th century. Among the final articles to be made was a colourful series of bread trenchers by Edwin Deakin, Peel Pottery, Longton. 'Eat thy Bread with Joy and Thankfulness' encircled the rim in hand-painted Gothic letters of blue on a pink ground. The centre of the platter was decorated with wheat-ears in gold on an egg-shell blue ground. In the 1840s the design had three wheat-ears, while from about 1850 there were eight and the rim was given a raised edge. Six ornate feet raised such a trencher above table level.

The firm of William Smith and Co., Stafford Pottery, Stockton-on-Tees, established in the late 1820s, made pearl ware impressed PATENT PEARL WHITE in a diamond. This was the patent taken out in 1845 (No. 101968) by George Skinner, who eventually became a partner in the firm.

Pearl ware was little used by its originator, although its introduction proved of considerable importance to the Potteries as being the precursor of inexpensive semi-chinas, opaque chinas and opaque porcelains, all early-19th-century names for improved versions of the pearl-ware body, by now a fine, white, close-textured porcellaneous earthenware coated with transparent glaze. All kinds of strong household equipment were made, such as vases, jugs, candlesticks, teapots, dinner, tea, toilet and other services. They are frequently found impressed or printed with the preferred term together with a trade-mark.

John Davenport, established at Longport in 1793, made all of these white earthenwares, including early pearl-ware dishes and plates with openwork rims. In 1860 the Davenport firm was advertising 'the hardest and most durable earthenware in white granite'. This was the final phase of pearl ware and was made by hundreds of potters from the 1840s, its very name suggesting great strength to its purchasers.

4

Staffordshire Blue

STAFFORDSHIRE BLUE china and earthenware claim an unshakable but remarkable position in the collector's affections. Much of it, post-dating 1830, is not yet even recognised as antique, yet the 'picturesque views' decorating plate and jug and soup tureen record an utterly vanished world. The familiar blue ornament ranges from Don Quixote illustrations to romantic Italian scenes, from Grecian, Persian and Oriental patterns to American landscapes, yet the results remain as essentially English as the rich, flower-laden borders which collectors recognise as the various makers' 'signatures'. Most of this ware was manufactured for a comparatively low-price market, and for tough everyday service, the very elaboration of pattern and border being planned to cover blemishes in the basic china or earthenware, yet how its value has soared.

A Staffordshire blue plate originally selling for as little as sixpence or at most two shillings, and made for daily service in the home, may command tens of pounds today. For instance, a soup plate bearing Andrew Stevenson's 'Governor's Island, New Jersey' engraved by W. G. Wall (see p. 30) has sold for £460. A plate with the arms of Connecticut bearing the trade-mark of Thomas Mayer has commanded the large sum of £600, and another, with the arms of Delaware, by the same potter, £400. The list of dishes that have sold for £50 apiece would include hundreds of different views.

The colour of these valuable pieces is rich, deep, cobalt blue, but the term Staffordshire blue covers all manner of ware transfer printed in innumerable tones and shades of cobalt blue and zaffre. Even the choice of blue began as a manufacturing necessity, for the heat required to fuse the glaze over the transferred ornament ruined other colours. The glaze was specially prepared to give a rich soft tone to the cobalt, which was partly absorbed in the biscuit ware.

Thomas Turner of Caughley initiated this revolutionary idea of printing the decoration on inexpensive earthenware in the way introduced for ornamenting such small objects as snuff-boxes in enamels and developed at Worcester for porcelain. In this way a design engraved on a copper plate could be printed, in a single colour, on to a huge number of transfer papers and thus conveyed to pieces of chinaware with a speed and cheapness previously unimagined.

In the 1780s Josiah Spode took the process its final step when he applied this printing under the glaze, so that many generations of scullery maids should not obliterate those dainty shepherdesses under April skies or the endless pursuit of Oriental lovers over the bridge of willow-pattern fantasy.

So perfect was the method by about 1810 that remarkably delicate effects of light and shade, of three-dimensional solidity and distance, could be achieved within the limits of the single colour by the use of line and stipple engraving.

From a purely technical point of view it is fascinating to note how cleverly the engravings were designed so that the transfer prints should cover the earthenware without leaving any large white spaces liable to reveal imperfections in the pottery itself. Puffy clouds soon filled the skies, and in the foreground figures and water appeared, while the borders were loaded with detail, mainly consisting of flowers and leaves and other naturalistic motifs in the exact, full manner of the early 19th century. On the backs, temptingly inaccessible during the meal, titles were frequently supplied, giving details both of the series and of the individual picture—but, unfortunately, not by any means always of the maker.

In blue transfer-printed table services, no matter whether made in Staffordshire, Yorkshire, Tyneside, South Wales or elsewhere, each flat piece—every dish, plate, saucer, gravy tray—carried a picture. Hollow-ware such as soup tureens, vegetable dishes, jugs, sugar bowls might each be decorated with three or four scenes with border reserves containing miniature views or portraits associated with the central theme.

To the collector these borders are of exceptional interest. The makers of many unmarked pieces have been identified by their border patterns, which appear to have been considered the original owner's exclusive property by competing potters even though the pirating of central pictures was frequent until the Registration of Designs Act came into force in 1842 (see p. 171).

Until about 1800 blue transfer-printed work followed the long-established convention for using designs derived from the Chinese, and the borders were in geometrical styles. Then the romantic pastoral mood of the late 18th century reached the Potteries and was quickly adapted to meet the more progressive ideas of the 19th century, which liked its romantic pictorial effects to be associated with the known contemporary scene, its figure subjects to be easily recognised celebrities. Then in 1802 William Brookes, an engraver of Tunstall, suggested to Stephen Crane, of Well Street Pottery, that beautiful borders would result by using reduced versions of the strip-borders then in fashionable use for paper-hangings. Almost immediately the geometrical style was outmoded. Borders might now be composed of flower and foliage festoons, fruiting vine, sea-shells, floreate scrolls interspersed with bell flowers or butterflies. As still further enrichment, the edges of dishes and plates might be moulded in relief with designs copied from late-18th-century dinner services. Some rims were given slightly escalloped outlines and others were perforated.

7, 8 and 9. Terra-cotta: 'Queen Victoria' and 'The Potter', statuettes modelled by John Broad for Henry Doulton, Lambeth, in the 1880s. (Below) Vase with decoration in black: jug with engine-turning and applied festoons; vase with engine-turning, dipped in black and scraped (all *c*. 1810); an early trial vase and a teapot with brown and white borders.

10, 11 and 12. (Above) Colour picture prints on pot lids, made by F. & R. Pratt, Fenton, Staffordshire. (Left) 'The Late Prince Consort'; hair, whiskers and moustache may be either black or sandy and border patterns vary. (Right) 'Lobster Sauce', a very rare early picture. (Below) Black basaltes: a pair of bulb pots pressed and glazed inside. Decorated in red and white encaustic colours and with applied motif of 'Cupids and Wreath'. Height $5\frac{3}{4}$ inches. Impressed WEDGWOOD (c. 1820).

A standard dinner service of blue-printed earthenware issued by Spode during the Regency years was made up of one hundred and thirty-four separate pieces: four fan-shaped dishes and covers, four square dishes and covers, one octagonal dish, liner and cover, two sauce tureens and stands with ladles, two oval egg stands each with twelve cups, six octagonal meat dishes, four oval dishes, a salad bowl, twenty-four each of soup, dinner and dessert plates.

Of the numerous Anglo-Chinese designs the willow pattern has continued unceasingly to this day. Hundreds of thousands of tons have been produced since Thomas Turner of Caughley originated the design in 1780. The pagoda is on the right of the picture surrounded by six types of conventional trees—willow, peach, fir, plum, the mysterious tree with dark circles, and the apple tree, tallest of all and bearing thirty-two apples arranged in three tiers. At first no figures were put on the little bridge spanning the river, but eventually one, two and finally three figures appeared. The wooden zigzag fence runs from the water to the right-hand edge of the picture. This design, with various adaptations in the design of the fence, the placement of the trees and ships, has since been used by hundreds of potters.

Staffordshire blue was often made by potters little known except for this class of work. The names most frequently encountered are Enoch Wood, Andrew Stevenson, Ralph Stevenson, T. Mayer, J. and R. Clews, J. and W. Ridgway, Charles Meigh and William Adams and Son. Josiah Spode II issued some of the finest work ever made in this medium.

The blue transfer-printed pottery from the factory of the Spodes and their successors the Copelands is now regarded by collectors as technically almost perfect. These have been grouped into five main classes by S. B. Williams in *Antique Blue and White Spode*, 1943: (1) Indian influence; (2) Caramanian pattern, (3) Italian patterns—Tiber, Castle, Tower, Lucano, Blue Italian; (4) Chinese patterns—Willow, Lange Lijsen, India, Marble or Mosaic, Two Birds, Hundred Antiques, Net, Nankin, Gothic Castle, Old Peacock; (5) General—Milkmaid, Woodman, Waterloo, Geranium, Warwick Vase, Filigree, Greek, Persian, Blue Rose, Union Wreath, Girl at the Well, Country Scene.

There are numerous variations in each group. The Indian series was undoubtedly one of the most interesting of these productions, engraving, colour and glaze all being outstanding. The forty subjects were taken from drawings by Samuel Howitt in the book *Oriental Field Sports*, showing hunters and such game as tiger, hog and bear. More typical of the period's mood was this firm's Italian series in the same tradition as the romantic views long expected of landscape painters. The elder Spode was an early maker of willow pattern, and it is a find indeed when one discovers a specimen of his first design.

Enoch Wood and his sons were probably the most prolific makers of Staffordshire blue; certainly the variety of their engravings exceeded that of any other potter. They produced a remarkable range of more than five hundred American, French and English views, the atter including scenes of London, of fashionable spas, of cathedrals, castles and country seats. In addition, more than three hundred miscellaneous pictures have been recorded. Sea-shells, in which the cockle was conspicuous, and flowers were Wood's favourite border motifs until about 1830, when a change was made to compositions of fruiting vine and oak leaves, edged with a narrow, twisted border. Frequent from the late 1830s was a flower and scroll border containing several reserves—usually six—separated from the central view by a narrow ornamental ribbon.

English views were displayed in an irregular opening encircled by a border of shells and flowers and included the name of the scene. The series of twelve 'London Views' were displayed in medallions bordered by fruiting vine motifs, ten of them picturing the Regent's Park district, the Bank of England and, oddly enough, the cliffs of Dover. French scenes were bordered with fruiting vine, hollyhocks and other flowers.

Wood's blue, in production until 1846, was always in dark shades, late examples being in a tint too dark to give perfect clarity to the pictures. Until 1818 the mark was merely the name WOOD impressed. The majority of blue transfer-printed ware, however, is of a later date and might be impressed variously E WOOD & SONS, ENOCH WOOD & SONS, or ENOCH WOOD & Co.

Rivalling Spode and Wood for delightful colours was Andrew Stevenson. In partnership with Bucknall he established a pottery at Cobridge in 1808, producing the ordinary range of domestic ware and blue transfer-printed earthenware. By 1812 Andrew Stevenson had become sole proprietor. He printed mainly in dark blue, occasionally in combinations of dark and light blues. His series of more than thirty English views was handsomely and variously bordered with designs of large flowers, roses predominating, and foliage. Among these views were Enville Hall, Staffordshire; Mereworth House, Kent; Walsingham Priory, Norfolk. He also issued American scenes, some of these being engraved from drawings made on the spot by W. G. Wall, a young artist who arrived in the United States during the early months of 1818, and began sending drawings to Stevenson immediately afterwards. Twelve of these appear to have been commissioned and are to be recognised by the presence of the artist's name on the back. Dishes and plates engraved with Wall's views are now highly priced: a soup plate engraved in dark and light blue with a view of Governor's Island, bearing Stevenson's name impressed and Wall's name in blue, has sold for £75. American views appear in borders of differing floral arrangements, scrolls, large flowers and small wreaths.

Staffordshire blue by Andrew Stevenson might be impressed with a crown surrounded by A STEVENSON WARRANTED STAFFORDSHIRE, and also imprinted in blue with the name of the scene accompanied by an eagle or a draped urn.

It is frequently stated that Andrew Stevenson's factory was taken over in 1818 by the Clews Brothers, who occupied the premises. There is little evidence of this, however, for the *Staffordshire Directory* of that year contains entries for Andrew Stevenson, Ralph Stevenson and Ralph and J. Clews, all of Cobridge.

Ralph Stevenson, a brother of Andrew, potted from 1815 until about 1840, but blue and white was produced only on a limited scale, some two dozen designs having been identified. They are in great demand and consequently are highly valued. He issued three short series of English scenes inscribed in blue on the back, 'Panorama Scenery', 'English Views' and 'British Lakes'. The first two series were enclosed in particularly handsome acorn and oak leaf borders, and rim edges might be raised in white relief. 'British Lakes' were bordered with elaborate flower motifs and scrollwork. American views were bordered in a design of hawthorn and vine leaves. Domestic ware might be printed in a combination of dark and medium blue transfers. A little of Ralph Stevenson's work was impressed STEVENSON or RS, but mostly lacked even those aids to identification.

In the late 1820s Ralph Stevenson was joined by W. Williams as partner. They marketed a further series of American views in borders composed of oak leaves and acorns, although one of them—'The Capitol, Washington'—is found in three alternative borders: the acorn and oak; four medallion portraits of Washington, Lafayette, Jefferson and Clinton; white embossed. Examples have been sold for sums varying from fifteen to a hundred guineas. Portrait and medallion plates included coronation souvenirs of William IV and Queen Caroline in 1831. The marks during this period were impressed RALPH STEVEN-SON AND WILLIAMS, or RSW.

Yet another firm known to have issued nearly two hundred popular views was Ralph and James Clews, established in Cobridge no later than 1817. Some of their engravings on earthenware are outstandingly picturesque in a blue rather less richly deep than that chosen by Spode. Today they are more especially associated with three series, each enormously popular at the time, and still to be found and treasured: 'The Pictures of Sir David Wilkie', a series of twelve, including the familiar 'Playing at Draughts', 'The Valentine' and 'The Rabbit on the Wall'; 'Don Quixote', which ran to about twenty subjects in borders with irregular inner edges and composed of flowers and scrolls with a scallop of beading; and 'The Three Tours of Dr. Syntax', covering some eighty easily identified Rowlandson engravings published between 1815 and 1821. The Syntax designs were bordered by large roses and other flowers, interspersed with small scrollwork. This is the firm's best-known border pattern, for they did not confine themselves to standard borders as did most potters. Each Syntax piece was marked in blue with the title of the picture in script enclosed in an ornamental rectangle.

More than a hundred English views have been recorded bearing the Clews mark, covering a very wide range such as 'Zoological Garden Views', 'Select Views' and 'Picturesque Views'. The cathedrals, abbeys and castles might be bordered in a composition of flowers and foliage, bell-flowers predominating, with intricate scrollwork. The borders of 'Select Views' consisted of large aster-like flowers and bell-flowers, the name of each view being impressed on the back in a ribbon scroll with a wreath of leaves.

'Picturesque Views' was a late Clews series found less frequently in blue than in colours.

These are mostly American scenes, and borders might consist of simple flower and leaf motifs, but more frequently the handsome border of passion flowers and four medallions was used. These were elaborately worked with a landscape scene showing a boat on a lake with a background of trees, through which passes a bar inscribed with the name of the view. A series labelled 'American Views' numbered twenty-four pictures, including three of the White House and five unnamed and now unknown. These are in scalloped borders bearing the names of fifteen States with a star between each.

The trade-mark of Ralph and James Clews was composed of a crown, CLEWS beneath, and below again, WARRANTED STAFFORDSHIRE.

The Clewses closed their Cobridge factory in 1834, James emigrating to America, where he established a pottery at Troy, Indiana. Here he endeavoured to make blue-printed earthenware equal in quality to the world-famed Staffordshire blue, impressing his productions JAMES CLEWS. The project failed, however, through lack of suitable materials and experienced labour. Years later it was discovered that deposits of fine-quality kaolin lay adjacent to the site.

In Cobridge they were succeeded by Wood and Brownfield, whose blue-printed ware was of very second-rate workmanship with pale-tinted decoration. This, marked W & B with the name of the pattern, was no doubt intended for a very cheap market. In 1850 the firm came under the control of William Brownfield, Jewitt recording in 1878 that their blue-printed patterns were well designed. The mark was WB in addition to the name of the pattern. After 1871 the name BROWNFIELD was impressed in full.

Josiah Wedgwood was printing his own transfers in blue and black by the mid-1780s and willow pattern was in production shortly before his death in 1795. This closely resembled Turner's original, with the difference that on plates the tree behind the pagoda carried thirty-four apples to Caughley's thirty-two: the fret on the fence was also re-designed. Wedgwood blue at this period was an intense cobalt. A much lighter blue was evolved by the firm in about 1820 by using a special glaze which gave a rich, almost glowing look to the colour. This effect delighted late Georgians and was imitated by other potters, but seldom, if ever, so successfully. The effect was produced by what was technically known as a 'flow': that is, by introducing a little volatising chloride in the sagger before firing. The blue melted into the surrounding glaze with a kind of halo effect. Almost invariably this effect was in blue, but rare examples in brown, green and yellow have been observed dating to the 1830s. Views were often enclosed in a border of rose sprays and vine leaves. The Wedgwood firm transfer-printed on cream ware and in pearl ware, impressing the name WEDGWOOD.

John Davenport, Longport, printed on fine-quality earthenware and from about 1810 on stone china and on bone china. Openwork rims in double rows were a feature, now difficult to acquire. His willow pattern, believed to have originated in Minton's engraving shops, usually bear thirty-three apples, but as few as twenty-five have been noted. These at first were impressed DAVENPORT, and from early in the 19th century were marked in blue, DAVENPORT or DAVENPORT LONGPORT, with or without an anchor, or with an anchor alone.

Thomas Minton, in May, 1796, established at Stoke-upon-Trent a pottery devoted to the production of blue-printed ware. He had learned the art of copperplate engraving for transfer work under Turner at Caughley, assisting in cutting the plates for the original willow-pattern design. Before embarking on his career as an outstandingly successful potter, Minton for several years operated as a master engraver of copperplates for transfer-printing. For Spode he had engraved a tea-ware pattern called the 'Buffalo', the 'Broseley' and the famous willow pattern. He adapted Turner's design for the use of other potters, including William Adams of Greengates and Hugh Williamson of Fenton, each of these varying in detail such as the fence patterns, number and style of trees and apples, placement of the boat and so on.

Minton's early earthenware obviously included willow pattern of fine colour and printing: in addition he issued a wide range of Anglo-Chinese engravings, all cut in his own engraving shops. No doubt, too, he issued the fashionable Regency all-over chintz patterns. Although Minton's output of blue-printed ware must have been large, no example of scenic work has been observed.

The name MINTON is found impressed. Early in the 19th century he marked good-quality transfer-printed earthenware with an expansive blue imprint displaying the name of the design, such as AMHERST in a cartouche.

John and George Rogers operated Dale Hall Pottery, Burslem, from 1802 until the death of George in 1815. The business was then carried on under the style of John Rogers and Son until 1842. Jewitt states that they produced 'table ware of a higher and better quality than most of their contemporaries, and were especially famed for their light blue "Broseley dragon" and "Willow" pattern services'. Their exceptionally radiant dark blue, however, was used for their English and American views bordered with a composition of roses and forget-me-nots, and also for their long series of romantic pictures such as 'Love in a Village' and 'The Maypole'. The mark was ROGERS impressed or printed in blue, sometimes with the addition of the sign of Mars.

The firm of Rogers was bought in 1842 by James Edwards, who modernised the works and within two years had increased production sixfold. Edwards continued using Rogers's copperplates and also introduced his 'Steamship' series with borders composed of medallions displaying steamships. At first the mark was EDWARDSDH impressed, followed from about 1848 by various printed marks all containing the name JAMES EDWARDS & SON or the script initials JE & S.

Thomas Mayer, Cliff Bank, Stoke-upon-Trent, who acquired his pottery as a going concern in the early 1820s, carried out excellently engraved transfer-printing in a very attractive shade of blue. His views, issued singly and not in unified series, included about thirty American scenes, while about a hundred English have been recorded. He edged his views with fine lace decoration set in borders of trumpet-shaped flowers and vine leaves. His table ware was rimmed with narrow edge decoration of overlapping scrolls interspersed with spoked wheels. Mayer's impressed mark resembled that of Enoch Wood, with the inscription surrounding the eagle altered to T MAYER STOKE STAFFORDSHIRE, and to this might be added the word WARRANTED. His printed mark, the largest found in English ceramics, consisted of an American eagle with a scroll flowing from its beak bearing the words E PLURIBUS UNUM.

The Ridgway family made a fortune from blue-printed wares—earthenware and china. Job and George Ridgway founded their pottery at Shelton in 1792 as specialists in the up-and-coming blue transfer-printed ware. In 1802 Job parted from his brother and with his sons John and William built the celebrated pottery at Cauldon Place, Hanley, trading as Job Ridgway and Sons. From 1808 they began blue-printing on bone china. After Job's death in 1813 the firm became J. and W. Ridgway, some outstanding transfer work being produced between then and 1830. The colour was rather paler than that of their leading competitors, but greater tone differentiation was visible and it is their name that appears on the highly priced Ridgway ware collected today.

Like many other contemporary potters they traded extensively with America, particularly popular being their 'Beauties of America' series, with borders consisting of conventional medallions containing roses. In these the engraving is exceptionally fine and the colour so rich against a smooth, pure white glaze that examples are rated at high values, although not at all rare. They also made a long series of Oxford and Cambridge University views set in eight-sided panels, bordered with medallions of children and flowers. These again are costly and seldom to be discovered as bargains. A series of Zoological Garden transfer prints was issued in the late 1820s, with elaborate borders of twisted scrolls. These are sometimes to be seen in green, red and black. All their blue-printed ware was impressed J & W RIDGWAY with the name of the view in blue.

The brothers parted in 1830, John going to Cauldon Place, while William established a series of specialist potteries until he owned six flourishing concerns turning out tons of blue-printed ware each month for the American market, much of it of poor quality and unmarked. The 'Beauties of America' series ceased to be made after their separation, for no examples have been found bearing their individual marks. William issued a ten-year series of American views printed in light blue and black, bordered with small sprays of moss, sometimes over a small scale pattern.

John Ridgway issued printed wares in all colours until 1836 and then reverted to blue: his favourite borders were a medley of flowers and rose leaves, with wide reserves containing children and goats. For some American views he favoured a border of large five-pointed stars, the space between them being filled with smaller stars. Ridgway's engravings on marked ware are all noteworthy as having been made from specially prepared sketches, rather than copied from engravings in books. Both William and John impressed their names in full.

Joseph Stubbs established the Dale Hall Works, Burslem, in the 1790s and later removed to Longport, and was responsible for some cleverly engraved views in dark blue, the English scenes bordered with a design of foliage and pointed scrolls; American views were bordered with a pattern containing eagles, flowers and scrollwork. Much of Stubbs's work is unmarked, but his border patterns have not been noted elsewhere. Some early blue and white was impressed STUBBS, probably from about 1810, but from 1816 his more commonly used trade-mark consisted of a ring centred with a star and encircled JOSEPH STUBBS LONGPORT, transfer-printed in blue. At one period, possibly at some time between 1810 and 1815, the firm was a partnership impressing the name STUBBS & KENT LONGPORT.

Heathcote and Co. established a pottery at Fenton during the early years of the 19th century, making good-quality blue transfer-printed earthenware. Their work, dating from 1811 and printed in blue, consisted of the Prince of Wales's feathers, the name C HEATH-COTE & Co above, and on a ribbon beneath the name of the view or series, such as LAKES. From 1859 they produced blue transfer-printed patterns on bone porcelain, one series being marked 'Old English Scenery'.

Ralph Hall, who potted at Swan Bank Works, Tunstall, from the early years of the 19th century until 1832, issued about twenty English views during the 1820s, including Conway Castle, Boughton Castle, Luscombe, and Wildernesse in Kent. These were framed in lace-edged borders of fruit and flowers and impressed R. HALL with a blue-printed scroll containing the name of the scene and the words SELECT VIEWS. A series of twelve views bordered with sprays of large flowers was similarly marked, but named PICTUR-ESQUE SCENERY. Hall's name was also impressed on willow pattern and on earthenware decorated in all-over designs adapted from chintz.

The celebrated Adams family of potters was responsible for a long and varied series of exceptionally well-engraved views between 1816 and 1840. The leading exponent was William Adams (1772—1829), who established a pottery at Stoke-upon-Trent in the mid-1790s to make blue transfer-printed ware, entering the bone-china trade in 1816. His blue transfer-work on both was extremely successful. English views followed the set fashion of the period, most of them adaptations from newly published books. His set of twelve London views was obviously by the same engraver as a similar series by Enoch Wood and Sons, eight of them scenes in Regent's Park, including Hanover Terrace and York Gate. None was duplicated by either firm. Other English views, which numbered at least a hundred marked examples, included Windsor Castle, Northumberland Castle, Beckenham Place, Kent and Morpeth Castle.

William Adams bordered his English views with designs composed of flowers, the fashionable bell-flower predominating. The London and American views were bordered with a foliage pattern which on any but the smallest plate was characterised by a pine tree placed to the left. After his death in 1829 the firm was styled W. Adams and Sons, and for a few years they printed in red, mulberry and black with border medallions containing animals and flowers.

William Adams impressed his early ware w ADAMS. By about 1805 the name might be printed, and soon afterwards the title of the picture was also included. His export ware from 1816 was marked with a blue-printed eagle, wings extended, grasping a twig in one claw and four arrows in the other, a foliated cartouche or festooned ribbon below containing the name of the subject. This mark, too, is found on English scenes intended for export. It is interesting to speculate on the reason why Adam's printed mark is found in identical form plus the name CLEWS. Possibly the Adams firm acquired J. and R. Clews's copperplates after their closure; such marks would then indicate a date later than 1834. After William Adams's death, more probably from a short time before this, blue transfer-printed ware was impressed w ADAMS & SONS or WA & S. The blue printed mark was continued.

Entries in *Parsons' and Bradshaw's Directory*, 1818, include William Adams and his cousin Benjamin Adams, who had succeeded his father William Adams (1745—1805) at Greengates, Tunstall. Benjamin printed a great quantity of willow pattern on stone china, the design closely resembling that of Caughley, except that the pattern on the rise is squarer. At first, until about 1810, there were thirty-two apples, but on new copperplates cut at that time the number was increased to fifty. His ware was impressed B ADAMS.

Omitted, however, from the *Directory* was another William Adams (1748—1831), then operating potteries at Brick House, Burslem, and at Cobridge, also producing printed earthenware in all-over chintz patterns of flown blue. The impressed mark until 1805 was ADAMS; then ADAMS & Co; finally W. ADAMS & Co.

The Old Hall Works, Hanley, was carried on by the Meigh family from 1770 until 1861, at first by Job, then from 1820 to 1840 by his son, and finally by his grandson Charles. Jewitt writes that 'the transfer printing at the Old Hall Works is more carefully done and the colours are clearer and brighter than at most manufactories'. English and American views were issued, the latter being notable for the only view of Yale College known on Staffordshire ware, and this was usually in red or green. The favourite border consisted of a medley of small flowers. The willow pattern noted has always been of poor colour and smudged, obviously for a very cheap market. Early pieces of good quality were impressed MEIGH, and from 1840 CHARLES MEIGH HANLEY.

John Aynsley, Lane End, operated as designer, engraver, printer of transfers and decorator from 1802 to 1826. He supplied transfers to potters and he himself bought earthenware in the white and applied the transfers. Careful examination of some transfer-printed views and romantic scenes will reveal the name J. AYNSLEY in microscopic script.

13, 14 and 15. Black basaltes and Egyptian black hollow-ware: (Top) Engine-turned capped teapot with widow knob to cover, impressed WEDGWOOD; ornamental ewer with pressed leaf decoration, impressed I NEALE HANLEY; cylindrical engine-turned teapot with widow knob cover, impressed E MAYER. (Above) Helmet-shaped cream jug with high loop handle, impressed HARTLEY GREENS & CO LEEDS ★ POTTERY; coffee pot with highly domed cover, the loop handle and spout decorated with leaf ornament, impressed LEEDS POTTERY; sugar basin decorated with bas reliefs, impressed LEEDS ★ POTTERY. (Left) Engine-turned cylindrical teapot, impressed SPODE, early 19th century.

16, 17 and 18. (Above) Drinking cans in black basaltes. Height 3½ inches. Marked WEDG-WOOD impressed. The left-hand example is sprigged with 'Bringing Home the Game' and has a silver rim. The other is embossed with beehive skip pattern (1830). (Below) Lithophane panel made by Mintons: it is shown on the left with the light falling upon it and revealing only its irregular surface; and on the right the same panel held with the light shining through it.

The potters of Rockingham (Swinton) issued blue-printed ware, all of it now rare. The willow pattern differs from others by positioning the boat in the water in the foreground, two men on the bridge, no fence, no fruit tree over the house. Until 1807 productions were not marked: then they were impressed, on earthenware, BRAMELD or ROCKINGHAM; from 1813 the name impressed was BRAMELD & Co. Bone china made from 1820 (see Chapter 5) was decorated, surprisingly in a flown blue. Examples have been seen decorated in the chintz styles, willow and Broseley patterns, and a few romantic pictures. These are marked in transfer blue with the griffin *passant* and the name 'ROCKINGHAM WORKS BRAMELD' in script.

Staffordshire blue, a term now used generically and including the productions of other pottery centres, was made by hundreds of potters during the 19th century, most of it intended for working-class markets. In addition to the potters mentioned above, the following made a certain amount of good-quality blue transfer-printed earthenware now collected.

Elkin, Knight and Bridgwood, Foley Potteries, made willow, Broseley and other blue patterns in the 1820s.

S. Tams and Co., Longton, made dark and medium blue of London buildings including Drury Lane Theatre, Somerset House, Opera House, in foliage borders marked with a large blue stamp bearing the title of the picture and the words 'semi-china'. They also issued portrait plates of American celebrities with line borders. Their productions, dating from about 1830 to 1850, were impressed S TAMS & Co.

Thomas Green, Fenton, issued poor-quality American scenes in geometric borders of ornate pointed design. These are highly valued, although dating to the mid-19th century.

Swansea, under changing proprietorship, produced vast quantities of willow and Broseley patterns in dark blue, light blue and flown blue. These patterns appear to have been made from the early 1800s until the factory closed in 1870, with variations in details, yet marked examples are rare. The willow plate in the Victoria and Albert Museum marked DILLWYN & Co and ascribed to 1825 has thirty-four apples, while another example impressed CAMBRIAN has but thirty.

Collectors must beware of the Staffordshire blue still being manufactured and 'aged' after leaving the factory. New pieces may be scratched with a small carborundum wheel to wear the glaze. The ware can then be yellowed all too easily by means of a salt bath and boiling fat. This occurs, of course, only with patterns that are valuable in their genuinely old state.

Genuine pre-1830 Staffordshire blue earthenware is not difficult to distinguish. In general the copies lack the surprising lightness of early-19th-century earthenware; most of the fakes are just about double the weight of early examples. If the glaze is examined with a light falling obliquely upon it, the surface of the old piece appears finely dappled after the style of smooth sea-sand after a shower of rain. Once recognised, this display is unmistakable and is a certain sign of age. It is not present on earthenware made after the 1820s.

The glaze is the transparent film of clear, hard glass applied over the decoration to protect it against wear and the effect of food acids. It often displays a faintly bluish tinge, seen best where the glaze has run into drops against an angle. The body, too, has a faintly cream tint, noticeably different from the chalky whiteness characterising Victorian ware. More important, copies fail to delight the eye with the subtle richness and beauty of colour which give old Staffordshire blue of the best years a glowing, unfading loveliness.

Then there are the stilt marks, small rough scars found on both upper and lower surfaces of flat-ware, usually in the margins, and caused by the pressure of little tripods called cockspurs or stilts between the plates when they were piled in the kiln. The stilts prevented damage to the glaze caused by contact before it hardened, but even such small points caused defects in its lustrous surface.

5

Bone China

THE ENGLISH potter's debt to the outflowing of earlier eastern culture is perpetuated in the use of the word 'china' to differentiate between translucent porcelain and opaque earthenware. There are really two sorts of china if classified by their chemical content—hard-paste porcelain and soft-paste artificial porcelain. Until bone china was manufactured on a commercial scale from the late 1790s, nearly all English porcelain potters made an artificial glassy ware; competing was the much more costly hard-paste porcelain of the Orient and the Continent.

The importation of porcelain was prohibited under an Act of 1794. The china-sellers of London and the big towns were unable to replace their depleted stocks of delicate, beautifully decorated hard-paste porcelain; sales were reduced to an unremunerative level. English artificial porcelain, fragile and covered with a softish lead glaze, was entirely unfitted for use with the steel of dinner table cutlery. Its faintly greyish hue, with surface flaws such as black specks, made it a poor substitute for the more costly porcelains of Sèvres, Meissen, Vienna and other Continental state-subsidised potteries. The china-sellers, too, preferred hard procelain and the queen's ware and fine stonewares evolved by Josiah Wedgwood because they stood up toughly to journeying. A fifty per cent excise duty had already been levied on imported porcelain from 1772; it could, then, be afforded only by the rich.

A monopoly had been created in the mining and preparation of Cornish china clay, capable of giving whiteness and plasticity to the paste, and Cornish china stone which caused vitrification and translucency. This monopoly had been brought about by extending until July 14th, 1796, a patent granted to William Cookworthy in 1768 and bought by Richard Champion in 1772. The potters of artificial porcelain were, therefore, effectively prevented from strengthening and whitening their wares.

The revolution in porcelain manufacture that would occur immediately the monopoly ceased had been foreseen by Josiah Spode, who carried out several years of tireless experiment. Using samples of the forbidden Cornish minerals—available in his pottery for the law permitted their use freely in opaque ware of which he was a master potter—he evolved a china of uniform translucency. He eliminated frit with its cost-increasing processes and mixed calcined bones direct with the heavier constituents. The resulting ceramic was the nearest approach to the true porcelain of the Orient yet devised for practical use.

Spode's account books for 1794 prove that limited quantities of bone china were marketed in that year. The Cornish ingredients must have been used under licence for Spode named the new porcelain 'British Cornish China'. It was an immediate success, merchants and china-sellers placing substantial orders on sight of samples.

The London sales warehouse managed by William Copeland at 45, Fore Street, Moorfields, could not accommodate the rapidly increasing trade and in 1796 the former Theatre Royal, Portugal Street, Lincoln's Inn Fields, London, was acquired. Spode's profits for that year exceeded £13,000, from which Copeland received a gift of £1,000.

In the same year Josiah Spode erected newly-patented Pepper kilns in his pottery at Stoke-upon-Trent. These possessed, among other advantages, that of more equally distributing the heat than former kilns, and were the first to be fitted with heat-regulating dampers, thus saving a substantial amount of fuel.

Spode's formula for bone china became a standard unaltered to this day, although methods of preparation and firing and the resulting ware have vastly improved. The mixture consisted of six parts bone ash, four parts Cornish stone, and three-and-a-half parts Cornish clay. The bone ash was responsible for its milky-white translucency, and also tended to prevent crazing of the biscuit in the event of over-firing. Because of its high shrinkage capacity, unusual care was required in drying and firing to prevent distortion and fire cracks. The glaze was a transparent glass made of silica, lead oxide and potash, sufficiently fusible for overglaze enamels to sink into and adhere without the hazard of subsequent flaking.

Bone china paste is much less plastic than potter's clay and required much longer to manipulate. In the early 19th century six hundred plates could be made from potter's clay in a twelve-hour day; the utmost possible in bone china was eighty, but more usually ranged between sixty and seventy. The modern moulding machine will produce thirty dozen in an eight-hour day.

There is no record of any potter making non-frit bone china until after July, 1796, although several competitors had entered the field before the turn of the century, including Thomas Minton, Stoke-upon-Trent from 1796; Duesbury and Kean, Derby, 1797; John Rose, Coalport, 1798; Chamberlain and Co., Worcester, 1798; Worthington, Humble and Holland, Liverpool, 1799; John Davenport, Longport, 1800. By 1812 they had been joined by the Wedgwood firm, New Hall and others.

No fewer than eighteen lesser-known Staffordshire potters manufacturing bone china were listed in *Parsons' & Bradshaw's Directory*, 1818:
Goldenhill, Tunstall, etc.:
Marsh and Haywood, Brownhills; W. S. and T. Rathbone, Tunstall.

Longport, Burslem, Cobridge, Hot Lane:

Philip Brookes and Co.; Sitch, Machin and Co., Holehouse; J. and R. Riley, Hill Works; Wood and Caldwell, Fountain Place.

Hanley and Shelton:

Hicks and Meigh, Shelton; Reuben Johnson, Miles Bank; Frederick Peover, High Street, Hanley.

Fenton (or Lower Lane), Lane Delph and Lane End:

Thomas Baggaley, Lane Delph; Charles Browne, Foley Pottery; Thomas Drury and Son, Daisy Bank; Hilditch and Martin, Lane End; George and Charles Mason, Lane Delph; Mathers and Newbould, Market Place; William Nutt, Lane End; Simkin and Waller, Lane End.

Much of the bone china issued by these firms was unmarked, but occasional examples are to be found with impressed initial; for instance, a comport and two dishes of an elaborately enamelled dessert service seen recently was impressed WS & TR. Unmarked bone china from these firms is usually, and without justification, classed collectively as Rockingham (bone china, 1820—1842), thus acquiring for it the value of that establishment's brilliant reputation.

The improvement in bone china over soft-paste porcelain is vividly illustrated in Eastbourne Museum. Here are shown a cup and very deep saucer and a tea basin enamelled in the highly colourful style known to early 19th-century potters as 'japan pattern'. The cup and saucer are in soft porcelain and each is marked in red with a crown, crossed batons and a cursive D, with the pattern number 42; the tea basin is in bone china and bears the same hand-painted Derby mark but with the number 41. W. B. Honey and other authorities ascribe this mark to the period 1786—1811. The contrast between the faintly greyish appearance of Derby soft-paste porcelain of the late 1790s and the sparkling white of bone china from the same factory is seen here to fine advantage.

Only a small proportion of the early bone china that emerged from the firing kilns was unflawed; much displayed minute black specks, particularly from the minor potters. These specks on costly pieces were concealed beneath a wealth of colourful opaque enamels, ground colours and gilding; on seconds the biscuit was thickly coated with white glaze. This china was also sensitive to sudden atmospheric changes and the white glaze was not entirely resistant to corrosion from food acids and industrial atmospheres.

A small dessert dish of uniform translucency made early in the 19th century hung as a wall plaque for several decades and the upper part of its undersurface became appreciably discoloured by sulphur-impregnated dust. Its tool-finished foot-ring was badly torn in the lathe, almost half having broken away owing to a concealed flaw in the biscuit. The fracture had been glazed, thus proving a market for badly flawed seconds. An unglazed portion of this dish shows the biscuit to be off-white in colour with many black specks rising above the surface of the paste; on the underside many of these emerge through the white glaze. The front of this dish is enamelled with an attractive but quickly produced design consisting of transferred outlines and stippled ornament in rusty black, overpainted with semi-transparent enamels in green, yellow, pink, Indian red and blue.

Much bone china was decorated by independent enamellers working for the china-sellers who bought from the potter in the white. Their customers selected patterns from folios of hand-painted designs and sample ware. From 1812 greater brilliance of hue was possible by the use of the high temperature enamelling kiln operating within the factory itself. This gradually replaced the small box muffle in which the enamels had been matured without exposing them to direct contact with the flames. Independent enamellers from about 1820 used such kilns which could be profitable only with a large output.

Ground colours became fashionable after the close of the Napoleonic wars and are found in dark blue, apple green, deep yellow, canary yellow, grey, turquoise, crimson, salmon, yellow-green, lavender, cane-colour, striped red and gold, marbled brown and blue. Until the early 1830s ground colours were rarely perfectly uniform in tint on a single piece. A process introduced by Henry Shelton in 1826 produced ground colours with an even glossy surface, easy to distinguish from the earlier methods and was carried out with colours less fusible than those used by the enamel painters and fired at a higher temperature. This meant that they were unaffected by the subsequent firings necessary to mature and fix the enamels.

Coloured grounds over patterns moulded in relief now came into use and by about 1840 the fashionable demand was for ground colours in Victoria green, crimson, turquoise and *rose du Barry*. The relief work was enriched with heavy gilding. Ground colours of exceptional beauty were evolved by various combinations of gold with salts of ammonia and other chemicals. Among the most fashionable were Sèvres green, Vincennes blue, ceramic purple, turquoise, and apple green richer than was formerly used. Tints varied with individual potters; such firms as Minton, Copeland, Rose of Coalport and several unknown independent decorators, for instance, produced ground colours of exceptional beauty.

Entertainment in the home at this time was on a lavish scale and in any event families were notably large. Extensive dinner, dessert and tea services, elaborately enamelled and gilded, were commissioned and might be a year in production. The fashion continued from silver plate of painting each piece with the family coat of arms in full colour. After about 1850 there was a thirty-year demand for services displaying bogus coats of arms.

Oriental designs adapted to the English taste were fashionable on bone china table services by 1805, an influence that declined during the 1820s. The effects were achieved by substituting English flowers for Chinese blossoms in floral patterns, and birds such as parrots and peacocks were Anglicised. Other patterns bearing a superficial resemblance to the Japanese *Imari*, with flowers and shrubbery in deep velvety blues, vivid patches of scarlet and gilded tracery, were termed japan patterns.

George IV began the widespread vogue for harlequin sets by ordering, from the Chamberlain firm at Worcester, dinner, dessert and tea services decorated in the current japan taste, but each piece enamelled with a different design. Other harlequin services were painted with a series of English castles, mansions or scenic views, each piece displaying one or more different scenes, the name painted on the underside of the ware. Representations of mythological legends were reproduced in full colour; a dinner service of 130 pieces has been noted bearing more than 200 such pictures. Paintings by eminent artists of the 18th century were copied. Naturalistic flower painting, less difficult of accomplishment, was popular from about 1815. Dinner services from the late 1820s copied the shapes of early 18th-century silver and were painted with delicate sprays of flowers in natural colours. By this time surface specks had been eliminated so that overcrowding with ornament was no longer necessary.

The well-modelled figures of soft porcelain which decorated dining and dessert tables of the second half of the 18th century became unfashionable, although Derby continued their production in bone china. There was little to recommend them, however, beyond a general gaudy splendour. Ostentatious vases became fashionable singly, in pairs, or in garnitures of four or five. For drawing rooms, entrance halls and passages there were massive covered vases, sometimes as much as forty inches in height, supported on ormolu rimmed pedestals. Later vases with a *bleu de roi* ground were enriched with reserves containing pictorial scenes or copies of French paintings.

The Spode pattern books and ledgers of the 1820s indicate the wide variety of ware made in bone china at that period. They include artichoke cups, asparagus trays, broth bowls, butter tubs and stands, card racks, chamber candlesticks with extinguishers, cheese dishes, cheese toasters, chestnut vases, chicken tureens, custard cups, cylinder pin-cases to screw, ice-pails, inkstands and pen trays, match-pots, mugs, radish trays, roll-trays, root-dishes, rouge-pots, salad bowls, sandwich sets, scent-jars, snuff-boxes, snuffer-trays, steak-dishes with compartments, strawberry baskets, sugar boxes, supper plates, syrup pots, toast-racks, turtle pans, violet baskets and wafer boxes. Punch and toddy bowls ranging from two gallons to quart capacity were decorated in matching sets.

Competition increased during the 1830s and the range of goods now included breakfast, toilet and trinket sets, ornamental ewers and tazzas. The vogue for naming patterns by means of a transferred back stamp, containing the potter's name or trade mark, dates from the 1840s although some earlier attributions have been made. In finer ware from about 1835 there were reproductions of 18th-century Dresden, Sèvres and Chelsea complete with those firms' marks. Many of these magnificent pieces now masquerade as originals although the bone china bears little resemblance to the 18th-century pastes, hard or soft.

Minton was marketing from 1848 a costly bone china whiter and more translucent than any being produced elsewhere. Shapes were now adapted from the styles of old Sèvres, but a wide range of ware was made purely English in character. Cabinet pieces of the late

1840s and 1850s were as highly regarded then as now and as worthy of their place in the collector's cabinet. Unfortunately few pieces were signed by the artists, who included such outstanding men as Hurten, the finest flower painter in Europe; Weaver, celebrated for his birds; R. F. Abraham, whose Etty-like figure subjects were adapted by others. Dress plates or high stands for desserts, and compotes composed of parian statuary with the dish units in bone china, were fashionable throughout the third quarter of the 19th century, and in the 1860s early Anglo-Chinese designs were revived under the name of Indian patterns.

19, 20 and 21. (Above) Herculaneum barrel-shaped jug typical of the Liverpool potters, in pearl ware, with black transfer-printed scroll-work and engraving of a marriage ceremony at the Gretna Green smithy; on the reverse is a scene of the chase by the lady's angry father. The dated inscription 'Jenny Taylor 1799' and the ornamental foliage are enamelled over the glaze. (Upper right) Pearl-ware jug painted on each face with a sailing warship and inscribed 'General Mercer and Captain Moores 1801' with the name James Gant. Impressed LEEDS POTTERY. (Right) A toddy warmer with socket for a tobacco taper, in Leeds cream-coloured earthenware, decorated on both sides with pierced ornament and a solid moulded mask. The loop handles have leaf finials.

22, 23 and 24. (Top left) A cabinet plate painted at Derby by Richard Askew, with lavishly gilded ornament on the rim. Marked crowned D with batons and dots in puce. Attributed to the early 19th century by the Victoria and Albert Museum. (Top right) Dessert dish with painted church scene in gilded border, rim of deep blue ground colour. By Copeland and Garrett *c*. 1840. (Below) Part of a Caughley-Coalport tea-set in bone china with views of English country seats. Painted in black stipple over the glaze.

6

Felspar Porcelain and Stone China

CHINA SHOPS were among the delights of fashionable Georgian London. Extravagantly lovely porcelains from the East rivalled the newest gilded beauties from Sèvres and the colourful radiance from Meissen. In 1794 this exotic pleasure received a blow from which it never recovered. The importation of porcelain from the Continent was prohibited, except from Holland, and even for this a special licence was required from the Treasury. Moreover, a duty of thirty per cent was levied upon all decorated porcelain whatever its origin.

Thus the monopoly in Oriental porcelain fell to the East India Company. Duty, war risks, breakages in transit and monopoly profits raised the cost of Oriental porcelains to a prohibitive level, and china-sellers were unwilling to renew their stocks of 'Indian Porcelain'. The result was a dearth of the dinner and dessert services particularly in demand for important formal occasions. They were preferable to most English porcelain dinner ware since this failed to hold its heat when warmed and was liable to fracture while in use and its glaze to suffer from crazing and the disfigurement of knife scars.

The Staffordshire potters seized the opportunity of evolving a more adequate substitute for the imported porcelain that would be hard, strong, durable under the strains of dinner-table use, and suitable for sumptuous enamelling. Miles Mason made hard porcelain in Liverpool from 1796 and in Fenton from 1800; William and John Turner, on January 9th, 1800, patented a method of manufacturing 'porcelain and earthenware' (No. 2367); and in the same year Josiah Spode II evolved felspar porcelain. The Turners' venture ended in bankruptcy; Mason and Spode became rich.

Spode's felspar porcelain, hard, tough, white, translucent and free from surface flaws, was an important addition to English ceramic techniques. It consisted of the bone-china formula with the addition of pure felspar and an equal reduction in the amount of china-stone which contained no more than thirty per cent of felspar. This was fired at a higher temperature than bone china and approximated Continental hard porcelain although less brittle. Wasters from the kiln were fewer than for ordinary hard porcelain.

The china-sellers welcomed Spode's felspar porcelain services and by 1806 he was producing magnificent table ware, perfectly potted, lavishly gilded and enamelled in brilliant unflakable colours. Owners of small services of late Chinese export porcelain could have them enlarged by ordering additional matching pieces in Spode's felspar porcelain.

Fine-quality enamels in green, yellow, blue, olive, purple, rose and brown, each in various tints, were used for the fashionable armorial dinner services in which each piece displayed an expansive coat of arms in full colour. Sometimes an old-gold colour was substituted for gilding, purposely omitted to create more harmonious effects. Dessert services might be painted with landscapes bordered by conventional flowers. As a wedding gift in 1826 W. T. Copeland received from Josiah Spode an expensive dessert service of felspar porcelain in the fashionable apple-green ground colour. Each piece had a deep, intricate openwork border with white rosette ornament in relief at each intersection. Cottage-shaped pastille burners and night-lights were made in felspar porcelain because it would model meticulously and would not crack under the prolonged heat of burning pastille or mortar.

Spode pattern books, still in existence, display a remarkable series of designs for table services, dressing-table ornaments, pastille burners, vases with landscapes and flower ornament, lavishly gilded by a method invented by Henry Daniel, their chief gilder.

Spode continued the manufacture of felspar porcelain, but under the Copeland-Garrett partnership of 1833 production was abandoned. The mark, printed in puce, consisted of SPODE in Gothic letters above a wreath of rose, thistle and shamrock containing 'Felspar Porcelain' in script. On felspar porcelain made during George IV's coronation year this mark was additionally encircled STOKE UPON TRENT STAFFORD AND PORTUGAL STREET LONDON and the date 1821 within the wreath. Spode, who had been potter to the King as Prince since 1806, supplied a Regent and Prince of Wales felspar porcelain service for the coronation banquet.

John Rose of Coalport made felspar porcelain from about 1815 until the 1840s. In 1818 he obtained felspar from a newly-discovered deposit in the near-by Breddon Hills, Welshpool. By incorporating this in the body he produced an 'Improved Feltspar Porcelain' rivalling that of Spode. It proved to be one of the whitest and most translucent ceramics ever to be made in England. Its fine quality delighted the London china-sellers, who urged Rose to imitate early Sèvres porcelain. George IV while Regent had set the fashion for collecting gorgeously decorated Sèvres, and demand became very great. Rose potted considerable quantities of pseudo-Sèvres porcelain marked with the crossed L's and on rare occasions accompanied by a naturalistic rose painted in puce.

Decorations in fine enamels included flowers, birds, animals, landscapes, garlands, bouquets, chinoiserie motifs, *fêtes galantes*, portraits—every subject associated with early Sèvres. They were displayed against beautiful backgrounds of dark blue, light blue, turquoise, apple green and soft pink, always slightly deeper in hue than the genuine Sèvres. It is interesting to remember in this connection that T. M. Randall at near-by Madeley was also copying Sèvres porcelain, and carrying on a considerable trade as a decorator of French porcelain.

Early Coalport felspar porcelain, pre-1820, was backstamped JRFP Co in red. The later mark, also printed in red, consisted of a circle two inches in diameter inscribed 'Coalport (Improved) Feltspar Porcelain' within a fruiting laurel wreath encircled 'Patronised by the Society of Arts. The Gold Medal awarded May 30th, 1820'. The central inscription might include the name 'J. Rose'.

To own a dinner and dessert service in felspar porcelain was a rich man's privilege, but Josiah Spode II evolved a less costly ceramic body which he named stone china. It is usually stated, wrongly, that Spode acquired the Turner brothers' patent and adapted it to his requirements. There is, however, little resemblance between the formulae of the Turners' stoneware and Spode's stone china.

The London china-sellers first displayed stone-china dinner-table ware in 1805. Its name is perhaps somewhat misleading technically, for stone china resembles hard porcelain only superficially and is not a porcelain in the usually accepted sense, but good-quality glazed earthenware with a dense opaque body which emits a clear ring when lightly tapped. It is double the weight of earthenware and displays a blue-grey tint. An improvement was made in stone china in about 1810 and for five years this was marketed as New Stone China. Spode had discovered that potash felspar vitrified more slowly than soda felspar and reduced the risk of warping. It also lessened the tendency to absorb smoke and thus the bluish-grey hue was lightened. No alteration occurred in weight or hardness, but the pores were filled more regularly and completely than formerly. This produced a smooth unflawed surface without undulations, perfect for blue transfer-printing under the glaze; unlike ordinary earthenware of the period it did not require close ornament to conceal specks and pitting. The delicate blue was an attractive ground for the colourful Anglo-Chinese designs which decorated it. The characteristic decorations were versions of the *famille rose* style developed on Chinese porcelain in the 18th century, executed in opaque enamels and named from the range of rose colours derived from purple of cassius.

Stone china at first was painted by artists in enamelling. Exact copies of East India patterns were produced, but adaptations more attractive to English taste were quickly evolved. Then, to speed production and reduce costs, outlines were printed underglaze and enamelled overglaze in a limited palette consisting mainly of flat washes of pink, blue and red with touches of gilding.

One outstanding success was the peacock and peony pattern, in which a pair of colourful peacocks confront a huge, pink peony flower and a spray of prunus blossom. This was thought by Jewitt to have been introduced in 1814. The parrot design was equally popular, showing an urn of flowers and a parrot against a background of mountain and lake. Spode's mosaic pattern continued until the mid-19th century, with grounds of various colours such as blue and deep yellow overprinted with a network of lines to suggest cracking ice. After being glazed the mosaic was enamelled with a single large spray of prunus blossom and a bird. The Chinese version signified the death of winter and the coming of spring. The cracked ice might be replaced by marbling.

The reddish-brown edges of Oriental hard porcelain were rough and sharp: Spode rounded the edges of his felspar porcelain and stone china. The Oriental paste and glaze did not permit the enamels to sink in, and thus gave a raised, slightly rough surface to decorations. In stone china the enamels sank into the surface and so did not flake in use.

Spode's stone china quickly established itself among the well-to-do, and its strength and attractive colours led to an extension of the fashion for huge dinner services, sometimes numbering as many as 250 pieces, that lasted for half a century to come.

Spode marked his stone china with a square seal containing pseudo-Chinese characters, the name SPODE across the middle and STONE CHINA below. This was usually printed in blue, but pre-1810 examples were in black. From 1810 to 1815 SPODES NEW STONE was impressed, but the firm then returned to the original mark. During the period 1833 to 1846 the mark was NEW JAPAN STONE; afterwards COPELAND STONE CHINA.

Spode's success prompted other potters to copy his new stone china. John Davenport of Longport was perhaps the first to do this, in dinner and dessert services of faultless quality. Like Spode he adopted Oriental patterns for many decorations, these closely resembling the originals. For others, he painted landscapes, flowers, fruit or birds in alternate compartments of blue and white. These were usually gilded lavishly. In stone china, too, he made jugs in the octagonal shapes now associated with Mason. Downman and Gunn refer to the fine quality of his plates with openwork rims. Two marks were used by Davenport on his stone china: DAVENPORT in a ribbon supported by a pair of pillars with an anchor between and STONE CHINA beneath, all impressed; and a circular garter bearing DAVENPORT LONGPORT STAFFORDSHIRE, encircling STONE CHINA in script, all printed in red, with an impressed anchor. To this mark the address 82 FLEET STREET might be added.

The celebrated Wedgwood firm made stone china for a few years, ceasing in about 1825. Examples are rare and should not be confused with the productions of E. Wedgwood and Co. who operated in the third quarter of the century and impressed domestic table ware STONE CHINA E. WEDGWOOD & Co.

Many other potters made stone china, most of them anonymously, merely impressing STONE CHINA without name or trade-mark. Such work is usually of mediocre quality. Among the potters who named their stone china was the firm of John and William Ridgway, of Bell Bank, Hanley. Their products, dating between 1814 and 1830, were transfer-printed with a lop-sided shield surrounded by scrollwork and containing the name of the pattern such as 'Indian Temple' with STONE CHINA JWR below. In 1830 John and William parted, John to carry on the family business at Cauldon Place. William continued at Bell Bank, still making stone china, enamelled and gilt, transfer-printed and flown. Examples have been noted impressed W RIDGWAY STONE CHINA. When William Ridgway failed in 1854, the pottery was acquired by J. W. Pankhurst and Co., who made fine-quality table services in stone china for the American market. These were printed with an adaptation of the royal arms above the inscription STONE CHINA J W PANK-HURST & Co.

John Edwards and Sons established a pottery at Dale Hall, Burslem, in 1842, installing the most up-to-date machinery then available, including among their productions stone china of good, firm, semi-transparent quality. Jewitt listed 'barley, rope, tulip, scroll and medieval' among their patterns. The printed mark was an adaptation of the royal arms above STONE CHINA and the firm's name: from about 1860 there was a dolphin entwined around an anchor beneath.

Anthony Shaw, Mersey Pottery, Burslem, specialised in stone china for the American market from 1850. It was of poor quality, crudely decorated, and marked with the royal arms heading the inscription WARRANTED/ANTHO NYSHAW/BURSLEM/STONE CHINA.

Stonewares were soon overtaken by several improved felspathic earthenwares marketed under such names as opaque porcelain, semi-porcelain, demi-porcelain and finally granite ware. These were all of considerable strength, moderately hard, of uniform texture, pure white and rather less transparent than bone china. Their opacity was due to deficiency of flux and to being fired at a temperature too low to produce translucency. The standard formula consisted of Cornish stone 40 parts, china clay 35, blue ball clay 18, calcined flint 7, but each potter varied this to suit his own convenience. Poor qualities were distinguished by their greater opacity and slightly yellowish tinge, which might be whitened by the addition of cobalt oxide. These felspars all emitted a clear ringing note when struck. Because of their cheapness, long-wearing qualities and gaudy colouring they were made by the ton for cottage use. Vast quantities were exported.

These felspathic earthenwares were notable to Victorians for the colourful results obtained by underglaze decoration. The white porous body was an extremely good ground upon which to apply colours protected from wear and food acids by the covering of transparent glaze. The fusibility of the glaze permitted a larger palette to be employed and produced brighter colours than was possible in underglaze decoration on porcelains.

The value of the colours used, and the absorptive quality of the body, necessitated the employment of highly skilled artists for this work, sure of touch, for once the colour was applied it was impossible for it to be removed. This freedom of brushwork gave decoration on these wares a freshness and beauty not found on other earthenwares.

After painting, the wares were fired to a red heat to drive off the oils used in the colours so that glazing would not be clouded. The colours that matured at the same temperature were purple, violet, brown, grey, black, red, orange, yellow, green, blue and a bluish green. These were all dull until glazed. The enamels for overglaze decoration were made by mixing stoneware glaze and adding colour and a little plastic clay of the same formula as the basic body to make them adhere. These earthenwares are also found decorated with colour-ful glazes, coloured engobes and lustres.

The term semi-porcelain used in connection with felspathic earthenware dates from 1850, when it was introduced by G. Grainger and Co., Worcester. Because of its low cost, durability and attractive appearance the china-sellers placed substantial orders. The sur-face is pure white with the superficial appearance of bone china, made more complete by enamelling and gilding. It has the advantage of being completely vitrified, so that in the event of chipping its original colour is displayed, not a disfiguring cream or brown flaw as with ordinary earthenware. At the Great Exhibition the Grainger firm showed dinner and dessert plates, soup tureens, vegetable dishes, ewers and basins in semi-porcelain. Semi-porcelain became especially demanded for dinner services, as it was found to retain heat longer than any other ceramic. Grainger continued production until 1889 when the firm amalgamated with the Royal Worcester Porcelain Company. John Edwards, Foley Pottery, was also a maker of semi-porcelain.

Opaque porcelain and opaque china were terms used for the finer felspathic earthen-wares. These were porcellaneous in appearance and glazed by the same methods then used for bone china. Because of this evenness and durability of glaze the ware became a success-ful competitor with French hard porcelain.

The earliest use of the term opaque china was by Baker, Bevan and Irwin, Swansea, who potted between 1814 and 1839. The mark B B & I OPAQUE CHINA has been found impressed on dinner services of the 1830s. Bates, Walker and Co., Burslem, potted out-standing opaque porcelain table ware, and jugs in an immense range of shapes, and were responsible for some of the most richly ornamented spirit barrels so fashionable during the 1860s and 1870s. Their printed mark was a nude figure kneeling and holding a ewer, based on a plinth inscribed 1790 above OPAQUE PORCELAIN, B W & Co.

Edward Clarke, Tunstall, was another outstanding potter in opaque porcelain from about 1860. The marks were: impressed, EDWARD CLARKE; printed, the royal arms above a ribbon inscribed EDWARD CLARKE/PORCELAIN OPAQUE/TUNSTALL. Opaque porcelain made by Bridgwood and Clarke, Churchyard Works, Burslem, dates between the mid-1850s and 1874. Cleverly decorated services of table ware were advertised, im-pressed with the name and bearing also a printed mark, the royal arms above PORCELAIN OPAQUE/B & C/BURSLEM. Among the fifty or more makers of this ware, most of it un-marked, were the productions of Isaac Wilson and Co., the Middlesbrough Pottery, three well-known patterns being named Convolvulus, Trent and Nunthorpe. The ware was impressed I W & Co.

The final phase of felspathic earthenware was potted under the name of white granite, its very name suggesting great strength to purchasers. This label was evolved by the American china-sellers who admired its hardness, evenness of surface and durability of glaze. The Staffordshire potters adopted the term granite in various forms from the late

1850s. In 1860 the Davenport firm advertised 'the hardest and most durable earthenware in white granite'. It was made chiefly in two qualities: pure white and light-weight for the city trade; bluish-tinted and heavy for the country trade. Its unusual strength made it suitable for transport, and vast markets were opened in the United States, Canada, India, Australia and many other countries. Granite ware was now used on ships, replacing pewter.

Some granite ware was potted in shapes and decorations imitating French hard-paste porcelain, less carefully finished but much lower in price. Sampson Bridgwood and Son, Fenton, named their version Parisian granite. This was a hard body, excellently glazed, and painted in the styles used on bone china. Dessert, dinner, tea and breakfast services were made, as well as toilet sets. Parisian granite was impressed with an oval enclosing the name LIMOGES P G, the initials indicating Parisian granite. This was accompanied by a printed mark consisting of an elaborate shield of arms with mantlings and sceptres above the inscription PORCELAIN OPAQUE/BRIDGWOOD & SON. This is proof that Victorian opaque porcelain and white granite were one and the same thing. J. and G. Meakin, Hanley, issued granite ware in imitation of French hard-paste porcelain, marked with their name printed in black.

The most handsome of granite ware is attributed to James Edwards, Burslem, his standard of excellence in all wares being the aim of his competitors. In 1842 he installed the most modern appliances in his factory, increasing his output sixfold without extending the premises. His impressed mark was EDWARDS DH, with a variety of printed marks all of which incorporated the name. The Old Hall Earthenware Co., Hanley, made white granite with a clear hard glaze upon which colours were highly brilliant. The mark of William and Thomas Adams, Tunstall, is found on granite ware decorated in relief. The firm issued excellent transfer-printed and sponged work. Several potters made only plain white granite, the majority bearing no mark. Among the exceptions were Henry Burgess, Burslem, and Wood and Co., Cobridge, who both marked their ware with an adaptation of the royal arms above the name printed in black.

7

Ironstone China

IRONSTONE CHINA was made in great quantity less than 130 years ago. Its name is coupled with the family of Mason and is thus one of the period's major success stories. More than this, the ware was patented and its formula and manufacturing details are thus available. Yet it appears that those who have studied the matter have entirely failed to appreciate one basic reason for its success. Indeed, some have even suggested that Charles James Mason deliberately supplied fictitious information to the Patent Office to protect his formula. Obviously his method of furnishing the necessary details was successfully misleading, but he never risked the legal consequences of providing false information. All he did was to detail a costly, laboratory method of producing one of the main ingredients which, in fact, he obtained from a Wolverhampton firm where it was produced under an earlier patent that termed it 'prepared iron stones'.

The story begins in the last years of the 18th century, when affluent Englishmen were fascinated by the magical delicacy and glowing colours of porcelains from China, from Sèvres and from Meissen. Suddenly in 1794 a high tariff was levied upon imported porcelains, a protective measure prompted by English potters competing with the subsidised state porcelains of Europe. One of the principal importers had been Miles Mason, 131, Fenchurch Street, London, who was now faced with sales reduced to an unremunerative level.

Twenty prosperous years as a china-seller had obviously familiarised Mason with fashionable porcelain styles. To stock his depleted showrooms with the radiantly enamelled domestic ware he had customarily sold and which he well knew was in continual demand, he found it necessary to establish himself as a potter. By 1796 he had entered into partnership with James Wolfe and John Lucock at the Islington China Manufactory, Liverpool, and with George Wolfe as an earthenware potter at Lane Delph, Staffordshire. The Wolfes were practical potters, while Mason became responsible for finance and sales management. In 1800 he appears to have withdrawn from the Liverpool venture and become sole proprietor of the pottery at Lane Delph. The *London Directory*, 1801, shows that he traded as Miles Mason and Co.

He now specialised in the newly developed bone china such as apparently had been

25. Rockingham bone china pastille burner in the form of a gabled house encrusted with creepers and flowers.

26. A dish in Chamberlain's Worcester bone china, the rim modelled and gilded with shells and scrolls in high relief, decorated in natural colours, the centre painted with a view of Buckingham Palace from the garden. Marked CHAMBER-LAINS in red.

27 and 28. (Below) Sunderland earthenware wall plaque shaped into an ornate 'frame' coloured with pink and copper lustres enclosing a sailing ship in black transfer printing. (Lower right) Staffordshire earthenware crime piece: 'A view of the Red Barn at Polestead', with figures of Maria Martin and William Corder at the doors.

29 and 30. (Left) A giant earthenware jug with decoration in blue transfer printing, showing the use of the same repetitive scenes and flower borders adapted to fit the areas to be decorated. Made by Bourne, Baker and Bourne, Fenton, Staffordshire. (Below) Blue and white teapot printed with the milkmaid pattern introduced by Josiah Spode II in 1814.

31 and 32. (Below) Spode plates in transfer printed blue and white. (Left) Soup plate decorated with 'Chase After a Wolf' from the series of 'Oriental Field Sports' after drawings by William Howitt. (Right) The Tower pattern adapted from an aquatint published in Merigot's *Views of Rome and its Vicinity*, 1798. The first date of manufacture was 1814.

produced at Liverpool, and by 1804 had evolved stone china, a tough felspathic earthen-ware with a glaze impervious even to dinner knives. These wares he decorated with enamels of exceptional brilliance, in designs that were Anglicised versions of the Oriental. Miles Mason now closed his London warehouse and concentrated entirely on production. Sales were phenomenal, and in June, 1813, he retired, a rich man.

The business he transferred to his sons George Miles (1789—1859) and Charles James (1791—1856), and within six weeks Charles James Mason was granted a patent for a new ceramic body. The brothers exploited this under the name of ironstone china, but it was described in the patent as 'English Porcelain' to distinguish it from bone china, then advertised by Spode as 'Stoke Porcelain'. The ironstone china contained 'prepared iron stone', an ingredient new to ceramics. J. Nicholson, in *Operating Mechanic*, 1825, des-cribed ironstone china as 'not very transparent; but possesses great strength, compactness, density and durability'.

Decoration in pseudo-Oriental designs was carried out in brightly coloured enamels. These were mechanically ground in a manner newly introduced to the pottery trade. This drastically cut costs, so that the colours could be applied lavishly and in flat washes, a method that was speedy and effective. The predominating colours were mazarine blue, brick red, pink and crimson—enamels that could be fired together. Other colours, such as green, yellow and gold could at that time be fired only individually. Much of this colour work was painted over black or blue transfer-printed patterns. Ironstone china, with its brilliant decoration, toughness and comparatively low cost, was tremendously successful. In 1815 George and Charles Mason moved to more extensive premises near by, eventually building a long row of four-storied workshops with mills and kilns at the rear.

Ceramic authorities have long discussed the composition of Mason's ironstone china at this period. In concluding that his formula was fictitious, however, they have overlooked the important fact that the specification supplied to the Patent Office by Charles James Mason was 'under my hand and seal'. It was illegal, then as now, to enter false specifica-tions, even if it were possible to deceive the officials concerned. Such a specification was invariably pronounced 'void', and such instances are recorded.

The specification begins:

'Charles James Mason of Lane Delph,
'near Newcastle-under-Line [*sic*] in the County of Stafford Potter.
'No. 3724 31st July 1813
'A process for the Improvement of the Manufacture of English Porcelain.'

The specification continues with a complicated description of a glassy frit produced by means of what was no more than a miniature of the kind of blast furnace then in use. Prepared in this way such a frit would inevitably be wasteful and costly: in any case the quantity required for a prosperous pottery, twenty per cent of each batch, could be produced only by means of a commercial blast furnace.

Mason was well aware that commercial blast furnaces were indeed then producing such a frit, which he described as 'scoria or slag'. Until 1813 it had been considered a useless dross to be thrown upon the waste heap. Then 'patent iron stones' were marketed by Aaron Manby, an iron-master of Wolverhampton in the same county. These were made under a patent granted in May, 1813, to John Mander, chemist, Aaron Manby, and Joseph Vernon, a furnace-man. These patent ironstones were composed of molten slag that flowed from iron furnaces. This was drawn off into moulds shortly before the puddlers tapped the iron and was gradually cooled in annealing flues.

The top layer of this slag was a glassy material, pale green in colour, closely resembling frit, and about as transparent. No doubt its resemblance to frit prompted Charles Mason to incorporate it in his patent as 'Prepared Iron Stone'. This material is not to be confused with the lava-coloured blast-furnace clinker or slag which under the Mander-Manby-Vernon patent was converted into 'Forms that may be used for any Purpose to which Brick, Quarry, Tile, Slate or Stone are now applied'.

Some at least of the transparent slag was obtained at a later date from the blast furnaces of Edward Giles, Wednesfield Heath, near Wolverhampton, who despatched it to the Potteries by canal. Mason saved much on the transport costs as compared with the carriage of material from Cornwall. Giles built an extensive rockery in his garden from large irregular blocks of this glassy slag, and when this was examined some years ago it was possible to discern objects through a block nine inches thick in spite of a 120-year film of smoke. Thin slivers were virtually transparent. This glassy slag was also used by Stourbridge glass-houses from the late 1830s, pressed into heavy ornamental ware.

In Mason's formula this glassy substance was 'pounded into small pieces and ground in water to the consistency of a fine paste at the slip mills. This paste is next evaporated to dryness on a slip kiln well known amongst potters. Thus evaporated to dryness it is used with other ingredients in the following proportions, viz.:

	cwt.	qr.	lb.
'Prepared Iron Stone	3	0	0
'Ground flint	4	0	0
'Ground Cornwall Stone	4	0	0
'Cornwall Clay	4	0	0
'Blue oxide of cobalt			1

'These, having been mixed together with water by the slip maker, are again evaporated on the slip kiln to the proper consistency for use. The clay thus prepared is, of course, used in the usual way in the fabrication of vessels.'

Some of the finer domestic ware in patent ironstone china was virtually covered with brilliant-hued enamels and gilding in patterns adapted from the Chinese, such as had been imported by Miles Mason. These included Anglicised versions of the beautiful *famille verte* in which clear green predominated, and the *famille rose* dominated by opaque shades from delicate pink to deep crimson. Flowers and foliage included 'Flowers of the Four Seasons': peony of spring, lotus of summer, chrysanthemum of autumn, prunus of winter. The peach, double cherry, magnolia and gardenia are among others seen. Fabulous birds, occasional animals, butterflies and insects are to be noted, as well as vivid scenes from Chinese domestic life with gardens and landscapes.

The Masons made jugs, octagonal on plan and with snake handles. These, with their sparkling brilliance of colours, immediately captured the imagination of a colour-starved public. The Tait collection contains a set of fourteen of these jugs in sizes ranging in height from two and a half to ten inches. These were rather crudely finished with a heavy, faintly blue glaze, and obviously produced to satisfy an inexpensive market. The colour, quickly applied over printed outlines, consisted chiefly of reds, blues and greens, with an occasional excursion into pink, puce, pale green, patches of black and brown. Many quaint, jumbled designs were used, particularly *Imari* patterns such as were decorating contemporary bone china. The motifs noted on a collection of twenty-three examples included the following, either singly or, more usually, in combination: large flowers resembling a peony and a full-blown rose, sprigs of prunus and daisies, all with foliage. Better-quality jugs were more meticulously enamelled and might display gilding. Mugs of all shapes were also made, some cylindrical, others octagonal, and perhaps containing a hollow toad.

George and Charles Mason potted immense quantities of this patent ironstone china, and after expiry of the patent in 1827 they met with competition from other potters. This possibly caused an accumulation of stock, for the brothers held periodic auction sales. A *Times* editorial in early May, 1828, commented that at a sale of patent ironstone china held in London, more than a thousand lots were sold at prices ranging from £20 to £30 each. This was probably the sale advertised in the *London Morning Herald* of April 21st, 1828: 'China of the most elegant description, embracing a great variety of splendid dinner services, numerous dessert services, tea, coffee and breakfast sets of neat and elegant patterns, ornaments of every description that can be manufactured in china, from the minutest article calculated to adorn pier table and cabinet, to the most noble, splendid, and magnificent jars some of which are nearly five feet high.' Two of these jars or vestibule vases, painted and gilded, and one with ornament in relief, are in the Hanley Museum. A further advertisement in *The Times*, May 24th, announced a sale of 'patent stoneware for coffee houses, tavern keepers and hotels'. In 1829 George Mason retired, to devote himself to politics, the firm then trading as Charles J. Mason and Co.

Charles Mason was responsible for some huge pieces of work in ironstone china, such as the so-called fish tank—really a wine cistern—in the Victoria and Albert Museum, and showily enamelled and gilded fireplaces of which a number remain, six different models having been noted. These are in two sizes, with forty-two-inch and twenty-two-inch openings. Decoration might be in the Chinese taste or rococo.

The rococo fireplaces are moulded in high relief, mainly with large, trailing acanthus-leaf patterns and masks thickly gilded and burnished and so designed as to provide smooth panels painted with flower and foliage sprays in pink, puce, pale green, apple green, vermilion and blue. Ground colours were also used and those noted include dark blue, apple-green and yellow. Three fireplaces have been inspected and all possess ground colours applied by a process introduced in 1826 by Henry Daniell of Shelton. These grounds were less fusible than those used by the enamellers, and were unaffected by firings required for subsequent decoration. Miniature models of ironstone fireplaces are known, distributed by Mason for shop-window display. For more than a century one has stood in a builder's office window behind Oxford Street in London.

Mason fireplaces are marked with a printed trade-mark in brown measuring about six inches across and four inches deep, composed mainly of the coat-of-arms of William IV, above which is the inscription 'China Chimney Pieces, Mason & Co., Patentees, Staffordshire Potteries' and below 'Patent Ironstone China'. This mark therefore dates after the retirement of George Mason in 1829 and before the accession of Queen Victoria in 1837. The use of the royal arms by potters other than warrant holders was forbidden by Queen Victoria in 1838.

The earliest trade-mark to be used by the brothers Mason was impressed in capitals, MASON'S PATENT IRONSTONE CHINA, in a line when convenient, in a circle without the name Mason on small ware. This was succeeded, probably from about 1815, by a mark transferred in red, blue, puce or jet black. This was composed of a crown with the name 'Mason's' above and 'Patent Ironstone China' in a cartouche below. There are numerous variations in the details of the crown: probably there was a chronological significance in these changes.

Improvements in puddling processes by the mid-1840s caused the glassy dross floating on the molten metal to display a deep purple tinge, thus making it useless for ceramic purposes. C. J. Mason then of necessity changed his formula, adding a proportion of flint-glass instead. The trade-mark was changed by substituting the word 'improved' for 'patent'.

The demand for ironstone china continued, and by the late 1840s several potters were producing huge quantities, much of it for export. It must be realised, of course, that this ware was not the real ironstone china but was comparable with the revised Mason formula. A typical firm was that of T. Furnival and Sons, who operated at Cobridge from the late 1840s. Jewitt in 1878 recorded that this firm produced 'beautiful patent ironstone dinner and other services of various qualities in point of decoration. Among their most recent productions are table services of rich Italian design, plain white with a china-like surface and glaze; the ornamentation, which is indented, is produced from an embossed mould, the lines being as fine and delicate as if cut by the graver, so as to have the appearance of chasing; and the lines being filled with glaze the surface is still even. Some of their ironstone china is attractively painted with grasses and insects. The mark is FURNIVAL impressed'.

T. and R. Boote made ironstone china from about 1850. Examples inspected have always been off-white, speedily hand-painted domestic ware impressed with the initials T & R B and printed in black with a greyhound between two laurel wreaths and the inscription T & R BOOTE/ROYAL PREMIUM/IRONSTONE. In 1857 this was superseded by the royal arms above the inscription ROYAL PATENT/IRONSTONE. The royal arms and reference to a patent have no association with ironstone, but concern a method of making inlaid mosaic ware for which the firm were granted a patent in 1857.

Collectors discovering ironstone china impressed WEDGWOOD & CO are often led into the belief that it is the production of Josiah Wedgwood and Sons, Etruria. It was the production of a firm operating at Tunstall from the late 1850s, the head being Enoch Wedgwood, J.P. Their ironstone china is notable for the excellence of its body, glaze and decoration: printed in various colours wholly or partially hand painted, enamelled and gilded. Wedgwood and Co's version of the Asiatic pheasant was much superior to the average in application and in colour. Ironstone services decorated with coats-of-arms and crests in full colours were a feature recorded by Jewitt. This ironstone was impressed IMPERIAL IRONSTONE CHINA in a ring encircling WEDGWOOD & Co.

The name Challinor is associated with a number of successful patterns on ironstone china, some of them evolved in the late 1850s and still popular in 1880, such as the embossed garland and vine-leaf, and wheat patterns. Names of designs transferred beneath jugs collated by Jewitt include wheat, barberry, lily, lotus, Paris, Versailles and Florence. The mark is a Staffordshire knot impressed, and in the case of ironstone this was accompanied by IRONSTONE/CHINA/E & C CHALLINOR. The printed mark consisted of the royal arms above a ribbon emblazoned IRONSTONE CHINA A & C CHALLINOR FENTON.

Among other makers of marked ironstone china were:

Thomas Hughes, Brownhills, from 1856 until the 1880s; impressed THOMAS HUGHES /IRONSTONE CHINA.

James and George Meakin, Tunstall, after succeeding their father in 1852, entered the ironstone-china trade; their printed mark was the royal arms and the words IRONSTONE CHINA/J & G MEAKIN.

Holland and Green acquired a long-established pottery in Longton during 1853 and made ironstone of excellent quality, some of it decorated with ground colours *rose du Barry* and brunswick green of outstanding clarity and brilliance. The printed mark was the royal arms above IRONSTONE/HOLLAND & GREEN.

8

Parian Ware

THE ENORMOUS gallery of parian statuary which garnished the vestibules and drawing rooms of the early Victorians was a triumph of the Staffordshire potters. Parian was introduced to the china-sellers of London in 1842 by the firm of Copeland and Garrett, the culmination of long, arduous and costly experimental work by Thomas Battam under the direction of Spencer Garrett, son of the partner Thomas Garrett. The first piece of parian statuary to be publicly released was 'Apollo as the Shepherd Boy of Admetus', by J. R. Wyatt, R.A. The original marble was in the collection of the Duke of Sutherland at nearby Trentham Park. The Duke showed his enthusiasm for the new porcelain by becoming Copeland's patron of parian ware on August 3rd, 1842. This date is important in the annals of the Staffordshire Potteries as establishing an English porcelain technique which continued in its finest expression for a full quarter-century.

Meanwhile, Herbert Minton, a near neighbour of Copeland's, was engaged in a similar project, the experiments being carried out under the control of John Mountford. Mountford, who always maintained that he was the inventor of parian, was himself a leading manufacturer of parian statuary by 1850.

The Jury of the Great Exhibition examining ceramic manufactures required William Taylor Copeland and Herbert Minton to submit statements regarding priority of production. Their report stated that they 'could not recommend an award of the Council Medal for the invention of parian without deciding on the disputed claim of priority... and have not felt it our duty to come to any such decision, especially as it would appear from the statement of each party, that whichever may have actually been first in publicly producing articles in this material, both were contemporaneously working with success towards the same result'.

Statuary parian is a highly vitrified biscuit porcelain, silky to the touch and notable for its lustrous transparency and for the delicacy of detail into which it can be modelled. The old ivory tint of early statuary, reminiscent of the marble of Paros and hence the name parian, was outmoded during the 1850s by pure white statuary, although the ivory tint continued throughout the period.

The introduction of parian statuary was well timed, harmonising as it did with the

Victorian desire for overcrowding in interior decoration. Its astonishing popularity, especially in nudes, attracted an army of outstanding sculptors, encouraged by William Taylor Copeland, who invited them to his London home to make models. Thus was inaugurated a period of artistic animation unknown to the Potteries since the days of Josiah Wedgwood.

Copeland himself commissioned models regardless of expense. At first these were reduced copies of existing statues: the original sculptor usually commissioned minor artists to do this work. An aid to the carver was soon found in a sculpturing machine patented in 1844 by Benjamin Cheverton (specification No. 10,015, January 16th, 1844).[1] With this it was possible to reduce three-dimensional statues or busts to similarly proportioned miniatures. Cheverton was continually called upon to produce alabaster copies of statuary for the parian potters: there is no evidence that he licensed his machine to others. This accounts for the cryptic 'Cheverton Sc' found impressed beneath some parian statuary obviously the work of others. One of these machines was operated daily at the Great Exhibition, the Jury awarding Cheverton a gold medal for his mechanised miniature in alabaster of 'Theseus' from the Eling collection in the British Museum. This was used 'for the purpose of casting in plaster with an accuracy which leaves the most fastidious critic nothing to desire'.

'Ino and the Infant Bacchus', by J. H. Foley, the original of which is now in the Victoria and Albert Museum, was copied for parian reproduction by Copeland and the alabaster model engraved with Cheverton's signature. This is illustrated on p. 711 of the catalogue of the Great Exhibition, where both the original marble and the parian reduction were on view. The latter bears the name Copeland impressed and a diamond-shaped pad with letters and numerals showing that the design was registered (see p. 171) at the Patent Office on December 4th, 1845. Among other registered statuary were 'Una and the Lion', by John Bell, October 4th, 1847, and 'Lady Clementina Villiers', by McDonald, December 4th, 1845.

At least six other marbles in the Sculpture Court had miniature counterparts among the Copeland exhibits. These included figures of the royal children represented as the Seasons modelled after originals commissioned by Queen Victoria from Mrs Thornycroft. These were Princess Alice as 'Spring', the Princess Royal as 'Summer', Prince Alfred as 'Autumn' and the Prince of Wales as 'Winter'. In addition there was a figure of Princess Helena. Others were 'Sabrina', by William Marshall, R.A.; 'Eve', by P. Macdowell; and 'Lady Godiva', by J. P. McBride.

'The Greek Slave', by American Hiram Powers created a sensation at the Exhibition, and Copeland acquired reproduction rights from the sculptor, who had secured for his masterpiece three years' protection against industrial piracy. Copeland sold a large number of this popular piece of parian statuary, measuring twenty inches in height and marked

[1] See *Wood Carving Machines,* by G. Bernard Hughes (*Country Life,* Vol. CXVI, p. 980).

'Published by W. T. Copeland late Spode 1 May 1852'. After mid-1855 inferior versions appeared, some cast directly from Copeland's copy. These measure about three-quarters the height of Copeland's: this feature distinguished other plagiarisms.

Venuses were highly popular with all potters of parian ware. Copeland issued at least six versions including 'Venus de Milo', 'Venus de Medici', Venus of the Capitol' and Venuses by Canova, Gibson and Thorwaldsen.

The list of Copeland's parian statuary at the 1851 Exhibition is useful to collectors in classifying early examples, for he seldom gave a figure more than a three-year run, although an exception was the best seller, 'Innocence'. This was made from an alabaster reduction carved by J. H. Foley, R.A., after his original statue in marble. The excellence of this model won Foley a prize of 100 guineas awarded by the Art Union of London. Copeland's parian copy, measuring sixteen and a half inches in height and dated 1847, was in production for ten years.

The portrait figures include Sir Robert Peel, by Westmacott; the Duke of Wellington and Lord George Bentinck, by Count D'Orsay; the Duke of Sutherland, by Francis; Jenny Lind, by John Durham, R.A.; Sir Walter Scott, by John Steel, R.S.A., 'from the original colossal statue on the Calton Hill'; and Baron Marochetti's equestrian statue of Emanuel Philibert, Duke of Savoy.

The remaining Copeland parian statuary were 'Venus and Narcissus', by John Gibson, R.A.; 'Rebecca' and 'The Prodigal's Return', both by W. Theed; 'Indian Girl', 'Nubian Girl', and 'Paul and Virginia', by Cumbersworth; and the groups 'Return from Vintage' and 'The Astragali Players'.

Herbert Minton and Co. produced some outstanding equestrian parian statuary, including 'Theseus', by Albert Carrier-Belleuse, the firm's own modeller, and 'Amazon', by Fauchère. Other celebrated modellers employed by Minton were Hugues Protat from 1848, and Emile Jeannest (*d.* 1857), who was instructor at Stoke School of Design.[1] The Minton display at the Exhibition consisted of 'Dorothea', 'Miranda', 'Clorinda', 'Una and the Lion', 'Triton and Nautilus', 'The Babes in the Wood', 'Shakespeare', busts of Michael Angelo and Raphael, a set of chessmen, all by John Bell; 'The Infant Neptune', by H. J. Townend; 'The Distressed Mother', by Sir R. Westmacott; 'Ariadne on a Panther', by Daneker; a pair of figure candlesticks in the costume of Louis XV, touched with gilt and mounted on pedestals enriched with gemstones. The works records include photographs of the following among other parian statuary: 'Autumn and Summer', by Carrier-Belleuse, and equestrian figures of Lady Godiva, Perseus and Andromeda, busts of Queen Victoria and the Prince Consort. Minton's continued parian statuary until the 1890s, when they produced a figure of the Princess May (later H.M. Queen Mary) on the occasion of her marriage to H.R.H. the Duke of York.

Herbert Minton was first to make dessert services in which parian statuary was combined

---

[1] *Staffordshire Chimney Ornaments*, by Reginald Haggar (1955).

33, 34 and 35. (Above) Staffordshire dishes transfer printed in underglaze blue, both 21½ inches long. (Left) An English version of the Oriental manner matched by a border in the same style. (Right) 'Triumphal Arch at Tripoli in Barbary' from the Caramanian series issued by Josiah Spode II, showing the brilliantly vivid three-dimensional effects obtainable with a single colour transfer print. (Below) A pair of Colebrookdale figure candlesticks and a figure, modelled with flowers in high relief.

36, 37 and 38. (Above) Leeds figures on square plinths, in pearl ware: left and right are a pair of musicians playing hurdy-gurdy and tambourine; in the centre is 'Mars', and flanking him are 'Spring' and 'Autumn' from a set of Seasons. (Left) Part of a tea and coffee service made at Derby early in the 19th century, each piece painted with landscape by John Brewer, surrounded by a frame of pearls and against a yellow ground marked with crown, crossed swords and dots, and DUESBURY DERBY.

with bone china. A dessert service, in which openwork baskets of bone china were supported by four cupids representing the seasons on plinths of bone china, was described
by the Jury of the Great Exhibition as of 'original design, presenting a high degree of
beauty and harmony of effect; design and modelling of the figures full of grace and spirit'.
Three dolphins might be used in place of the cupids. The parian was usually entirely plain
but might be touched with gilding. Pairs of wall brackets in the form of eagles or mask
heads are to be found bearing the impressed mark M and a date-letter.

Carrara was the name given by Josiah Wedgwood and Sons to their parian statuary,
considered by the firm to resemble the white statuary marble of Tuscany. The Jury of
the Great Exhibition recorded that carrara was less translucent than parian statuary.
Their entry in the Exhibition catalogue names no modellers, although it is known that the
firm commissioned fashionable models of Venus, nymphs and cupids, while employing
such outstanding modellers as Edward Keys during the late 1840s and Thomas Great-
bach from 1844 to 1864.

Sixteen examples were on view at the Exhibition: 'Figures from the Antique, Venus
and Cupid, 27 inches high; Cupid 24 inches; Infant Hercules 28 inches; Venus 19 inches;
Mercury 17 inches; Faun with Flute 17 inches. Busts of Washington, Shakespeare and
Venus. Figures: The Preacher on the Mount; Crouching Venus; Nymph at the Fountain;
Cupid and Psyche group; Cupid with bow.'

Some exceptionally fine parian statuary came from Charles Meigh and Son, Hanley,
whose entry in the Great Exhibition catalogue included 'Templar and Companion'. This,
no doubt, was the eighteen-inch group illustrated by Mr. Geoffrey Bemrose, impressed
on the plinth 'Vision of the Redcrosse Knight' and marked 'Joseph Pitts 1851'.[1] This
firm also exhibited: 'Falconer and Companion', 'Bather and Companion', 'Dancer and
Companion', 'Flora', 'Prometheus' and an ornamental clock case chased in gold.

The amazing success of parian statuary made by the great potters urged lesser firms to
enter this branch of potting, but no more than half a dozen achieved the fine surface
texture and sharpness of detail, the distinguishing features of perfect statuary. One was
John Rose and Co., Coalbrook Dale, Ironbridge, Shropshire—such is their address in the
catalogue of the Great Exhibition, where their parian entries were: 'Clock-case, gilt, with
figures of Time and Cupid. Elevated flower-vase, supported by Dolphins. Pair of wrestling
figures. Group of figures: "The Pleiades adorning Night". Basket supported by three
female figures. Ornamental Ewers. Group of figures: "Puck and Companions".'

Keys and Mountford, John Street, Stoke-upon-Trent, described themselves as
designers, inventors and manufacturers and referred to their parian productions as
'porcelain statuary'. Their catalogue entry is: 'Statuettes of Flora; Prometheus tormented
by the vulture; Venus unrobed at the bath; Two Circassian slaves. Group of three boys
with perforated baskets for dessert, centre piece. Statuette of Venus extracting a thorn.

[1] Plate 76, *19th-Century English Pottery and Porcelain*, 1952.

Group of two dogs, setter and pointer with game. Group of three greyhound dogs. Bacchanalian ewer from the antique.' These were impressed K & M. The partnership was dissolved in the late 1850s, Mountford continuing alone, impressing his figures J MOUNTFORD STOKE.

T. and R. Boote, Burslem, began making statuary in 1850 and at the Exhibition were able to display a number of excellent statuettes measuring twenty inches in height and including Venus, Bacchus, Shakespeare and Milton, as well as a bust of Sir Robert Peel modelled from his portrait by Sir Thomas Lawrence. These and later statuary were impressed T & R B.

J. Simpson, 28, Theobalds Road, London, issued a number of finely modelled nudes about eight inches high, sold within glass domes and all marked with his name in script around the base. Bell and Co., Glasgow, made bas-reliefs from the Elgin marbles in statuary parian. A bell is impressed on the back.

Haggar lists nearly thirty other Staffordshire potters who made parian statuary, ranging from Turton and Gregg, established in Hanley *c.* 1851, to the Harrops of Tinkersclough, who operated in 1889 and 1890. These include Samuel Alcock, Burslem: a figure of Venus has been noted impressed S A & Co.

The formula for making parian statuary was obviously well known by 1850, for Alderman Copeland published it below his entry in the catalogue of the Great Exhibition. This called for 40 parts felspar, 36 parts china-clay and 24 parts frit. The frit was prepared from 57 parts white sand, 11 parts Cornish stone, and 8 parts potash. Because this glassy frit is incorporated, parian statuary is included in the category of soft porcelain. Other potters might deviate from these proportions. The distinctive ivory tint of early statuary was due to traces of iron silicate in the felspar. This might be counteracted to some extent by the addition of cobalt, but pure white statuary was obtained by the use of Swedish felspar which proved to be free of iron silicate. In 1851 vast deposits of pure felspar were found in Ireland (see Chapter 23). The Royal Worcester Porcelain Co. at once took this into use and in the spring of 1853 were advertising 'Irish Statuary Porcelain'. They designed and made a magnificent dessert service modelled by W. B. Kirk, showing scenes from Shakespeare's *Midsummer Night's Dream.* This was displayed at the Dublin Exhibition, 1853, and described in the catalogue as 'from materials the produce of Ireland'. Staffordshire potters at once demanded the finer and less expensive Irish felspar.

The American potters quickly acquired the technique of making parian statuary, for early in 1844 John Harrison, a china-paste mixer from Copeland's, well provided with practical knowledge, was attracted to the United States.

The making of parian was a highly skilled branch of the potter's craft. The figures were cast in moulds from a slip of creamy consistency, several moulds being required for each figure. These casts were assembled into an exact copy of the original model, all parts being attached by a slip similar to that used for the castings. All parts liable to warp or move during firing were supported by an elaborate network of props made of the same material and therefore subject to similar contraction in the kiln. The ends of the props were coated with powdered calcined flint to prevent adhesion.

After standing for two or three days to ensure that no moisture remained, the assembled statuary was ready for firing in the biscuit oven, being by then sufficiently dry not to crack in the heat. Baking continued for sixty to seventy hours at a low temperature: the fires were then drawn and the oven gradually cooled. When the ware was cold the network of props was removed and the surface cleared of scars and flaws. The figures were then embedded in sand-filled saggers and refired at a greater heat. This sand-bedding adequately supported the figures during vitrification.

While progressing through the ovens parian figures contracted to about three-quarters of their original size. A figure made from a twenty-four-inch model measured about eighteen inches when finished, having lost one and a half inches by contraction of slip in the mould, another one and a half inches through evaporation in the drying oven, and a further three inches during vitrification.

A parian evolved during the late 1840s was found suitable for making hollow and other table ware. T. J. and J. Mayer have previously been credited with originating this paste, ideal for domestic ware, in about 1847. This has been set aside by the recent discovery of a set of three bacchante jugs by Charles Meigh, Hanley. These are impressed with the date September 10th, 1844, and a registration mark for September 30th, 1844. This became known as standard parian, differing from statuary parian in that it was a hard porcelain containing a much larger proportion of felspar and no frit. Composed of 67 parts felspar and 33 parts china-clay, it was capable of withstanding sudden changes of temperature caused by boiling water.

Standard parian was ideal for casting and resulted in much hollow-ware decoration in high relief. Unlike statuary parian, it did not automatically acquire a delicate surface glaze in the firing. A glaze was essential, but dipping into even the thinnest of lead glaze obscured the details of the clear-cut relief work which were so important a feature in the eyes of the purchaser. Smear glazing was therefore used. This was not applied directly to the parian, but introduced with it in a tightly sealed sagger. Whether placed in a small cup or thickly coated over the interior walls of the sagger, the glaze melted as the temperature rose and its vapour settled as a fine mist upon the surface of the parian. Hollow-ware intended to contain liquids was lead-glazed within, but the exterior was subjected to the volatisation process.

In addition to the usual range of domestic ware some large pieces were made. At the Great Exhibition, Herbert Minton displayed a chimneypiece of parian, enriched with gilding. He also exhibited a ewer and stand, now in the Victoria and Albert Museum, moulded in high relief and decorated with gilding; this is believed to have been modelled by Emile Jeannest.

63

Mayer also applied colour to parian, giving a rich, bright blue ground against which the moulded ornament stood out in white relief. The smooth areas to which the colour was to be applied were often stippled, the indentations suggesting a thimble. This pitting was brought about by carving raised points within the mould. This effect, known to some collectors as cameo parian, formed a fair imitation of Wedgwood's jasper, for which it is often mistaken by amateur collectors, even though process, texture, colour and appearance generally are entirely different.

The coloured background was produced by brush-applying slip to the parts of the mould where it was required. A slip for the body was then poured into the mould. The two slips immediately united by adhesion and without intermingling. Firing completed the union. From the mid-1850s brown or sage-green might be used. Usually the whole surface was smear glazed, but examples have been noted with the coloured ground lead-glazed, the figures in white relief remaining unglazed and standing out as if carved in marble. Other colours were occasionally used. A small bust decorated with blue, pink and green has been observed impressed with Mayer's name and a registration mark for 1855.

Harder standard parian ware might be sold uncoloured. Flat-ware was produced with a drier slip than normally used, from which the water had been removed until it was of a doughy consistency. This was rolled into flat sheets and then hand-pressed against the sides of the mould. Colour was never applied to the surface of hand-pressed parian.

Contemporary criticism[1] was made that 'the fine granular surface of parian has a positive attraction for dirt, and we do not like to be compelled to remember the inevitable impurities of parian tea-cups, butter dishes and beer jugs, in connection with the divine creations of art fitly enshrined in the same material'. For this reason fine statuary was preserved from dust beneath glass domes.

Silliman and Goodrich also deplored the use of 'this exquisite material, this happy substitute for marble in statuettes and works purely ornamental, being misapplied and degraded by being moulded into jugs, cups and candlesticks. One strange jug has an inverted pear-shaped body, with a spray of delicate flowers on each side, the opening is in the body of a swan with upstretched wings to form a spout—handle formed of the bird's neck attempting to swallow a rush from a group growing curiously out of the side and around the base of the jug, with sharp projecting leaves, a perpetual danger to the fingers.' Such a jug, recently sold for ten guineas, bore the 1850 registration mark.

The majority of standard parian was unmarked. The Copeland mark, however, proved the firm to have made some outstandingly attractive candlesticks and jugs; the Minton mark has been noted on a wide range of cleverly designed ware with discreetly applied gilding.

At Coalport, under John Rose and Co., parian ware was in considerable production. In 1850 they first marketed what proved to be a popular breakfast set consisting of a three-

[1] Silliman and Goodrich, 1854.

lobed tray with teapot, jug, sugar basin, two cups and saucers, ornamented with flowers and foliage in high relief. These sets continued in production until about 1860. The firm became celebrated for wall brackets catalogued as 'in the Raffaelesque style'. T. and R. Boote, Burslem, made tall vases, as much as three feet in height, in blue cameo parian with trailing vine leaves and bunches of grapes in relief, and others with flowers hand modelled. Their ornamental jugs, bulbous of body, slender of neck, with a high pedestal foot, were exquisitely worked with high-relief flowers and foliage against a blue ground and enclosed in oval panels. The deep undercutting carried out by hand after casting made them difficult to clean, and examples are uncommon.

A few of the firms whose impressed names have been noted on standard parian are: Bell and Co., Glasgow, who made ewers and stands after Cellini, sea-horse tazzas and sets of chessmen; William Brownfield and Sons, Cobridge, whose statuary figures were modelled by Albert Carrier-Belleuse; Moore Brothers, Longton; G. Grainger and Co., Worcester; Livesay, Powell and Co., Hanley; Robertson and Leadbeater, Stoke; Samuel Alcock and Co., Burslem; Turner, Hassall and Pearce, Stoke-upon-Trent.

9

Slip Ware and Welsh Ware

POTTER'S CLAY in a liquid, cream-like consistency offers the potter one of the simplest and most satisfying media for forthright ornament on everyday earthenwares. As a result, there is a tendency to give a date in the 18th century, if not earlier, to any piece of coarse ware made in reddish-burning clay and decorated with this clay slip. Yet such slip ware was being produced by many provincial potters in the 19th century, often using the old method of applying the slip by letting it trickle through a quill to make lines and dots, geometrical patterns, borders, conventional designs and so on. All slip ware dating earlier than the 1760s, and much that may be dated to a later period, was glazed by dusting finely powdered sulphide of lead over the unfired surface. The clay was then fired at a moderate temperature, baking the clay and melting the lead into glaze at one operation. If powdered calcined lead were used, blended with manganese, a range of highly glossy purples and browns was obtained; various shades of green by adding copper oxide. Slip ware of the 19th century was dipped into liquid lead glaze easily distinguished from the older glaze.

Slip ware was made by small potters working local clays, and each producing an individual type of goods. Three other types of ware were made in the 19th century: marbled slip ware; mocha ware; banded ware. In these the slip was applied mechanically.

Slip marbling was recorded by several writers in the late 17th century and continued unceasingly in production until late Victorian times. The marbled effect was obtained on the shaped earthenware by the application of thin lines or splashes of light-coloured slips in two or more shades, such as red and white, buff and brown, light red and buff, dark red and brown. While fairly moist these slips were worked singly or mingled together over the surface with a wire, leather or hook comb and a sponge, using the same technique as the paper marbler. Nineteenth-century marbling on jugs, mugs and dishes was carried out in Staffordshire, Yorkshire and Tyneside.

Granite marbling was an effect obtained by spraying earthenware with a grey or bluish mottled liquid lead glaze. This was evolved in the late 18th century by Josiah Wedgwood in imitation of granite. It was made also by Neale and Co. In the early 19th century Enoch Wood issued granite marbling, as also did small potters in Staffordshire.

Painted marbling ornamented cream-coloured earthenware and pearl ware from about 1815 to 1855. From Yorkshire came tankards and mugs, often with sharply fluted moulding at neck or foot, thinly coated with bright green glaze. The marbling resembled the freer type of paper marbling and covered the ware in streaks of yellow, reddish brown and chocolate colour. An example has been seen impressed with the name of the Don Pottery. Staffordshire and Swansea potted similar ware.

Marbling was later produced on earthenware and porcelain by a method patented in 1845 by C. J. Hullmandel. Upon a specially prepared bath of gum tragacanth and other constituents were floated unmingled colours such as could be drawn into any desired shape by the ordinary process of marbling. The ware, either glazed or unglazed, was immersed in the bath and took up colour, thus producing marbled patterns similar to those found on marbled paper. The method is fully described in Hullmandel's patent specification, No. 10,675, May 22nd, 1845. Usually such ware has been attributed wrongly to the early years of the century.

Mocha ware was so named because of its superficial resemblance to the quartz known as mocha-stone, and appears to have been evolved in the 1780s. Jewitt possessed a Lakin and Poole bill dated 1792 in which 'Mocha tumblers' are specified. The impressed mark of William Adams, Greengates, has been noted on several mocha mugs made before his death in 1805.

Early mocha decoration was applied to a creamware body, while by 1820 pearl ware might be used, and buff-coloured stoneware from about 1830. In earthenware a ground of coloured slip covered the shaped clay, various shades of yellow being usual: chestnut brown is invariably present on early earthenware. Over this was applied a pigment— usually brown, but blue, green and black were also used—mixed with a saturated infusion of tobacco and hops. This spread into the markings, suggesting trees, bushes, feathers or moss.

Mugs decorated in this way might be used for public-house service; those made from 1824 onwards might bear the excise mark applied by the Weights and Measures Officer to a white oval pad. In buff-coloured stoneware they were made as shop measures for such commodities as dried peas, shrimps and winkles.

Mocha ware was a considerable production in Staffordshire and the North of England until mid-Victorian days, but continued to be made in the present century. A cheaper substitute was known as Moko. This was a buff or red terra-cotta mottled by splashing various coloured slips over the biscuit and then glazing.

Earthenware encircled with three or four coloured bands was made throughout the 19th century, marked early examples being collected. The decoration is composed of slips of similar texture to the basic earthenware, and rises slightly above its surface. The biscuit was rotated horizontally in the lathe, skilful operators applying the slip at considerable speed. Slips were prepared in three colours—blue, brown and yellow formed a frequent combination—and poured into a three-section funnel, emerging from adjoining openings. The potter held the funnel over the revolving earthenware in such a way that a fine stream of tri-coloured slip flowed out. Manipulation of funnel and lathe speed produced a wide range of bands, strips, spots, curves and spirals. Although the three slips left the funnel in a united stream they were received upon the ware in entirely separate positions. The ware was then dried, fired and glazed.

Several of the more important Staffordshire potters such as Copeland, Davenport, William Adams of Greenfield, and J. and R. Riley made much of the ware for export, as did many of the smaller potters between about 1815 and 1850.

Ornament made by the application of two layers of slip in different colours was patented by William Clark in 1861 and licensed to others. The slip-covered article was then engine-turned, the removal of parts of the outer coating of slip producing attractive designs.

Welsh or streaked ware was the 18th-century term for large near-oval meat dishes of coarse earthenware covered with slip combed and feathered in zigzag patterns and coloured with streaks of glaze, usually yellow and brown. It is usually assumed that examples are of 18th-century origin. The great majority of specimens, however, were potted in the 19th century, production continuing unceasingly until the early 1880s. They were a staple production of Shore and Co's Pottery, Isleworth, from 1795, and when the firm moved to Hounslow in 1810 Welsh ware was made until about 1830. The Hounslow dishes were impressed with the initials HN.

Welsh ware must have been a country-wide manufacture of potters in 1811, for in that year Richard Waters, Fore Street, Lambeth, was granted a patent (No. 3457) for 'making cloudy or Welsh ware by using a number of pipes for distributing the colour, instead of one as formerly'. A patent at that time cost about £300, suggesting that the sale of many of these devices was anticipated.

An example in the museum of the Yorkshire Philosophical Society is described in the catalogue as a 'Welsh tray of yellow earthenware, glazed, 12.75 inches, by 9.9 inches, by 1.8 inches high. Oblong with rounded corners, the underside convex—flat base: the upper side combed in black, blue and white. Mark impressed, HARWOOD STOCKTON. C. 1850'. This was made at the Clarence Pottery, Norton, Durham, founded in the early 1840s and closed in 1877.

39 and 40. (Above) Cream-coloured earthenware vases made by Slees Modern Pottery, Leeds, impressed LEEDS * POTTERY: (*left*) base of body moulded in relief, a winged figure springing from base to shoulder on each side, cover finial in form of a fish; (*right*) hexagonal with all-over piercing, low foot, high-domed cover with fish finial. (Below) Collection of Coalport bone china of the mid 19th century; a pair of vases and covers; a pair of spill vases and (*centre*) a vase with a blue ground and gilded ornament.

41 and 42. (Above) Coalport bone china: fruit coolers, sucriers, pedestal dish and centre dishes from a dessert service of forty-two pieces decorated with burnished gold circles against a light sage-green ground, white reserves painted with flowers in full colour and with lavish gilding. (Left) Belleek parian ware: a double-spouted teapot in white glazed with pearly lustre. This design was protected from piracy by registration at the Patent Office in London, on 9th March, 1880. Height 14 inches. Mark in black transfer: wolfhound, harp and round tower.

10

Decoration

A GREAT DEAL of china and earthenware of the 19th century lacks the potter's name or trade-mark, although symbols used for reference purposes in the factory warehouse are often mistaken for marks of origin. The dates of anonymous pieces may be attributed with reasonable accuracy by associating the type and quality of paste or body with form and decoration. Improvements were made in processes associated with enamelling, transfer-printing (Chapter 4), gilding, lithography, lustre (Chapter 11) and dipping, and these were in chronological sequence, with the dates of their first introduction known at least approximately.

Enamelling in the early 19th century was carried out on a commercial scale in the potter's own decorating workshops, where brilliance of colour and speed of production were the main considerations. Enamelling of cabinet quality was carried out by independent enamellers operating their own workshops and painting to the order of china-sellers, some of whom also employed an enameller on the premises. Customers selected their earthenware and china in the white from dealers' stocks, and their preference in decoration from enamelled patterns and books of hand-painted designs in full colours.

Newspaper announcements and directory entries from the 1760s to the mid-19th century prove independent enamellers to have been numerous, often emphasising their skill as painters of coats-of-arms and crests. A water-colour in the Victoria and Albert Museum painted by Thomas Baxter in about 1810 shows the interior of his father's workshops at 1, Goldsmith Street, Clerkenwell, London. A printed bill headed 'New Price List / Coalport White China' is nailed to the wall. Most of the decorated china seen is for domestic use, but in the foreground there is an exquisitely enamelled cabinet plate.

Enamels were composed basically of metallic oxides and transparent lead-oxide glaze which, under high-temperature treatment, formed what is no more than coloured glass. The colours for commercial enamelling were not costly and were mechanically ground; cabinet enamels, laboriously hand ground with a pebble muller on a marble slab, might cost as much as twenty shillings an ounce.

Crimson, rose and purple were produced from gold oxide precipitated by tin; other reds were obtained from oxides of iron and chrome, oxides which also yielded black and brown although these could be obtained from manganese and cobalt; orange was made from uranium, chrome, iron and antimony; green from oxides of chrome and copper; blue from cobalt and zinc. These were painted over the glaze and, after 1812, fired in an earthenware muffle kiln designed by Samuel Walker while he was employed by Barr, Flight and Barr at Worcester. Although the kiln was coal burning, neither glaze nor enamels were tinged by smoke fumes, the result being that the surface of commercial enamels displayed a greater brilliance than formerly.

These round-topped kilns, in general use at potteries by the early 1820s, measured about forty-two inches in width, fifty-four inches in height, seventy-eight inches in length and contained many more pieces than did former enamelling kilns. After each use the interior walls were scrubbed to remove acid accumulations from fumes emitted by the ware, glaze and enamels. These enamels are always raised slightly above the glazed surface and are liable to be worn away and acted upon by food acids. Cabinet pieces needing individual attention continued to be fired in box muffles as formerly.

Refractory colours capable of withstanding the great heat of a glazing kiln were painted direct to the biscuit without injury to the smoothness, brilliancy or hardness of the glaze which protected them from the effects of wear and acid foods. These colours were blue from cobalt; green from chrome; brown from oxide of iron; yellow from oxide of titanium; black from uranium oxide.

The prepared colours were tied in bladders which at first were perforated with a nail that was afterwards used as a stopper. After about 1820, instead of drawing the neck of the bladder close and tying it, a slender cylindrical stick was inserted and the bladder bound closely around it. This when dry formed a tube, and when the stick was withdrawn the colour could be squeezed as required, the tube being closed by replacing the stick.

Painters of enamels on ceramics laboured under a great disadvantage for the colours as seen on the palette bore no resemblance to the desired tints which appeared during firing. The muffle kiln not only enhanced the final colour but partially softened the glaze, so that the enamel sank into it and became permanently fixed. Over-firing and under-firing were equally damaging. Rose colour or crimson, for instance, when painted on the glaze was a drab violet; the gradual increase of temperature in the muffle kiln changed the metallic oxide from brown to a dull reddish hue, and from that it progressed slowly to its final tint. If the heat continued beyond that point, beauty and brilliancy of colour were destroyed and the enamel emerged a dull purple. This disadvantage was particularly disconcerting when delicacy of tint was required, such as a flesh tone. There was an ever-present risk of the ware cracking as the heat was intensified, or if it was withdrawn too quickly from the kiln. Large pieces were particularly liable to this misfortune, rendering fine enamel painting a disheartening process.

Ground colours were fashionable on early-19th-century bone china in dark blue, apple-green, deep yellow, canary-yellow, turquoise, crimson, salmon, yellow-green, lavender, cane colour. These provided an even background of colour for gilded ornament, with enamelling and transfer-printing in white reserves.

Ground laying was a simple process but required a light, delicate touch. The colours were less fusible than enamels, and required firing at a much higher temperature to produce a level glassy surface unaffected by subsequent firings in the muffle kiln. Reserves for decoration were secured by protecting the surface of the glaze with a liquid composed of sugar and water tinted rose-pink to make it visible. A coating of boiled oil was laid over the glaze and levelled with a boss made of soft leather. Any variations in the thickness of the oil film affected the colour, producing undulations in tint. Finely powdered colour was dusted over the oil and the piece set aside until the oil hardened. It was then immersed in water to remove the coating of sugar, which brought with it any oil or colour that might have spread to the reserve, thus leaving it with a perfect, clear outline. When great depth of colour was required this operation was repeated several times.

Sponging was a method of decorating inexpensive domestic ware in bright colours, carried out over a thick glaze with a sponge impregnated with pigment. For the most part this was applied to thick, heavy granite ware, chiefly tea-sets consisting of teapot, covered sugar basin, jug, plates, cups and saucers. Hexagonal hollow-ware was frequent, and highly domed hexagonal lids with knob finials usual. Sponged ware was in great demand between the 1840s and the 1880s, but is now extremely scarce owing to breakage in every-day use; it was rarely stored as 'best'.

The colours used were various shades of blue, pink, green, brown and purple, with an occasional dash of yellow. Sponging might be in monochrome or polychrome. The collector will find three types of decoration:

1. Sponging intended to give the effect of all-over stippling; in bands of varying width; in swirls; in splotches.

2. Sponging in association with hand-painted decoration, speedily produced and very effective in contrasting—but seldom harmonising—colours. Flowers, fruits, houses, birds are the most frequent motifs. The houses are crudely painted in brilliant enamels and commonly surrounded by sponged work in deep blue. The bird had a great vogue. It was a quickly painted backward-glancing creature known to Victorian potters as the Asiatic pheasant, depicted in mere outlines with a plumed tail and usually standing upon a branch of sponged work. The bird might be in yellow, red or green, with outlines of black and a ground of deep blue sponging. These pigments are capable of maturing with a single firing.

3. Transfer-printing combined with sponging was a speciality of William and Thomas Adams, Greenfields, Tunstall. The Asiatic bird is found in this medium also, usually in underglaze blue.

Comparatively little sponged ware was marked, but the following have been recorded, all impressed.

ADAMS: this was the firm of William and Thomas Adams, whose entire output was exported.

HARVEY: Charles and W. K. Harvey, who traded until 1853.

ELSMORE & FISHER TUNSTALL: later Thomas Elsmore and Son.

BB: Barker Brothers, Gold Street Pottery, Longton, made 'fancy sponged' in the 1870s.

BEECH: James Beech, Swan Bank Works, succeeded Beech and Hancock in about 1870. Jewitt notes that their sponged ware was for the home trade.

BRIDGWOOD & CLARKE: usually accompanied by a printed mark PORCELAIN OPAQUE.

B & C BURSLEM below a coat-of-arms: this firm occupied the Churchyard Works, where Josiah Wedgwood worked as an apprentice to his brother. After 1858 their entire production was exported to America.

STONEWARE B & F; B & T; IRONSTONE P W & Co; L D: these also have been noted.

Among the popular novelties in sponge-decorated granite ware was the double-spouted teapot. These were a vogue of the early Victorian period which continued until about 1880. One spout extended from the bottom of the pot, its opening covered with a strainer in the usual way, while the other matching spout opened directly from the top of the pot. At this time it had not yet proved possible to clear tea of its dust, which floated on the surface of the liquid in what Georgians and Victorians termed 'motes'. Formerly a spoon with an almost flat strainer bowl and a spear handle, known as a mote skimmer, had been used to clear the dust floating on the surface of the tea. The secondary spout enabled the server to remove motes much more quickly by pouring the surface tea into the basin. The tea was then served from the other spout.

Lithography was first used to decorate earthenware and bone china by A. Ducote, who patented the process in November, 1839 (No. 8278). This produced single-colour designs. At first only light blue was possible, carried out with artificial ultramarine. Licencees seem to have been few until 1845, when lithographs appeared in pink, green, purple, mulberry, grey and black. Great skill was required with these or the lithograph emerged from the firing kiln dull and uninteresting, owing to the infinitesimal amount of colour used.

The design from which the transfer was made was drawn on lithographic stone in an acid-resistant wax and the background then removed with dilute nitric acid, so that every detail to appear in the decoration stood in relief. The stone was then 'inked' with potter's varnish and impressed upon transfer paper coated with lithographic size. This was transferred to the surface of glazed ware and dusted with powdered colour. Underglaze lithography was carried out in the same way, but vegetable gluten replaced potter's size. Two processes of chromo-lithography on ceramics were given provisional protection by the Patent Office in 1856 (Nos. 360 and 1833). These do not appear to have been confirmed, but on May 7th of the following year a patent (No. 1296) was granted to L. C. Dollean for 'the reproduction of paintings on porcelain'. A stone was lithographed for each colour contained in the design and impressions in varnish taken upon specially prepared transfer paper. Each successive impression, taken in a sequence from dark to light, was sprinkled with finely ground porcelain enamel and dried before the next application. The colours were in metallic oxides capable of maturing at the same temperature.

Chromo-lithography, less costly than ordinary transfer-printing in colours because of the infinitesimal amount of colour used, was not perfected until the 1870s. Early examples are collected as uncommon and interesting expressions of an imperfect process.

The finest gilding of the 19th century was carried out by the mercury process, recorded by Professor Church as having been introduced to this country from Meissen in about 1790. Formerly English potters had gilded porcelain by laying gold leaf over the glaze, attaching it with an adhesive such as resin or printer's size, and firing it; mercury gilding was harder and more brilliant. Porcelain gilded in the 1790s is as perfect today as when it left the factory.

The original method of mercury gilding differs little from that used today. The gilder was supplied with an amalgam of grain gold in the form of a black dust. This was worked to a paste with turpentine and oils in the same way as enamels, and skilfully painted over the glaze with a pencil brush. The gilder supported his working arm on a rest and steadied the piece with his other hand. The gold flowed freely and was equally well adapted for groundwork and broad bands or the finest details of a complicated design. The cost of drawing intricate patterns on every piece of a service was dispensed with by using a perforated pounce, through which the outline of the design was dusted with charcoal. The gilded ware was later fired in the enamel kilns, driving off the mercury in the form of vapour, and fixing to the glaze a coating of pure gold with a dead surface.

Brilliance was restored by burnishing. The gold was first scoured with fine wet sand, with a smooth motion that avoided scratching. This was a test for permanency. If under-fired or insufficiently hardened, the gold would not adhere under this treatment, remedied by refiring. If over-fired, brilliancy was destroyed and the piece needed regilding. Burnishing was continued by polishing with a bloodstone; high lights on moulded surfaces were obtained with agate fitted into a handle and applied with considerable pressure. This immediately produced a polish which increased in brilliancy the more it was burnished.

When a matt finish was desired, leaf gold was rubbed in a pestle with powdered gum. This was applied by means of a brush and fired.

Raised gilding in scrollwork and other patterns was obtained by modelling the desired pattern in relief. This was fired, gilded and refired, the final effect suggesting solid gold.

Brown gold, a paste evolved for gilding by William Cornelius in 1853, but little used until the late 1860s, produced gilding of richer brilliance than was formerly possible.

A thin paste was made of gold chloride, bismuth oxide, borax and gum water. After firing, the dull surface was burnished.

In the same year Charles Breeze invented and patented (No. 361) a method of gilding porcelain with complicated filigree patterns in gold, or even engravings with gold lines. Gold leaf was laid upon isinglass painted over the glaze and dried. The required pattern was printed on to a transfer paper in an ink composed of asphalt, oil and gold size and thus conveyed to the gold upon the porcelain. When dry, superfluous gold leaf was washed away with water, leaving only what was covered by the protective transferred pattern. When this protective covering was removed with turpentine it left the pattern in bright gold. This was fired in the normal way.

A process of transfer gilding patented (No. 6817) in 1835 by Godwin Embrey does not appear to have been widely used and examples are rare. Marks noted on such ware have included Davenport and Rose of Coalport.

Brilliant or liquid gold was little used by English potters until the early 1850s, when it began to be applied to the felspathic earthenwares. Formulae are secret, but are based on the power of various sulphur-impregnated oils to dissolve gold or retain it in suspension. The resulting brilliant gloss needs no burnishing, but does not wear well.

Underglaze gilding occasionally decorated early-19th-century earthenwares, usually unmarked. The gold was cut to shape from the leaf, attached to the ware by adhesive such as resin and fired. It was then brightened by covering with a thin film of glaze dusted over with sand, and refired. The pattern was again gilded and the whole piece glazed in the normal way.

The introduction of machine-made lace brought with it a new method of decorating china and earthenware with detailed designs in white. This was very popular for a few years during the early Victorian period. The process was patented (No. 9424) by Charles Ayers in 1842. The ware was covered with essence of lavender, and on this was laid openwork lace which adhered to it closely. Dry colour was dusted over it and adhered to the uncovered parts of the essence of lavender. The ware was fired to fix the colours. This burned away the lace, leaving the design in clear white against a coloured ground.

The bat-printing process of decorating porcelain and earthenware was introduced to England in 1765 by W. W. Ryland and was used extensively by soft-paste potters. The *Technical Repository*, 1823, recorded a revival of such decoration. The advantage of the process was the extreme fineness of the engraved line, especially successful for small motifs such as flowers, foliage, fruit, shells, inscriptions and the cartouches for painted coats-of-arms and crests. Considerable use was made of bat printing during the 1830s to 1870s.

W. T. Copeland exhibited in 1851 'specimens of "Bat printing" on the glaze, and of tinting'. The catalogue entry describes the process above the initials T.B., possibly those of Thomas Battam, Copeland's chief decorator. 'The engravings for bat printing are extremely fine, and no greater depth is required than for ordinary book engravings. The impression is not submitted to the heat necessary for press printing, and the medium of conveying it to the ware is also much purer. The copperplate is first charged with linseed oil, and cleaned off by hand, so that the engraved portion alone retains it. A preparation of glue being run upon flat dishes, about a quarter of an inch thick, is cut to the size required for the subject, and then pressed upon it, and being immediately removed, prints on its surface the oil with which the engraving was filled. The gum is then pressed upon the ware, with the oiled part next the glaze, and being again removed, the design remains, though, being in pure oil, scarcely perceptible. Colour finely ground is then dusted upon it with cotton-wool, and a sufficiency adhering to the oil leaves the impression perfect, and ready to be fired in the enamel kilns.'

Silver ornament on porcelain enjoyed a brief vogue during the 1860s, but was un-popular as it oxidised to black very quickly, and if cleaned the metal tended to be rubbed away. Silver was used by Harvey, Adams and Co., Longton, from early in the 1860s, both as a ground and as a heightening to embossed leaf decoration. The silver might be matt or burnished, and in association with gilding and overglaze enamels provided hand-some and unusual ornament. Tea services were chiefly made, and dishes with openwork rims interlaced with ribbon, and their silvered centres painted with naturalistic flowers.

Inlay decoration on earthenware was a welcome change to Victorians satiated with painting, printing and lustre. The earliest inlay followed the St Porchaire style, often termed Henri Deux ware. The pattern was impressed in the wet clay from a metal wheel, the depressions then being filled with slip of contrasting colour. The surface was then turned or scraped level, revealing the inlaid design upon the body of the ware. A method of carrying out this process in reverse was patented (No. 1893) by Horatio Wareham in 1853. The casting moulds were made with embossed or raised patterns, the depressions then being filled with plastic material and finished by turning or scraping. In the following year Charles Toft patented (No. 2268) a method of inlay by turning grooves, cutting incisions or indentations in pottery, filling them with coloured slip and finishing on the lathe. This was stated in the specification to be a less costly decoration than either painting or transfer-printing.

Pottery and terra-cotta inlaid with colourful mosaic designs in the manner of Berlin woolwork or Tunbridge wood mosaic were favourite decorations from about 1840 until the 1870s. The earliest of these was produced under the Nickels-Greenwood patent (No. 8090) of 1839. Prepared blocks of coloured clay were cut into thin veneers and set into recesses cast into the body of the ware. This was particularly effective on terra-cotta ware. Many potters decorated china and earthenware with inlaid mosaic designs during the third quarter of the 19th century, such as James Dudson, Hanley, who advertised 'white, drab, and blue earthenware inlaid with a variety of colours: tea and coffee pots, sugar bowls, jugs'. These were impressed with the name or initials. Mosaic stoneware was made by G. Hodgkinson, Hanley.

Pictorial and figure inlay work was achieved by a process patented by Richard Boote, Burslem, October, 1843. The specification states that 'compositions of the required varieties of colour are fixed inside the moulds, the halves of the moulds fastened together, and slip suited for the ground work poured in. The excess of liquid is withdrawn when the necessary thickness is attained'. This invention seems to have been particularly suitable for jugs. Matching sets in black, blue, sage-green and fawn were inlaid with mosaic designs and figures in white traced with gilding. A bill dated August, 1848, shows that 'one pair of Coptic vases with fancy leaves and other ornament in mazarine blue, traced in gold, by the patent process' cost one guinea. This process appears to have been licensed to other potters. In 1851 the firm of Cork and Edge, Burslem, recorded in the *Art-Journal Illustrated Catalogue* that 'a patented branch of their business is devoted to the ornamentation of earthenware by inlaying clays of various tints, thus producing an indestructible colouring for leaves and other ornaments.... It must be borne in mind that these articles are constructed only for the cheapest market'.

Three examples were illustrated, two teapots and a water jug.

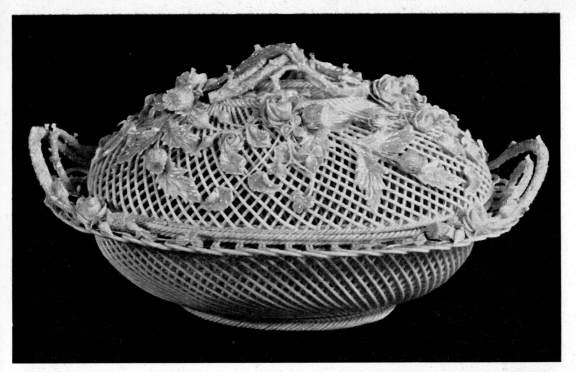

43, 44 and 45. (Above) Belleek basket ware dish and cover in parian ware decorated with hand-modelled roses, thistles and shamrock, glazed with iridescent pearly lustre. Mark impressed on ribbon label: BELLEEK CO FERMANAGH. (Below) Two ornate covered vases on square plinths: (*left*) Worcester painted with views of Kirkstall Abbey and Morpeth Castle, marked FLIGHT BARR & BARR in red script, 1813—1840; (*right*) Swansea porcelain, body and lid enriched with painted roses and other English flowers by Thomas Pardoe, relief work and flat surfaces gilded: marked SWANSEA in red.

46 and 47. (Above) Doulton salt-glazed stoneware vases of the late 19th century, designed and decorated by (*left to right*) Florence E. Barlow, dated 1883; Arthur Bolton Barlow, dated 1873; George Hugo Tabor, dated 1883. (Below) Salt-glazed Lambeth figures by Henry Doulton (*left to right*) Queen Caroline, the Duke of York, Queen Victoria, Prince Albert.

11

Lustre Ware

ENGLISH LUSTRE ware has always been well loved. Neither high prices nor the wealth of shoddy modern reproductions have deterred its enthusiasts, most of whom would never claim to be serious collectors or connoisseurs. The earliest specimens are probably barely a hundred and sixty years old, and there is no secret about the manufacturing methods that achieved its unique brilliance. Yet when one gets down to the facts a lack of basic information is encountered which is as surprising as it is discouraging.

Lustre ware defies description. Its metallic surface—silver and a hundred shades of gold and copper from delicate pink to richest purple—is sometimes shot with all the colours of the rainbow. The finest specimens are lavishly and often beautifully decorated, and their present-day value is high. Yet a piece of antique lustre ware bearing its maker's name is almost as rare as a piece of labelled furniture, and although the ware was produced by nearly every pottery of consequence in Staffordshire and the northern districts, as well as by many makers of bone china, contemporary chronicles scarcely acknowledge its existence.

English lustre ware was a commercial adaptation of the resplendent Hispano-Moresque pottery, which had fascinated connoisseurs for centuries and in the late 18th century was a fashionable importation from Spain. The fiery radiance of the metallic surface as rays of candlelight struck the plate, bowl or jar made such specimens enviable possessions, but costly. In no other species of ceramics is this metallic gleam more beautiful; in some lights the pieces are fiery red, in others copper, in others golden, blue or rosy pink.

The development of lustre ware in England stemmed from the potter's desire to commercialise Hispano-Moresque effects, not on tin-enamelled earthenware but on the newly evolved creamware which was bringing wealth to the Staffordshire master potters with transfer decorations in blue. Little success was achieved in the production of lustred earthenware, however, until the early years of the 19th century.

John Hancock, an enameller employed by Josiah Spode at Stoke, and later a 'flowerer' of Derby porcelain, claimed to have produced lustre ware in 1789. In a letter to the *Staffordshire Mercury* in 1846 Hancock declared that he had indeed 'discovered and put into practice the gold, silver and steel lustre at Spode's factory during 1789'. This statement remained unchallenged. No evidence has yet come to light proving that Josiah Spode I marketed either gold or silver lustre. It is possible that such brilliance was found to be impermanent.

Gold lustre was not produced successfully until early in the 19th century. In 1801 Lewis Weston Dillwyn had bought the Cambrian Pottery, Swansea, which was then producing a superior kind of earthenware sold under the name of opaque china. This had a fine, hard body, and when suitably glazed was found to be an ideal base for gold lustre. In 1807 the Cambrian Pottery Warehouse, 64, Fleet Street, London, was advertising 'Ware ornamented with an entire new Golden Lustre'. This suggests that Swansea made the first commercially profitable gold lustre. Because of the war-time scarcity and the high price of gold, however, potters turned their attention to the production of silver lustre, obtained by using platinum oxide. Less expensively other potters decorated with thinly applied pink lustre prepared from the gold chloride and tin chloride mixture known as 'purple of cassius'.

The film of lustre was so thin that diffracting effects were produced by firing the ware in a reducing atmosphere for eight or twelve hours. The basic metallic oxides or chlorides were usually mixed with balsam of sulphur and oil of turpentine, then thinned to the required consistency with oil of lavender. This liquid, with the metal held in suspension, was brush-applied to the ware. Most writers wrongly state that the ware was dipped: this would have produced too thick and variable a coating. After partial drying, the coated ware was placed in the muffle of a reverberating furnace where flames and heat passing over a brick firebridge were reflected downward to the protecting muffle which prevented the products of combustion from coming into contact with the lustre.

The heat dissipated the oxygen and destroyed organic matter contained in the metallic coating. This left remaining on the surface of the ware a hard, fast deposit of lustrous metal. Large furnaces were found unsuitable for firing lustre ware, brilliance being lost in the necessarily slow heating and cooling. Some lustres needed rubbing with the hand immediately after being drawn from the muffle, as otherwise the surface became dark and unattractive.

Silver lustre was an English invention obtained by using platinum oxide. By adding manganese oxide to the platinum a lustre resembling polished steel was obtained. Silver oxide was never used, as its lustre dulled quickly on exposure to air. The fact that platinum was used excludes the possibility of a date for such lustre before 1784, when Achard introduced the first crucible in which the metallic oxide could be made. But a comprehensive technical work devoted to platinum published as late as 1800 by Knight of London, and a paper on the subject read to the Society of Arts in 1803, still make no mention of the metal's association with ceramics. The Wedgwood firm have records proving that they began to use silver lustre on a commercial scale in 1805 in the form of encircling narrow bandings, often in association with coloured enamels.

Lustre, both gold and silver, was introduced in delicate patternings set off by the white or creamy white glazed ground. The earliest method of achieving such effects was somewhat elaborate, and this stencilled lustre was soon ousted by the more familiar work known as resist lustre. In this the opposite effect was achieved, the patterns appearing, in equally delicate detail, in the white against the lustred ground. The earlier, stencilled lustre ware was produced by a technique evolved in 1806 by John Davenport of Longport, Staffordshire. Cut-out paper patterns were pasted upon the glazed ware and the entire surface then waxed. When the wax-coated patterns were removed, the design remained exposed on the glaze. This was coated with lustre; when dry, the wax was removed from the background with benzine and the ware fired. Silhouettists were employed as paper-pattern makers, cutting with scissors and penknife so skilfully that hair-line details were of pen-and-ink fineness.

Resist lustre dates from about 1810. The design was painted on the glaze with a resist material such as finely pulverised china-clay mixed with glycerine or honey. This repelled or resisted the metallic-oxide solution with which the entire exterior surface was painted. When this had dried, the resist was removed by washing in water. The white glaze of the pattern showed boldly against the lustred background in this resist ware, which many collectors consider the finest lustre work. Designs included the grape and vine-leaf, geometric or scroll patterns, and the purely English inspirations featuring song-birds, roses, strawberries, thistles, ivy, fuchsias (late), even sporting scenes and so on.

Until the late 1820s the ground colour was almost invariably a white, cream or buff glaze, the exceptions being hand-painted grounds distinguishable by their slightly uneven finish. Buff, pink, apricot, blue and canary-yellow grounds then appeared, the rarest of all being a true rose colour, superb for lustre. The ground-laying process for such ware was introduced in 1826 by Henry Daniell of Shelton. In order to secure a level glassy surface, ground laying or colour dusting involved firing at a higher temperature than was required for the metallic lustres.

First a coating of boiled oil was smeared over the glaze, and when hardened by drying had to be 'bossed' with a soft leather until perfectly level or tint variations might occur during firing. The colour, in the form of a fine powder, was dressed over the oiled ground with cotton-wool. After firing, the surface was again bossed. Ground laying brought early death to those actively engaged in the process, even though they worked with bandages over nose and mouth in an ineffectual effort to avoid inhaling the poisonous colour dust.

Silver lustre ware in forms resembling solid silver plate were made, but there is no evidence that such pottery was issued in quantity until after 1823. Earlier, such lustre was inclined to exhibit a dull greyish-black hue except when used on Wedgwood's pearl ware. This was a white earthenware containing more flint and white clay than was usual on creamware. A trace of smalt in its composition contributed to its whiteness (see Chapter 3).

In all-over lustring the ware received two coats of platinum solution. The first, applied to the biscuit, consisted of platinum dissolved in aqua regia with a rather smaller quantity of spirits of tar added. This was fired and a further coating applied in which the platinum oxide was prepared with the aid of sal-ammoniac. The ware was then refired at a lower temperature. The difference in appearance between silver lustre ware and burnished sterling silver plate was that the lustre displayed a slightly darker hue, but was usually more lustrous than the precious metal.

Such earthenware was silvered inside and outside, thereby assisting the illusion that it was either silver or Sheffield plate. The potters prepared special moulds copying the three-piece tea-sets then being issued by the manufacturing silversmiths. These were rectangular in plan and comprised tea-pot, sugar bowl and cream jug. In addition to domestic ware, silver lustre goblets in this style were used at funerals, and chalices, patens and plates in small places of worship.

Early all-over silver lustre table ware is of excellent quality. No relief work was used apart from a beaded edge, which reflected high lights, and the fluting then expected of silver ware. Examples from 1845 were less well designed, however, and no longer attempted an illusion of silver, being lined with white glaze and painted with gaudy flowers or banded in horizontal rings of blue, cream or pink.

The extent to which silver lustre ware was made may be gauged by the exhibits of Edward Deakin, Longton, at the Great Exhibition of 1851. These were detailed in the catalogue as 'Mouth ewer and basin; coffee and tea-pots, sugar-box and cream jugs; tea and breakfast cups and saucers; toast rack and egg-frame with cups; communion cups with handles, plate, jug and cover; sauce tureen with cover, stand and ladle complete; candlestick and extinguisher; broth bowl with stand and cover; mustard pots and salts'.

A less costly method of silver lustring was invented in 1852 by John Ridgway and Co., Cauldon Place. This was a chemical process known as 'electro-metallurgy', its development being prompted by the success of electro-plated silver. The film of platinum was so thin, however, that it was unable to withstand even a normal amount of washing. A considerable quantity was issued until the early 1860s.

The well-known purple lustre thinly painted in designs over white glaze was a popular ornament for inexpensive ware until the 1860s. This lustre is often classed in a group as pink, although in point of fact it was produced from the purple powder of cassius and displays a distinct tinge of purple even at its palest. The first successful version originated with the Wedgwood firm. It appears that shortly before the death of Josiah Wedgwood, in 1796, his friend, Dr Fothergill, had suggested to him that purple powder of cassius, long used as a colour for enamelling, might be prepared to make a commercially profitable metallic lustre. The powder, a precipitate from a mixture of gold chloride and tin chloride, was thoroughly cleansed to remove acid traces, then put into suspension in an oily fluid prepared by dissolving sulphur and venetian turpentine in ordinary turpentine. Oil of lavender was added as required to thin the fluid to a working consistency: it was then painted on the glazed ware and fired at a low red heat in a muffle kiln. The tint of the resulting colour varied with the gold-tin ratio, one to four producing light purple, one to five a rose shade. Several years elapsed before this lustre could be guaranteed to retain its brilliance. It was used chiefly for ornamental banding, conventional motifs and painted scenic pictures.

A vast quantity of glazed earthenware was decorated with this inexpensive lustre by the Sunderland potters (see Chapter 21). Marbled effects evolved by mingling various tints of it were introduced by the Wedgwood firm before 1810. Styled moonlight lustre, this was soon copied by other potters. The only one known to have equalled Wedgwood was Turner of Lane End.

Splashing or mottling was a variant also introduced by the Wedgwood firm. Among today's collectors it is more particularly associated with Sunderland, but the potters of Staffordshire, Liverpool and Bristol produced precisely the same effects. The purple lustre was applied to the glaze and sprayed with oil blown through a tube, the far end of which was covered with fine muslin. The oil expanded in the muffle, forming tiny bubbles which burst upon the surface of the ware, producing irregular spots, waves and splashes. In most instances panels were reserved for printed or painted decoration over the glaze.

Gold lustres varying from guinea gold to reddish gold and the not very durable ruby were produced with gold oxides. The widely different hues were the result of using gold in various carats. Early gold lustre may be recognised by its distinctive guinea-yellow colour derived from the guineas which the potters found a useful source of gold. The more copper there was in the gold alloy the darker and more bronze-like was the lustre. These gold lustres decorated glazed ware and were applied in styles similar to those described in connection with silver lustre.

Dr S. Shaw, in *The Chemistry of Pottery*, 1828, named John Hancock, together with John Gardner and William Henning, as the originators in 1823 of gold and copper lustring direct to a specially prepared reddish-brown clay. This clay was capable of being finished with a smooth, mirror-like surface, giving consistent depth and richness of tone to low-carat gold lustre. But in high-quality work the biscuit was covered with a glaze stained purplish-pink with purple of cassius; this made the lustre sparkle like shot silk. In other ware a first coating of purple lustre might be given for the purpose of increasing brilliance.

An attractive reddish-brown lustre with a greenish hue was made at this time by mixing oxides of gold, iron and ochre with lavender oil and applying this to the ware with a brush. This was gently fired in a reducing atmosphere. The lustre was revealed only by well rubbing the ware to remove an obscuring film.

In about 1840 a less expensive range of lustre made from copper oxide was issued. This ware, liable to be disfigured with specks, pin-holes, pimples and bubbles, is distinctly heavier than the earlier gold-lustred ware, which is conspicuously light in weight.

The colour of the basic earthenware was found to have a considerable effect upon the colour of lustre applied direct to the biscuit. White, yellow or light grey clay mixtures were preferred for silver lustres, and reddish brown gave a warm glow to the metallic yellow brilliance of high-carat gold. Resist and stencilled lustre work, and that produced with the purple of cassius, continued to be applied to glazed surfaces. Where lustres from gold oxide and from the purple of cassius formed decorations on a single piece, red-brown earthenware was used and the parts to be painted were coated with a thick white glaze.

A purplish lustre on a deep chocolate-coloured biscuit resulted in either a bronzed gold lustre or a bronzed purple lustre. A purple reminiscent of ripe blackberry juice was introduced at this time by Wilson of Hanley and quickly copied by other potters. But some of the most delightful effects in gold lustre were brought out by experimental techniques which were not developed.

One of the usual methods of introducing lustre was in association with reserves in white or colour treated as other contemporary ceramics. They might display blue-printed transfer designs; paintings in sepia or in purple lustre; decoration in coloured enamels; black transfer work including views of country mansions and portraits, sometimes overpainted with colours or thin purple lustre. Another method was to use a printed-transfer design before lustring. When dry it was coated with a weak solution and fired. The resulting lustre was so thin that the transfer printing showed through. Like other 19th-century earthenware productions, the subjects displayed not an amateurish air so much as an indication that their decorators were working at high pressure for piecework rates.

Towards 1820 there was a renewed demand for ceramics with the sprigged ornament in relief so popular during the third quarter of the 18th century. At first this appeared on lustre ware in the form of continuous scenic bands, such as huntsmen, hounds and fox, encircling jugs and other hollow-ware. These pictorial effects were enriched by colouring with purple lustre and enamels, usually broadly banded top and bottom with lustre. Early sprig work was meticulously modelled and sprigged on with a brass tool, each motif being applied without overlapping its neighbour. Enoch Wood and E. Mayer were probably the first potters to cast such decoration in relief directly on the ware, from the early 1820s. Such relief work was decorated in colour. Wilson of Hanley is credited with lustre ware bearing ivory-white ornament in relief, against a jasper-blue ground, but only fine examples were produced by this potter.

Copper lustre hollow-ware was usually lustred inside, while the exterior might be banded with colourful motifs painted directly on the lustre, or upon glazed bands, some of which were ground coloured, forming a background for relief moulding. The series of jugs decorated with brilliant yellow bands and floral patterns, first issued by Thomas Barlow of Longton, were marked with a large impressed B.

Lustre decoration on bone china and hard-fired earthenware was often outstandingly beautiful, particularly in silver-resist and in gold-resist designs showing geometrical outlines in white against the gold lustre. New Hall, Swansea, and Minton issued some exceptionally lovely tea services slightly touched with lustre. One excellent pattern, noted with both New Hall and Swansea marks, is known to collectors as the strawberry lustre design, with berries in red, green hulls and leaves, and pink stems and tendrils. A set would comprise teapot, cream jug, sugar bowl, slop basin and six cups and saucers.

Peter Warburton of New Hall, in February, 1810, patented (No. 3304) a method of decorating bone china and earthenware with 'gold, silver and platina' transfers. The use of silver and platinum suggests that it had not yet been realised by potters that lustre made from silver oxide quickly tarnished in stock. An impression in oil was taken from a copperplate by means of a bat composed of glue and isinglass. The oil impression was transferred to the ware and sprinkled with the powdered preparation of gold or platinum, no mention of copper being made in the patent. It was then fired.

Chronological classification of lustre ware is peculiarly difficult, aided only by the few dates associated with the introduction of certain processes. A very few pieces bear a maker's name or mark printed or impressed in the paste; a few more may be recognised by their close resemblance to marked pieces of ordinary earthenware, but even of these the number is discouragingly small. And, to add to the complexity of the problem, later potters have used old moulds and revived old models obtained from factories that have gone out of production. Indeed, classification in detail has so far proved impossible.

The list of makers is extensive and more than three dozen different marks have been recorded. The principal makers of marked specimens, in addition to those already noted, were Charles Allerton, Longton; John Aynsley, Lane End; Bailey and Batkin, Longton; Lakin and Poole, Hanley; C. Meigh and Sons, Hanley; Thomas Minton, Stoke-upon-Trent; J. F. Wileman, Longton—a late maker of lustre.

During the early and mid-Victorian periods much lustre ware was bought by peddlers and sold for a few pence each; others found a place at country fairs where they made attractive prizes. It is therefore advisable to examine specimens for hidden defects, particularly in the case of copper lustre.

One firm established in 1831 has continued making silver lustre and resist lustre ever since, using the original formulae, processes and shapes. Other potters were making gold and copper lustres, the latter easily recognised by absence of a smooth mirror-like surface. More than fifty years ago J. F. Blacker told his readers to beware of the lustre ware which the Staffordshire potters were even then 'distributing to the antique shops of the world'. Arthur Hayden warned against frequent washing of lustre ware as warm water tended to detract from its brilliance. He advised the use of a soft cloth and nothing more.

12

Colour Picture Prints on Staffordshire Pottery

To EARLY Victorians multi-coloured ornament on ceramics still meant laborious hand painting. On the cheap wares in everyday use it meant little more than dabs of colour enlivening a one-colour transfer print, and this was a far cry indeed from the elaborate ornament in the detailed, story-telling manner admired at the period. George Baxter showed them that printing processes could reproduce on paper something of the rich colour harmony of oil paintings, but on ceramics a comparable achievement was made through quite remarkably humble channels. This is perhaps unfortunate, for the process was applied largely under circumstances where extreme cheapness was essential. Ceramic collectors today who have seen only late, poorly finished 'pot-lids' tend to condemn an interesting by-way of ceramic decoration that for a short period was applied ex tremely attractively and with practical success to a much wider range of table and toilet ware.

The story of this development begins, nevertheless, with what have come to be known as pot-lids. The late Georgian dandy deluged his hair with bear's-grease pomade bought in shallow, wide-mouthed pots of hard felspathic earthenware, with labels printed in black on the flat-topped lids. The specialist potters concerned were F. and R. Pratt and Co., Fenton. When hairdressers required more colourful, decorative lids, this was accomplished by using outline transfers and filling in colours by hand.

At about this time George Baxter had perfected his now celebrated method of printing in radiant colours, and Jesse Austin (1806—1879), the Pratts' chief decorator, felt the urge to decorate earthenware lids by comparable methods. He had been apprenticed to John Davenport as an engraver of copperplates for transfer-printing in blue, and at the age of twenty he established himself in Burslem as a designer and copperplate engraver to the pottery industry. The transfer-printing trade declined in the late 1830s, and he closed his workshops in 1840.

A year or so later, Austin was employed by the Pratt brothers, and in 1845 he hit upon the idea of decorating vitreous earthenware, non-absorbent and impermeable, with colour engravings under the glaze. The printing enamels could not sink into the close-textured surface of this newly evolved ceramic, the result being that the inked lines from transfer-printing received their full emphasis of colour, accentuated by the film of glaze. Austin was a water-colour artist of outstanding ability and painted the original pictures in colours capable of being broken down into their component colours for reproduction by transfer from stippled copperplates. A portfolio containing about a hundred and fifty paintings made for copying still exists.

At first Austin experimented with two colours, and since bear's grease was contained in the pots his first thought was to produce pictures featuring various bears: by early in 1846 'Polar Bears' in two colours was on the market. The now rare bear series ran to sixteen subjects, including 'Bears at School', 'Performing Bears', 'Bear Hunting' and 'Bear Pit', Austin progressively improving his printing methods until the later bear subjects were in four colours. On early issues the picture extended over the entire lid. From about 1850 a white border encircled the picture and this might be printed with the maker's name and address.

For instance, there is a bear hunting scene accompanied by the words 'Ross and Sons' Genuine Bear's Grease Perfumed. 119—120, Bishopsgate Street, London'. It was then fashionable for London hairdressers to keep a live bear in their shops, a notice informing customers that it was to be fattened and killed for its grease. Ross and Sons in 1855 paid £20 for four brown bears from the sale of surplus animals at the Royal Surrey Zoological Gardens.

Thus the English potter's first efforts at multi-colour printing could scarcely have been humbler, but their success was such that makers of meat and fish pastes placed orders. It was difficult to obtain a smoothly flat surface free from dappling on the flat-topped lids of these early pots, now rare and highly valued. On the last day of December, 1847, Felix Pratt was granted a patent for a method he had devised by which pot-lids could be shaped mechanically and given a smooth, slightly convex surface, a perfect base for developing the craft of multi-colour transfer-printed pictures.

The Pratt firm's entry in the catalogue of the Great Exhibition, 1851, plainly indicates that for fine work a single multi-colour transfer was used. Here it records that 'each colour is produced from a separate engraving, and *the transfer requires to be carefully registered*'. This means that the picture was applied from a single multi-colour transfer made under the hitherto overlooked patent No. 12097 granted to Frederick William Collins and Alfred Reynolds on March 18th, 1848. The picture transfer was built up by printing the different colours upon the transfer tissue one by one from separate copperplates applied with meticulous accuracy. The really important detail in making a multi-colour transfer was the perfect placement of each colour so that blurring was avoided. This was ensured by engraving register marks in the form of tiny rings to the sides of each plate. These were applied to the transfer so that the dots on each were exactly superimposed. Occasionally three or four register marks are noted, usually faintly visible beneath the ornamental or plain gilt border that generally surrounds a lid.

The colours blue, red, yellow and brown were used in various tints, capable of maturing with a single firing, printed one over the other on specially prepared transfer tissue paper. This is confirmed in a further patent (No. 2576, 1856), where reference is made to 'the order in which the colours are ordinarily printed upon the transfer paper'. Hitherto it has always been stated that the copperplate impressions were transferred one above the other direct to the earthenware in its biscuit state. When a complete coloured transfer had been prepared it was applied to the unglazed biscuit surface in the ordinary way, the transfer paper being washed off when the colours had been transferred to the lid and time allowed for drying. A finer result was obtained by allowing the colours to dry upon the transfer paper. The ware was coated with varnish and when nearly dry the transfer was pressed upon it.

When the colour work was complete the decorated biscuit was placed in the hardening kilns at a temperature high enough to burn all oil from the coloured inks, which were so constituted that the metallic oxides matured into their final colours at approximately the same temperature. They were then ready for the final process of glazing, which gave the pictures brilliance and permanence.

The catalogue of the Great Exhibition shows F. and R. Pratt and Co. to have displayed 'earthenware printed in various colours, under glaze, after pictures in the Vernon Gallery'. This included dessert ware colour-printed with the following subjects: 'The Last In', by W. Mulready, R.A.; 'Highland Music', by Sir Edwin Landseer, R.A.; 'The Blind Fiddler', by Sir David Wilkie, R.A; 'The Truant', by T. Webster, R.A.; 'The Hop Queen', by W. Witherington, R.A.; 'The Cottage Children', by Thomas Gainsborough, R.A. Also exhibited were a pair of pictures in gilded earthenware frames, a pair of ornamental vases painted to resemble malachite, and 'a variety of box covers'. The latter was a series of twenty-six lids for toilet-table pots encircled with gold borders one-quarter inch wide. A complete set of these was sold for £206 as long ago as 1925. The Jury's Report described these as 'remarkable specimens of a process they have greatly improved, viz., that of coloured printing under the glaze. The freshness and truth of the colouring are excellent.'

The success of these prompted F. and R. Pratt to market tea services with pictures on both sides of the cups, and teapots rimmed with burnished gold against a ground colour of blue, red, green or yellow. Trinket boxes, toilet jars and bottles, tobacco jars and jugs were also issued. Plates with 'pot-lid' centres and wide rims decorated with elaborate borders in Staffordshire blue were made as cabinet pieces. The majority of this ware was exported to America, where it enjoyed a long and profitable vogue.

Jesse Austin fortunately possessed the ability to separate a picture into its component primary colours. In all the remarkably colourful pictures he produced he never exceeded five copperplates—four in different colours and a keyplate in brown. The keyplate, which sharpened the detail of the picture, was printed first, stippling only being used for the flesh portions, the remainder being in line. Over this, one at a time, were printed the colour plates.

It was long surmised that the Pratt firm were the only makers of colour picture prints. The entry of T. J. and J. Mayer, Longport, in the catalogue of the Great Exhibition, however, shows them to have displayed 'various designs for meat pots, printed in colour under the glaze'. H. G. Clarke has recorded more than fifty prints from this source, many of them on table ware. Yet another firm to make colour prints was T. C. Brown-West-head, Moore and Co., Hanley, successors to John Ridgway and Co. This appears to have been during the early 1860s—probably 1861—when Austin was employed by them for about a year, following a disagreement with the younger of the Pratt partners. The Pratt patent had expired and lids with domed tops could be made freely. The Pratts were quickly aware of a falling demand for their 'coloured pictures on pottery' in face of this new competition, and Austin was persuaded to return at a salary of £175 a year, later increased to £200.

The manufacture of potted meats and fish pastes was being developed as an industry at this time and the Pratts secured long-term contracts from Crosse and Blackwell, E. Lazenby and Son and John Burgess. These three firms between them used tens of thousands of colourfully lidded meat pots each year, eventually covering more than five hundred different subjects. These were, obviously, less expensive productions than those formerly made, the pictures being designed to permit speedy printing of the transfers.

This was assisted by the Lander process of preparing copperplates, patented (No. 2161) in September, 1858. The entire design was engraved on the copper and copies made by the galvano-plastics method. Parts of the pattern were removed from these so that the portion of the engraving present on each plate was absent from the remainder, each restricted to a single colour. When the successive impressions were made on special tissue the subject was complete for transferring.

These commercial pot-lids were usually issued in series with an eye to customers who might collect complete sets. Among these are pictures of the Queen's residences—Buckingham Palace (rare), Windsor, Sandringham, Balmoral and Osborne. The London series consists of about twenty views, four of which are marked 'Entered at Stationers' Hall': St Paul's Cathedral, Westminster Abbey, the Tower, the Houses of Parliament. No other lids possess this inscription, and examples are valued accordingly. In some instances the date of issue is indicated by the picture itself, such as the Embankment, built in the late 1860s; Holborn Viaduct, constructed 1867—9; the Albert Memorial, completed 1872; Osborne House, a royal residence from 1875.

The earliest pot-lids to be decorated for the fish-paste trade were commissioned by S. Banger, and Tatnell and Son, both of Pegwell Bay near Ramsgate. They appreciated that customers would delight in taking their well-known shrimp pastes in attractive containers and issued eighteen coloured lids all displaying pictures of the Pegwell Bay district, one of them illustrating their 'Shrimp Sauce Manufactory' with bottles of sauce displayed in the windows.

I am indebted to Mr E. Timperley of Merton Park for the following glimpse into the Pegwell Bay series of pot-lids. 'Forty years ago in Pegwell Bay I met a fisherman named Sam Banger (pronounced Ban-jer), who said that although the business had closed he still possessed some of the old pots. He told me that his family began to sell shrimp paste in 1804 and that the business was later carried on by his grandfather and aunt: a pot of paste guaranteed to keep in good condition for three weeks was sold for a shilling. The copperplates for their series of Pegwell Bay lids, Ramsgate Harbour and Walmer Castle cost Banger more than £20. They remained his property and when a fresh supply of pots was needed they were sent to F. and R. Pratt and Co. They also used pots printed by other firms including the "Marriage of the Prince of Wales to the Princess of Wales in 1863".'

The finest of these colour prints bear Jesse Austin's signature: 'J. Austin Sculp'; 'J. Austin Sc'; or 'J A Sc'. These are invariably of high-quality craftsmanship, and may be distinguished at a glance from the pictures produced for commercial purposes. About fifty sets of plates bearing his name have been recorded by H. G. Clarke. A diamond-shaped registration mark was occasionally incorporated into the picture design such as 'The Village Wedding', adapted by Austin from the painting by David Teniers the younger, now in the Bridgwater Art Gallery. Austin's version was registered at the Patent Office by F. and R. Pratt and Co. on January 15th, 1857. The name Thomas Jackson has been noted on four-colour prints. A maker's trade-mark is infrequent, but when present it is usually on table ware which may be backstamped with the royal crown /'Manufacturers to H.R.H. Prince Albert/ F & R Pratt'. After June, 1857, the inscription was changed to 'Patronised by the Prince Consort'.

Colours on the printed ceramics made under Austin's management are notable for their velvety brilliance and body depth, and for meticulous detail. The glazed surface of a pot-lid is usually crazed—that is, covered with a network of thin, irregular hair lines resembling fine cracks. Pot-lids of the original vitreous earthenware may be recognised by their tone. An uncracked lid hanging from the little finger and tapped with another lid will emit a dull note, indicative of the genuine example. Lids of more recent manufacture give a clear, bell-like note; if artificially crazed or otherwise 'antiqued' the ring is less distinct. Exceptions to this rule are those made in bone china by John Ridgway and Sons during the 1850s, these having a clear ring.

Some two hundred of the original sets of copperplates used by the Pratt firm were rediscovered by their successors early in the present century. When pottery decorated with colour prints began to be collected, re-issues from some of the original plates were made, but on a harder vitreous earthenware.

13

Lithophane Pictures

EARLY VICTORIANS were puzzled and enchanted by very simple marvels. They were thrilled by the spectacle of paper-weights aglow with tiny beds of 'flowers' in brilliant, unfading colours set beneath rounded domes of clear glass, and they thought that a slab of irregular-surfaced porcelain was wonderful indeed when a light placed behind transformed it into a vivid, detailed picture wholly in accord with the artistic canons of the day. In the deeply shadowed parts of the picture the glassy porcelain was thick enough to resist the passage of light in degrees varying with the volume of shade required; thin areas produced contrasting translucency. Viewed directly the surface of the porcelain was barely suggestive of any pictorial effect at all, yet, with a light passing through from behind, delicate and precise variations in opacity formed a perfect detailed picture resembling finely finished mezzotints. Because manufacture was slow, expert work, examples are now infrequent. These panels were usually pierced for hanging.

Lampshades might become alive with an encircling hunting scene or fascinating with a panoramic view such as the City of London from St Paul's; uninteresting boxes became charming night-light shelters resembling cottages when a candle-mortar burned within; hand fire-screens revealed celebrated paintings when held protectingly against the fire-light; panels hung against windows displayed copies of contemporary paintings or portraits of celebrities. Tea-cups apparently decorated in the ordinary way with coloured enamels and gilding might surprise the tea-time visitor when a picture became visible at the bottom as the cup was tilted against the light.

These decorations, known as lithophanes, were the invention of Baron de Bourgoing of Paris, who was granted patent rights in 1827 and licensed his formula and methods to potters in England, Holland, and Germany, where further patents were granted. The English purchaser was Robert Griffiths Jones, Brewer Street, London, who disposed of the manufacturing rights to the firm of Grainger, Lee and Co., Worcester. Their name has been recorded as impressed on panels, night-light shelters and lanterns. Jones termed this ware 'lithophanic translucid' and referred to the pictures as 'shadowed drawings'. To potters, however, the patent was known as 'Jones's method of ornamenting china'.

The processes involved in the production of lithophanes have caused much speculation, some authorities suggesting photography as the basis, in spite of the fact that lithophanes were being sold long before the invention of photography. None of the conjectured methods, however, bears any relation to the facts, which are fully specified in Patent No. 5626, dated March 3rd, 1828. Lithophanes were made from a thin, glassy species of hard porcelain composed of china-clay, quartz and felspar.

The projections and indentations upon the surface of lithophanic porcelain were not shaped to display the subjects in their actual forms, as in the case of common embossing and relief modelling. The subtle differences in thickness were planned wholly with a view to the intensities of light they would transmit. The exaggerated shapings thus required presented an irregular surface, indistinct and unfinished-looking, displaying little of the effect of the design.

The work involved in producing a lithophane picture was considerable, and much of it highly skilled. A model of the ornamental design was first prepared, a slow and costly undertaking. For this, white wax was tinted until its translucency corresponded with that of the porcelain to be used in the lithophane. This was melted and a layer poured upon the smooth surface of a sheet of plate-glass bordered with putty. Craftsmen, formerly portrait artists in wax, using only a few simple ivory tools, carved the wax until the desired effects of light and shade were secured. First they reduced the thickness of the wax where high lights would appear in the picture, full thickness remaining for shadows. More wax might be added to produce deep shadow effects. High-light concavities were accentuated by impressing metal profiles into the wax.

In a landscape, for instance, the wax modeller would pour a thin layer of hot wax upon the plate-glass. By gently swaying the glass he agitated the fluid, making it possible to manipulate the general flow as required. Blowing upon the cooling wax produced waves of graduated thicknesses which were quickly modelled into cloud effects. Slightly 'darker' distant mountains were suggested by applying additional fluid wax to the original layer, this being spread into suitable forms by blowing and then shaping with a tool, being laid most thinly where high lights were required, such as on distant peaks.

The wax was now ready for the foreground to be modelled. Men and animals, buildings and trees were produced by cutting suitable shapes in laminae of hard wax and fixing them into position. Alternatively, fresh layers of fluid wax might be added and the surface carved as required. Where such figures formed the principal subjects in the design they were scraped to reduce their thickness for lighter tones and raised considerably for dark shadows. This greater emphasis of contrast in the foreground details was most essential to ensure clarity in the transmitted picture, but gave the porcelain a rough, incoherent appearance. By holding the wax model, on its clear glass foundation, against the light, the modeller could examine the progress and effect of his work.

A plaster-of-paris mould was taken from the finished wax pattern, this being in reverse of the actual model. Greater delicacy and sharp contrasts were ensured by retouching the plaster cast, the bare branches of trees, fences and similar details represented by dark lines being sharply carved. From this mould was taken a second cast, a counterpart of the original, but more perfect and in higher relief at all the shadowed parts and along dark outlines. This in its turn was retouched with a graver to reduce thin parts still further where necessary and thus improve and emphasise the high lights.

From this pattern a mould was cast in pewter, tin or type-metal. Even then the mould was not ready for use until it had been engraved with the finishing touches that gave the porcelain picture its surprising, photographic vividness. Delicate lines such as facial features and needlework on garments were achieved in this way. Moulds were made from this pattern and the lithophanes produced by the normal processes of porcelain making. The piece was finally smear-glazed.

In its final effect the lithophane bore a close resemblance to a mezzotint. The introduction of colour into such work tended to confuse the clarity of the design and few examples are known in which lithophanes were tinted before glazing. After the 1850s lithophanes might be tinted throughout their texture by incorporating high-temperature metallic oxides into the paste. Smalt was used to give a rich blue tint.

When the patent expired a few other potters produced competing lithophanes. Herbert Minton issued a number; panels measuring five inches by four inches have been noted impressed 'South Wales Pottery'; W. T. Copeland made some imposing lithophanes, such as the copy of a religious painting in Hanley Museum, with an arch top and measuring twelve and a half inches in height; Adderley and Lawson, Burslem, are recorded as makers. The picturesque lampshades, gems of this branch of the ceramic arts, are unfortunately not marked. That production continued into the present century is proved by the existence of pairs of panels depicting Edward VII and Queen Alexandra shortly after their coronation in 1902.

Some exquisite lithophanes are impressed P P M followed by a serial number, these being of German origin. The Kennedy Porcelain Manufactory, Burslem, developed the idea of impressing glassy porcelain in such a way that pictures were made visible by transmitted light.

The original rights in Germany were patented by the Meissen factory, and the French rights acquired for the Rubelles porcelain works by Baron A. du Tremblay, whose lithophanes are impressed A du T. It was he who developed by 1842 another method of porcelain decoration by utilising deep relief depressions. Known as *émail ombrant*, exhibits of dessert and table services in this medium at the Great Exhibition were awarded a gold medal by the Jury, who commented upon its beauty and low price. This new process was licensed in 1873 to the Wedgwood firm.

The design was impressed in sharp relief as in the lithophane work, but in reverse, the high lights appearing as projections and the shadows as cavities, as in the variety of decorative enamel known as *basse-taille*. This irregular surface was then flooded with coloured transparent glaze, usually green, to level the surface once more. As a result the cavities of the design appeared as deep green shadows of various intensities, while the parts in highest relief came nearest to the surface of the glaze and produced the effects of the high lights in the picture.

14

Worcester

WORCESTER TONQUIN MANUFACTORY, founded in 1751 by Dr Wall and fourteen associates, passed into the hands of Thomas Flight in 1783. Flight was not only London agent for the firm but also jeweller to the royal family. Under the control of his sons, John and Joseph, the original soapstone paste and glaze were altered. Translucency was lessened, and if held to the light a faintly yellow tint was visible. Flight's improved soft-paste porcelain was commercially successful, for wasters were drastically reduced. George III, with Queen Charlotte and a retinue of princesses, visited the Worcester factory in 1788 and as a token of appreciation granted permission for the pottery to be known as the Royal Porcelain Works. This patronage inaugurated an era of sumptuous production for the nobility, even while the main bulk of the firm's manufacture was designed for those less wealthy.

Martin Barr joined the concern in 1793 and they traded as Flight and Barr until 1807, when Martin Barr II became a partner, the firm then being styled Barr, Flight and Barr. In about 1800, heedful of competition from the numerous newly established bone-china potters, they entered this branch of the industry. Their early bone china possessed a faintly greyish hue, was hard-looking and less attractive than their porcelain. Not until about 1820 were pure whiteness and high translucency achieved. Meanwhile, soapstone porcelain continued in production.

In about 1808 William Billingsley and Samuel Walker (see Chapter 17) began experimental work for the firm with a view to developing a fine soft-paste porcelain. In 1810 Martin Barr I was able to report a 'great improvement in the texture, whiteness and beauty of our porcelain'. Shortly afterwards Walker developed a coal-burning muffle kiln which gave finer results and greater brilliance to the enamels.

Flight and Barr's dress services emblazoned with armorial bearings in full colour and consisting of as many as fifteen hundred pieces were splendidly painted. Seldom was there a year without at least one order for an important dress service, in addition to many smaller services, and in 1833 William IV himself ordered an heraldic service.

Less costly decorations were very simple at first, often no more than blue painted or printed flowers encircled by a blue band, with or without sprigs and with some gilding.

Round fluted cups and cylindrical cans were made in large numbers, often decorated with the 'royal lily'. In colour there was naturalistic, though mechanical, flower painting. Designs were also adapted from architectural pattern books. The japan taste was followed by classic borders and plain bands of colours and gadroon edges. More care was given to details of potting and ornament than by most competing potters. Flight's style differed from that of the near-by Chamberlain firm—colours were more subdued, there was a less lavish use of gilding.

Until 1789 the mark was 'Flight' pencilled in script, sometimes alone or accompanied by an open crescent above or below, in blue, red or gold. From 1789 to 1793 this was accompanied by a crown. The name FLIGHTS impressed dates from 1783 to 1793. 'Flight & Barr / Worcester' below a crown was pencilled in script between 1793 and 1807. The name BARR, FLIGHT & BARR printed in red or blue underglaze, accompanied by the Worcester and London addresses, was used from 1807 to 1813. Also there was use of B F B impressed, surmounted by a crown. From 1813 to 1840 the printed mark was FLIGHT BARR & BARR printed in red or black script, or F B B impressed, or a more elaborate mark including the royal arms and Prince of Wales's feathers, their Worcester and London addresses, and the date 1751.

The Chamberlain porcelain factory at Worcester had been established in 1786 by Robert Chamberlain, then an independent decorator of porcelain buying in the white from Caughley, New Hall, Lowestoft, and elsewhere, including France until 1794. He died in 1798, but before then, with his two sons, he had begun to manufacture bone china. Orders quickly became too heavy for their limited resources, and from 1804 until 1811 they were financed by G. E. Boulton of Kemsley. During these seven years wages averaged £4,500, and gold for decorating purposes cost £900 per annum. From 1828 the firm was under the control of Walter Chamberlain and John Lilley, who in 1840 acquired the Royal Porcelain Works of Flight, Barr and Barr.

Chamberlain's early bone china, like that of many another potter of the period, was slightly grey and flawed with specks. By 1815, however, translucency was equal to that of Spode's bone china, but the paste less white. A very translucent soft-paste porcelain with a hard, durable glaze that gave brilliance to the colours was introduced in 1811 under the name of Regent china. The Regent himself was delighted with the new paste and ordered harlequin dinner, dessert and tea services decorated in the japan taste, but every piece with a different motif. These, which cost the Regent £4,047 19s., started a twenty-year vogue for very elaborate table services of lavish dimensions, particularly among English and foreign nobility. Princess Charlotte commissioned a dessert service decorated in old Sèvres style, the scrolls being raised to form panels in which were rose, thistle and shamrock in relief; the ground was drab colour, and the centres of the plates and dishes painted with bouquets of English, Scottish and Irish flowers.

A prosperous trade in bone china was built up during this period, the japan patterns completely covering the ware and hiding minor defects in the paste. This type of decoration was quickly executed and its price proportionately low. Chamberlain's paste was lighter in weight and more translucent than that of Flight, Barr and Barr, and enamelling more brilliant. Table services from 1820 were decorated with English castles and country mansions, each invididual piece displaying at least one different scene, its name printed or painted beneath.

Representations of mythological legends were produced in full colour, and pictures after eminent Georgian artists became fashionable. Decorators expert in naturalistic flower painting were employed throughout the period. Coloured backgrounds were infrequent, a gilded meandering vermicular pattern being preferred. Armorial services were in continual demand from Chamberlain throughout the first half of the 19th century.

Virtually all productions were marked, and from these it is possible to attribute examples to well-defined periods.

Until 1808: CHAMBERLAIN'S or CHAMBERLAIN'S / WORCESTER in red script and sometimes accompanied by the pattern number.

1808–1824: same marks in purple, occasionally in gold.

1814–1816: CHAMBERLAIN'S / WORCESTER / & 63 PICCADILLY / LONDON in red script.

1814–1820, on Regent china: a crown above CHAMBERLAIN'S / REGENT CHINA/ WORCESTER / & 155 / NEW BOND STREET / LONDON / ROYAL PORCELAIN MANU-FACTURERS printed in red.

1820—1840: a crown or royal coat-of-arms above CHAMBERLAIN'S / WORCESTER / & 155 / NEW BOND STREET, LONDON / ROYAL PORCELAIN MANUFACTURERS printed in red or black.

In 1840 the Chamberlain firm absorbed the Royal Porcelain Works, a joint-stock company being formed with Walter Chamberlain, John Lilley, Martin Barr, George Barr and Fleming St John as directors. They introduced a wide range of models and designs appealing to the popular taste. Potting and decoration deteriorated, the firm living mainly upon its past reputation and a new class of customer. This policy appears to have set the combined businesses firmly upon their feet, the marks during the period being:

1840—1845: a crown above CHAMBERLAIN & Co/WORCESTER/155 NEW BOND STREET/& NO I/COVENTRY ST/LONDON printed in red.

1847: 'Chamberlain & Co Worcester' in printed script letters.

1847—1850: CHAMBERLAINS printed or impressed.

1850—1851: CHAMBERLAIN & Co WORCESTER enclosed in the border of an oval containing a crown.

Chamberlain and Co. was acquired in 1852 by W. H. Binns and R. W. Kerr, their policy being to raise the Royal Porcelain Works to its former glory. The factory was enlarged and modernised, first-class workmen and decorators engaged, new and costly models designed, porcelain formulae improved. By the mid-1850s the number of employees exceeded six hundred. In 1862 the firm became the Royal Worcester Porcelain Co., Ltd., under which name it still operates.

Under the new régime ivory porcelain, a paste evolved from parian, was introduced in 1856. Groups, figures, busts and ornaments were made in the biscuit state which exactly matched the natural tint of ivory. Other goods in this porcelain were coated with a soft glaze, and from the mid-1860s might be decorated with a film of silver, bronze or other metal. Ivory porcelain also formed the basis of other ornamental ware such as Worcester's 'Raphaelesque' porcelain, made from 1862, in which the bold relief surface was coloured in the style of old Capo di Monti ware and Buen Retro porcelain. Cabinet porcelain was made in the style of Limoges enamels, a translucent white slip being painted on a royal blue porcelain.

A Japanese style of ornament dating from 1873 was also in ivory porcelain. A set of vases noted by Jewitt was decorated in relief to 'represent the various processes of the potter's art as followed in the East; and these pictures are so minutely and exquisitely painted and gilded that it requires a good lens to bring out their many and very minute beauties'. Jewelled porcelain far finer than that of Sèvres was also made.

The mark used by Binns and Kerr until 1862 was a circle containing four script Ws radiating from a centrally placed crescent with the numeral 51 between its horns—Dr Wall's mark and the year of Worcester's establishment at Warmstrey Hall in the mid-18th century. On cabinet pieces the mark was a shield bearing the inscription K & B/ WORCESTER. From 1862 the circular mark was crowned.

The Royal Worcester Porcelain Co. in 1889 absorbed the neighbouring Grainger Pottery, founded in 1801 by Thomas Grainger, a nephew of Humphrey Chamberlain and a former decorator in his workshops. For several years Grainger operated as an independent decorator, buying bone china in the white from Coalport and Staffordshire. In about 1812 he was joined by a Mr Lee. When the Napoleonic war ended in 1815 they entered the production branch of the trade, making a soft-paste porcelain. The firm was styled Grainger, Lee and Co., their address, the Royal China Works, Worcester. The Sèvres-like soft-paste porcelain they produced was unprofitable because of wastage in the kiln. In 1820 they abandoned this in favour of bone china, and for the next decade they made table ware embossed with sprigs of wild roses and foliage, birds, butterflies, flower posies. An intensely deep opaque *gros bleu* was characteristic in sprays and stripes. In 1829 Grainger, Lee and Co. introduced lithophanes to England (see Chapter 13). The style of decoration on bone china from about 1830 closely followed that of the Chamberlain firm.

Lee retired in the early 1830s, and upon Grainger's death in 1839 the pottery was inherited by his son George, who traded as G. Grainger and Co., described as 'inventors, designers and manufacturers'. At the Great Exhibition they displayed parian statuary and domestic ware, and 'a new ware called Semi, or Chemical porcelain' (see p. 50), for which there became a great demand. A critic in 1851 wrote that 'though presenting the appearance of costly porcelain, it is manufactured at a comparatively small cost; indeed this remark will apply to the generality of works issued from the extensive manufactory of Messrs Grainger'. In about 1860 Grainger improved his parian paste and issued a great variety of finely perforated vases.

Figures decked in elaborate lace drapery came from Grainger and Co. These were already being made by Alfred Singer and Co., Vauxhall Potteries, from about 1840. The fragile lace was made by soaking real lace in china slip made to the consistency of cream and filtered through lawn. Firing in the kiln burnt away the threads of the textile, leaving the filigree china. Then little blossoms were attached, each petal being shaped by a girl in the palm of her hand, a process which impressed the paste with skin markings. The figure was then coloured. Those by Singer bear the monogram A S in crimson.

The name 'Grainger' appears in the firm's marks. From 1812 until 1840, GRAINGER LEE / & Co / WORCESTER was painted in script. The mark from 1840 was printed—a scalloped rimmed dish inscribed G. GRAINGER & CO/MANUFACTURERS/WORCESTER. From 1850 this might have the addition of CHEMICAL PORCELAIN. After 1889 the Royal Worcester Porcelain Co. continued the semi-porcelain department, the printed mark being a shield containing G & Co /| ESTABLISHED / 1801 within a circle reading ROYAL CHINA WORKS WORCESTER. After 1891 the word ENGLAND was added.

A short-lived pottery at Worcester was the firm of James Hadley and Sons, Ltd., established in 1896 and incorporated with the Royal Worcester Porcelain Works in 1905. Productions were mainly of the art pottery group tending towards the *art nouveau* decorative effects, relying on the use of coloured clays in relief. The early mark was J H in monogram painted or stamped with a rubber, and from February, 1897, to June, 1900, with the addition of ' & S'.

15

Derby, Rockingham, Coalport and Madeley

DERBY UNDER the three Duesburys was celebrated for its figures and still more for its colours. This reputation continued until early in the 19th century, when under the Duesbury-Kean partnership, 1796—1811, production necessarily changed from soft-paste porcelain to a whiter, stronger, far more opaque bone china displaying a faintly green translucency when held to the light. The thin, hard glaze did not absorb the enamel which, therefore, could be applied more economically.

Productions consisted mainly of dessert services, tea equipages, cabinet pieces, ornaments and figures. There was a considerable trade in cabinet coffee cans, these being painted with excellent pictorial panels or groups of classical figures. During this period, until 1810, John Brewer, a former miniaturist, painted landscapes in natural colours against backgrounds of chrome green and burnished gilding. He painted exotic birds equally well. Thomas Steele painted realistic fruit in richly transparent colours, obtaining delicate effects by dabbing the wet colour with his fingers. During this period, too, biscuit figures continued to be made, in a smear-glazed frit porcelain.

Kean retired in 1811, selling his share to William Sheffield, Duesbury's father-in-law, and until 1815 the firm traded as Duesbury and Shefield. The mark during these periods was the well-known crown, crossed batons, and script D painted in vermilion, and incised on figures and vases. This mark was continued on best-quality bone china until about 1830.

At the close of the Napoleonic wars in 1815 the Derby factory came into the possession of Robert Bloor, who for many years had been the commercial manager. The purchase price was £5,000, payable by instalments, and certain annuities. Within seven years Bloor had paid off the debt. The Duesburys had always adopted a policy of allowing none but perfect ware to be decorated or leave the factory. The seconds, many of them scarcely flawed, had been stored for more than half a century in the warehouses, and vast stocks had accumulated. Bloor found in this ware an almost inexhaustible source of easy money. By decorating these goods he was able to meet his commitments with the Duesbury family and also become rich.

This porcelain puzzles many collectors who are inclined to suspect its genuineness. The larger proportion was in 18th-century soft paste, but decorated with enamels obviously of 19th-century origin and fired by Walker's muffle kiln introduced to Derby in about 1816. Having discovered a large and ready market for porcelain 'with imperfections thick upon them', Bloor naturally began to reduce production costs and quality to cater for the lower-price markets. This bone china is distinguished from others by its heavy appearance and lack of translucency. Its hard, thick glaze is usually crazed and discoloured.

Bloor soon began to supply much of the demand for highly colourful all-over decoration in the Japanese taste, introduced by Josiah Spode II before 1803, when examples in full colour appeared in the Spode pattern books. In 1817 Bloor advertised in the *Birmingham Gazette* for 'twenty good enamel painters who could paint different japan patterns'. Three different styles of Crown Derby japan decoration were produced—Rock Japan, Grecian Japan and Witches Japan, with the sprawling red and blue patterns often wrongly stated to imitate Japanese *Imari*. Derby japan colours include a foxy red, deep orange, deep blue, sharp pink, green and gold, the latter sometimes forming the outline of the design. The poor-quality china used for gaudy japan decoration was inclined to be flawed with black specks, and this all-over decoration was so arranged that these were concealed.

Simultaneously Bloor manufactured sumptuous table ware in lesser quantity and was appointed potter to George IV in 1821 after making a magnificent dessert service for the coronation. This remains fully intact in the Household Breakfast Room at Buckingham Palace. Twenty years later Bloor was commanded by Queen Victoria to make another handsome and extensive dessert service.

Derby introduced a costly new style of decoration in 1817, ornamenting enamelled trays, dishes and other flat-ware in the style of the oil paintings already fashionable on japanned iron and papier-mâché. The early examples were painted by William Corden. Figures continued to be made, now mainly for the popular market, such as the long series of Dr Syntax figures by Edward Keys, one of Bloor's chief modellers. Bloor made biscuit ware until 1830, but in a non-frit porcelain, the forerunner of parian. At first this had a dry-looking chalky surface, but by about 1821 Derby biscuit was little different from ordinary unglazed china biscuit. A demand for such ware did exist, although the figures were carelessly modelled even when Duesbury's original models were brought into use.

Bloor at once closed the costly London showrooms opened in the 1760s by William Duesbury of 33, Bedford Street, Covent Garden, and appointed Thomas Courtney of Old Bond Street as his London agent. The mark on commissioned ware from this source was 'Messrs. Robert Bloor & Co., 34, Old Bond St.', in red painted script. When Derby ceased production, Courtney bought his bone china from other potters, possibly Locker and Co., Derby, this being marked COURTNEY LATE BLOOR. After Bloor's death in

1845 the Derby factory was operated by a relative for three years, and then closed in face of increasing competition from Staffordshire. The models and moulds, including those taken over by William Duesbury from Chelsea and Bow, were sold to Samuel Boyle of Fenton, who later disposed of them to W. T. Copeland.

All marks by the older firm were hand painted, as were Bloor's early marks. The Bloor mark from 1815 to 1820 was a carelessly painted crown, smaller than the Duesbury version and without jewels on its bows, two brush strokes to represent crossed batons, and a pattern number below. This was in vermilion enamel, occasionally in grey. Early in the 1820s Bloor adopted his own marks, all printed in vermilion. About a dozen have been established, including two concentric circles enclosing the name BLOOR DERBY and encircling a jewelled crown; a crown with BLOOR above and DERBY below; a crown over a Gothic D or over the word DERBY on an expansive ribbon.

In 1848 six of Bloor's former leading employees established a small pottery for the manufacture of bone china at King Street, Derby. These men—William Locker, James Hill, Samuel Fearn, Samuel Sharp, John Henson and Sampson Hancock—traded as Locker and Co., late Bloor, and advertised 'Derby China'. Their productions were marked in red transfer with the name of the firm in a ribbon enclosing the name Derby. In 1851 the firm became Stevenson, Sharp and Co., the mark being the name in full, enclosing KING ST. DERBY. Upon the death of Sharp in 1859 the firm became Stevenson and Hancock, the mark reverting to the old Derby jewelled crown and the script D with the batons and six dots, the batons being transformed into swords with hilts flanked by the initials s and H in large capitals. This mark was continued by Hancock when he became sole proprietor. The firm was in production as late as 1910.

Another Derby pottery, Cocker and Whitaker, was established in 1826. Jewitt quotes the following announcement of their opening: 'DERBY NEW CHINA WORKS. For the Manufacture of Porcelain Figures, Ornaments, &c.—MESSRS. COCKER and WHITAKER beg most respectfully to inform the nobility, gentry and the public, that they have commenced the above business in FRIAR GATE, DERBY, where they manufacture, and have now ready for inspection, and sale, a numerous assortment of Goods in Biscuit and Enamel, such as they hope will be found not inferior to any thing of the kind at present produced in this kingdom.

'Messrs. C. and W. have also a variety of tea and dessert services of modern and approved patterns.

'N.B. Ladies or Gentlemen may have Figures, Ornaments, &c. executed from models or drawings of their own.

'Friar Gate, Derby, Feb 28, 1826.'

The partnership soon ended, and Cocker continued on his own until 1840, making a variety of figures and busts, both in biscuit and enamelled. His biscuit figures have the dry, chalky appearance associated with Bloor, but were marked COCKER incised or bore

48. Collection of 19th-century Worcester china in the Victoria and Albert Museum with the following attributions: pastille burner (*second row*) 1820; pair of candlesticks, 1840; bowl (*third row*) 1845; bottle and stopper (*fourth row*) 1845; ewer (*top row*) 1859; plate (*lower right*) 1861.

49. (Left) Collection of Coalport china in the Victoria and Albert Museum with the following attributions: (*top row*) teapot and sugar basin, 1820s; tazza painted with woodland scene and gilded, 1840; candlestick, 1820s: (*middle row*) plates, late 1840s; jardinière, 1850: (*lowest row*) two ewers, 1830; flower vase and cover, 1865.

50. (Right) A collection of bone china mainly potted by John Davenport, now in the Victoria and Albert Museum with the following attributions: (*top row*) jug with panels containing sprigged motifs, 1810; urn-shaped vase, 1820; Rockingham jug, 1830: (*middle row*) pair of flower pots and stands, 1820; plate, 1810: (*lowest row*) plates, *c*. 1830; vase 1820.

an incised cross below the plinth. He also made exquisite flower-encrusted baskets, as well as brooches and other trinkets.

The Crown Derby Porcelain Co. established in Derby during 1877 was an entirely new business specialising in high-quality china. The mark until 1890 was a crown surmounting two crossed Ds, one in reverse. After a visit by Queen Victoria in 1889 the works became a royal factory by letters patent and the words 'Royal Crown Derby' were added to the mark. Writing in 1910, J. F. Blacker noted that the firm 'manufactures immense quantities of tea, breakfast, dessert and dinner services and it s pecialises in japan patterns and in reproductions of Old Crown Derby designs... Dr. Syntax figures and the "Mansion House Dwarfs" are again produced... Eggshell china is made of wonderfully delicate porcelain, yet so tough as to withstand the highest temperature of liquids better than the thicker china'.

Among the establishments associated with ceramics manufactured in the 19th century none is more highly regarded by collectors than Rockingham, on the Swinton estate of Earl Fitzwilliam. From 1820 until 1841 this factory was the source of much outstanding bone china. The factory, established as a pottery in 1745, had come into the possession of four brothers, Thomas, George, Frederick and John Wager Brameld, by whom production costs were recklessly disregarded. They searched England for suitable materials, selecting only the finest from Cornwall, Devon, Sussex and Kent. Experienced craftsmen were attracted from Staffordshire and Derby.

Their bone china in its more luxurious forms displayed more advanced potting technique and finer decoration than other contemporary china, notwithstanding a taste in design which today may appear execrable. In spite of a continuation of the pottery's profitable earthenware manufacture, the Bramelds' bone-china products were so costly that financial resources proved unequal to the strain. Instead of bankruptcy, however, they obtained aid from Earl Fitzwilliam in 1826, when the business was re-named the Rockingham Works and the Fitzwilliam crest, a griffin *passant*, was introduced as the factory trademark.

Enamelling technique was of a high quality and colours superb. The Bramelds were renowned for resplendent ground colours throughout the 1830s. Outstanding was the thick, smooth opaque apple-green peculiar to Rockingham, although apple-green was used by competing potters. The harder shade of green sometimes met with by collectors was brought about by the inadvertent use of impure metallic oxide; the tint would not mature until fired. Blue grounds in a palette of several tones invariably display rich shadings and include a deep *gros bleu* verging on violet, and particularly soft mazarines and *bleu de ciel*. Reds range from a deep pink to the maroon usually associated with Chelsea. Rockingham yellow is considerably darker than that of Derby, with which it is liable to be confused on unmarked pieces. The delicate characteristic peach tint is rare. A favourite decoration of the 1830s was a pink ground gilded in diaper patterns.

The Bramelds were lavish in their application of gilding, much of their china being notable for areas of solid gold such as wide borders, handles and knobs, brilliantly burnished. They also featured delicate lace-like patterns in gilding. Rockingham gold has often acquired a faintly coppery tinge through long exposure to the atmosphere. Such work is marked. Many unmarked dessert services of lesser quality have been attributed to Rockingham. Comports, dishes and plates are characterised by moulded edges in relief, usually radiant with gilded scrollwork and with gilded veins to the leaf-shaped handles.

Dinner services, like those of other great potters in bone china, were based on patterns evolved by contemporary silversmiths. Sprays of naturalistic flowers and lifelike butterflies and other insects in full colour against a yellowish ground appear to have been in great demand. Tiny flower sprays, recognised by their artist's feather-like touch in their details, were the work of Edwin Steele who, however, worked in a similar style at Derby and in Staffordshire. Tea-cup interiors might be painted with cleverly composed views and exteriors enriched with gilded patterns. The Rockingham artists originated the resplendent style of painting a tray or dish with a gilded cartouche in the centre garnished with a skilfully executed miniature painting in each corner.

Rockingham issued much flower-encrusted ornamental ware, including baskets woven from straws of bone china, coloured white, off-white or cane-yellow, and handsome pot-pourri bowls massed with tiny flowers modelled in the round. The firm also made a splendid series of wall plaques, many of which have been preserved uninjured because they were framed and glazed. In these, bouquets of brilliant flowers such as tulips, dahlias, primulas, roses and other garden favourites were cleverly arranged against highly glazed white grounds.

When Victoria became queen she removed the royal patronage held by Rockingham throughout the reign of William IV. Fashionable society followed the monarch's lead, and in spite of their high standards the Bramelds were soon facing financial disaster. In 1840 Earl Fitzwilliam appears to have withdrawn his support. They then negotiated with L. L. Dillwyn regarding a partnership and the establishment of a china works at Swansea. Nothing came of this, however, and Rockingham closed in 1842.

It is seldom realised that Rockingham bone china continued in production until 1854. John Wager Brameld in 1843 established a bone-china pottery at Coburg Place, Bayswater, London. The paste was less subject to variations in transparency than any bone china yet made. This London Rockingham included much cabinet ware, splendidly enamelled and gilded, and some impressively delicate flower encrustations. Brameld's entry in the catalogue of the Great Exhibition was: 'Ice pail of Rockingham china, gilt, with enamel painting of "Bird-trap" and "Charity" with snow scenes at the foot, and berries; Vase with painting of "Champion" after Webster; Grape basket, with guava cup for pineapple, and wreath of gilded union flowers in china; Pattern cabinet cups and saucer; Breakfast cup and saucer of the original Rockingham glaze, painted with flowers and the rose, shamrock and thistle, gilt.'

Rockingham bone china made before 1826 was seldom marked. An oval medallion impressed with the name Brameld encircled with a wreath of national emblems might be applied to better-quality ware. The name BRAMELD might be impressed, or printed in red or purple. The re-organised firm from 1826 invariably used printed marks. First came a griffin *passant* above the copperplate inscription ROCKINGHAM WORKS. BRAMELD. This might be in red, purple or brown. In 1830 the griffin was surmounted by the royal crown with the inscription 'MANUFACTURER TO THE KING' below the factory name. After 1837 the word 'KING' was altered to 'QUEEN'. By 1840 marks containing royal references were no longer permissible, the mark reverting to the griffin as used between 1829 and 1830. John Wager Brameld in London marked his china with the printed griffin and the name BRAMELD from 1844 to 1854.

The Coalport china works in Shropshire owed its distinction to the far-seeing genius of John Rose, formerly an apprentice at Caughley. In 1796 he, his brother and a partner named Blakeway decided to manufacture bone china, selecting a site at Coalport connected to the Severn by a newly cut canal. This permitted supplies of china-clay and china-stone to be shipped direct from the Cornish coast, and finished goods to be seaborne to other parts. Immediately upon its introduction bone china became in great demand and in 1798 Rose and his associates opened a London warehouse in Red Lion Place, Giltspur Street, London. In the following year they acquired the Caughley pottery on the other side of the canal at Coalport. By 1802 they were trading as Rose, Blakeway, Winter and Co., and in 1810 the firm's entry in the London *Post Office Directory* was 'John Rose & Co., Colebrook-dale Porcelain Manufacturers, 9, Thanet Place, Temple Bar'. Throughout the 19th century the firm traded as John Rose and Co., although there were many changes in partnership.

The London warehouse carried on a wholesale trade. In 1802 retail agents were appointed, shown in the *Post Office Directory* as 'Mortlock & Sons, Colebrook-dale China Warehouse, 250, Oxford Street, London'. To this china, bought in the white and decorated for the most part by independent enamellers, was added the name MORTLOCK in gold script above the Colebrook-dale mark. Factory-decorated ware was sold unmarked.

For a quarter of a century Coalport was largely engaged in supplying glazed bone china in the white to independent enamellers and china-sellers. To begin with the china was less purely white than Spode's, it possessed little translucency, was flawed with a multitude of tiny specks, and the glaze was soft. The paste was gradually whitened, and by 1820 its texture had become clearly translucent and the surface smooth and unflawed. Then Rose, fascinated by the lovely translucent frit porcelain of Nantgarw (Chapter 17), invited William Billingsley and Samuel Walker to Coalport to improve his bone china. This proved immediately successful and simultaneously Rose himself developed a felspar porcelain (Chapter 6) intensely white, hard and very translucent. For this he invented a hard, white, highly lustrous leadless glaze. This discovery won him a gold medal and valuable publicity from the Society of Arts.

Rose's early domestic ware in bone china was transfer-printed in pink or purple outline and over-painted by hand, some parts of the transfer remaining unpainted. Blue printing under the glaze in all-over patterns included most of the designs evolved by Caughley, where they had been used on soapstone porcelain, such as the willow pattern and Broseley dragon. It was the development of the stronger, cheaper bone china that prompted Rose to close the Caughley works and enlarge Coalport. Some bat printing was done at this period, and a considerable amount of ornament was carried out in moulded relief. Enamelling from about 1820 was more sparse than that of his competitors, the intention being to display to its greatest advantage the brilliant whiteness and high translucency of his paste. Flower painting was mannered and obviously designed for mass production and gilding was thin and light in hue.

John Rose died in 1828 and was succeeded by his son. It was he who raised the quality of Coalport decoration to a high level. At great expense he evolved superb ground colours in imitation of Sèvres. The lovely turquoise that appeared in about 1840 was preceded by a pale imitation catalogued as 'céleste'. Rose's versions of the claret of Chelsea and the deep velvety mazarine of Duesbury's Derby were highly successful. Splendid dinner, dessert and tea services were made with these ground colours, exceptionally clever flower, fruit and other painting, and thick, brilliantly burnished gilding. Moulded relief work enriched with gilding was plentifully employed against ground colours. Intricate, more expensive patterns were in raised gold or chased on grounds of solid gold. Vases, pastille burners, pot-pourri bowls, inkstands, clock cases and other ornamental ware might be encrusted with masses of tiny flowers. The largest of these, representing carnations, sweet peas and ranunculus, were Coalport characteristics.

As with the productions of most other potters of this period there is no typical Coalport style of decoration. Each potter acquired the best-selling ideas of his competitors for immediate marketing. Unmarked Coalport of this period may be recognised by clear decoration in bright fresh colouring.

John Rose II died in 1841 and was succeeded by his nephew William. Under his management the exquisite pink or rose colour of Sèvres, known to Victorians as *rose-du-Barry*, was evolved in 1849. This attracted world-wide commissions when dessert services and small coffee sets were shown at the Great Exhibition. The Jury's Report records that 'Messrs. Rose holds a high place for form and colour; and some of the more successful of the larger efforts at enamel-painting on china in England are exhibited by artists in the employ of the manufacturer, as well as some excellently finished statuettes'.

Reproductions of Sèvres, Chelsea and Meissen were made in bone china under John Rose II. The brilliance of the gilding, however, contrasts with the thick, dull gilding found on genuine pieces. So many of these reproductions have been submitted to the writer that the following quotations are given to emphasise their existence in large numbers. *The British Museum Guide*, 1905, notes that the 'marks of other factories such as Sèvres and Chelsea were not uncommonly used on careful copies of the wares of these factories made at Coalport'. J. F. Blacker confirmed this in 1910: 'With the exception of Madeley no factory ever made finer imitations of Sèvres porcelain, and when these imitations were marked with the Sèvres mark it is difficult to discover the forgery.' Professor Church wrote in as early as 1885: 'Coalport vases are often coarse imitations of Chelsea porcelain, and sometimes bear what must be looked upon as the forged mark of an anchor in gold. Cups and saucers are also found having the two L's crossed, in imitation of Sèvres; marks of other factories, English and foreign, are also found upon Coalport porcelain and earthenware.'

Sardinian green, a rich deep enamel, became a characteristic colour during this period. From about 1850 there was a revived fashion for japan patterns, the craftsmanship being distinguished from earlier work by its extreme precision and regularity. Colours, especially the deep reds and a blue with a purplish cast, were fuller than formerly. Examples, including magnificently coloured pilgrim bottles, have been noted bearing bogus Japanese marks.

After the retirement of William Rose in the early 1860s the firm appears to have made ordinary domestic ware, for which there was an immense demand. More interesting to the collector is the fact that Coalport produced what may appear anachronistic ware at this period for the same reason that has caused collectors to look doubtfully at some of Bloor's late Regency Derby work. It was in 1865 that the Coalport establishment began to work through half a century's accumulation of biscuit china, glazing and decorating it in the mid-Victorian style, although the forms and the various qualities of the paste were of earlier periods. Such pieces were marked COALPORT AD 1750.

Not until late in the 1880s did Coalport display revived interest in fine china. This followed a few years after the business was acquired by Peter Schuyler Bruff. The *Wolverhampton Chronicle*, at the beginning of the present century, wrote of Bruff: 'An inherent love of art, a quick eye for the beautiful, and a keen business instinct formed the only apparent equipment which Mr Charles Bruff possessed for his task when, in 1889, he undertook to reorganise his father's business.... Mr Bruff gathered round him talented artists including Mr T. J. Bott, skilled craftsmen, capable men of business, and a new vitality was breathed into both the art and commercial sides of the undertaking. Old designs were revived with all the old beauty and grace; new designs and patterns were introduced. Imitations were studiously avoided, originality was encouraged, and with this spirit of fostering care the highest results possible were once more achieved.... The works have been extended and give employment to five hundred people.'

Until about 1815, so far as is known, Coalport bone china was not marked. Then from 1815 to 1828 'Coalport' was painted in blue script under the glaze. During this period felspar porcelain was marked in red (see p. 47). The marks on bone china from 1828 until about 1850 included 'Coalport' in script letters not joined; JOHN ROSE & Co.; COLEBROOK DALE; C.D.; C. DALE; C B D; in various styles of blue script. The blue or gold monogram C B D was used from the late 1840s to the early 1860s. This was succeeded until 1875 by a C combined with an s-scroll forming three loops containing the letters C S N in gold, occasionally in red or blue. The mark COALPORT AD 1750 was used on biscuit taken from stock after 1865 and on productions between 1875 and 1881. The misleading date purported to be that of the pottery's foundation, as Caughley was started that year and was acquired later by Coalport. From 1881 until 1892 this mark was used with the addition of a crown. The word ENGLAND might then be added in compliance with the McKinley Tariff Act.

The Prince Regent was an extravagant collector of Sèvres soft-paste porcelain, setting a fashion that made prices soar to fabulous heights. Dealers searched in vain for a potter willing and able to make soft-paste porcelain of the Sèvres type and also capable of decorating in styles that could not be distinguished from *vieux Sèvres*. The man who most nearly fulfilled all these requirements was Thomas Martin Randall, former gilder at Coalport, decorator at Derby and at Pinxton, who in 1812 set up as an independent decorator in London, employing more than forty decorators after the close of the Napoleonic wars. It is probable that here he was engaged in decorating, for Mortlock, of Oxford Street, the vast stocks of biscuit porcelain found stored in the warehouses of Sèvres and acquired by the victors.

In 1825 he returned to his home town of Broseley and at near-by Madeley established a small pottery on the canal bank a mile or so above the Coalport factory. Here, for fifteen years, he produced the finest soft-paste porcelain ever made in England. Randall was at first occupied in re-decorating Sèvres porcelain sent to him by agents in London and Paris. This included table services, magnificently potted vases and many other articles sparsely ornamented with gilding, sprays of flowers, linework and other simple motifs. This decoration was removed from the glaze by means of fluoric acid. The gold was applied so thickly that Randall peeled it off with a knife and sold it to London refiners. The glaze was so blended with the paste that, after re-passing through Randall's higher-temperature enamelling kiln, a new surface was created. This was lavishly enamelled and gilded in the old Sèvres tradition.

There is no doubt that he consulted his old friend William Billingsley, who lived at Kimberton, no more than a mile away, before erecting kilns and producing this soft-paste porcelain. Like Billingsley's Nantgarw porcelain it had an unfortunate tendency to fuse and collapse in the kiln, causing an unprofitable number of wasters. The extent of Madeley's productions may be gauged by the fact that Randall possessed no flint-mill, buying the ready-crushed powder from Stoke-upon-Trent.

Two kinds of paste were made at Madeley—the soft-paste made from a frit formula and bone china of a quality closely resembling Copeland's of the late 1830s. Randall's soft-paste porcelain had a mellow, creamy hue very nearly matching Sèvres, but it was slightly thicker in section, only dimly translucent, easily abraded with a file and coated with a thin, hard glaze tinged faintly green. Flaws in the body were many, such as specks and fine hair cracks, but these could be concealed beneath ground colours and lavishly applied enamels.

The ground colours were all slightly deeper in hue than comparable Sèvres and had a slightly granular appearance caused by using powdered enamel over the glaze. They included dark and light blue, turquoise, apple-green and soft pink. *Bleu de roi* was usually enriched with delicate designs in gold tracery. *Oeil de perdrix* was one of Randall's favourite backgrounds, consisting of near-circular sea-green or bright blue spots centred with points of black against a white ground. Raised gilded moulding encircled the reserves of the more important paintings. Alternatively, little rosettes surrounded by blue and gold circles might be scattered over the surface. Gold was used either in flat touches or on relief work, made brilliant by burnishing.

The general decoration for Madeley ware included every subject known to have been issued on Sèvres soft paste before 1768. This was the year in which hard paste was intro-duced at Sèvres, the two qualities being made concurrently until 1802. Soft paste was then abandoned, but was revived in 1854 in response to a demand created by the closing of Madeley. *Fêtes galantes*, cupids, flowers, coastal views with figures, female figures, children, animals, landscapes, chinoiserie patterns, portraits are all found on Madeley porcelain. Articles included teapots, comports, sweetmeat stands, cabinet cups and covers, plaques for inlaying in furniture, wine coolers and coasters, toilet-table accessories, dishes and plates. Figures were modelled but few were issued, as they rarely emerged undistorted from the kiln.

Randall was a Quaker with scruples forbidding him to apply Sèvres marks to his own productions. His nephew John Randall, in *The History of Madeley,* has recorded that after 'repeated and persevering experiments Madeley succeeded in producing a frit body with a rich glaze bearing such a close resemblance to Sèvres porcelain that connoisseurs and famous judges failed to distinguish them. Thomas Randall refused, however, from conscientious motives to apply the Sèvres mark'. The close resemblance is demonstrated by the fact that F. W. Rose of Coalport, himself to become a Sèvres copyist, failed to recognise a piece of Madeley Sèvres. He called upon Randall, carrying a vase sold to him in London as Sèvres, and asked if it could be reproduced. He was astonished to be told that the specimen he held had been made at Madeley and decorated by Randall himself.

So rich were Madeley's paintings, grounds and gilding that the London dealers offered, unavailingly, to contract for Randall's entire output of porcelain, no matter how great, if only he would mark it with the double-L monogram of Sèvres. His refusal led some dealers to boycott his porcelain. No porcelain made at Madeley was marked although the original Sèvres mark remained on re-decorated ware.

The supply of genuine Sèvres suitable for re-decorating gradually lessened and had virtually ceased by the late 1830s, although demand showed no sign of diminishing. Randall's porcelain-making venture had always been subsidised by the decorating department. He now began to manufacture bone-china domestic ware decorated in the Coalport style. This may have been unprofitable, for in 1840 he ceased production and moved to Shelton, where he again established himself as an independent decorator. A probable alternative is that he found decorating the more profitable. At Shelton he decorated his Madeley reserve stock, hard porcelain imported from France, and Burslem bone china. Herbert Minton offered him a partnership on condition that he divulged his methods for making the Madeley paste, glaze and ground colour. Randall, however, declined on the pretext of age.

51. Collection of Bloor's Derby china in the Victoria and Albert Museum: (*top shelf*)
mug and jug, 1830; flower pot and stand, 1820: (*second shelf*) tray or wall plaque, 1820:
(*third shelf*) teacups and saucers, 1820s; fruit dish, 1840: (*fourth shelf*) plates, 1820s;
bell-pulls, 1820.

52. Collection of Spode bone china illustrating forms and decorations originated in the Regency and George IV periods, including (*third shelf*) enamelled plates; potpourri bowl and cover; teacup and saucer: (*lowest shelf*) gilded coffee cup and saucer; porringer, cover and stand; chamber candlestick,

16

Leeds and other Yorkshire Potteries

OF ALL English pottery none is more sought after, more difficult to obtain, or more satisfying to possess when acquired than Leeds creamware. Admittedly it was made, at first, merely in imitation of Wedgwood's queen's ware. But the great Leeds firm of Hartley, Greens and Co. so improved in their methods as actually to surpass their formidable rival, especially in their manufacture of vessels patterned with perforations.

The history of the firm has been outlined briefly by Mr A. Hurst[1]: 'Leeds Old Pottery, in Jack Lane, said to have been founded in 1760, by two brothers named Green; before 1774, the firm was Humble, Green & Co., when the products would probably be red ware, yellow or black-glazed, brown ware, and later perhaps white and cream-coloured wares. As Humble, Hartley, Greens and Co., great progress was made and from 1781 to 1820 as Hartley, Greens and Co., its finest productions were made in white, cream-coloured, painted, printed domestic ware, figures; Egyptian black, white felspathic stoneware; silver, gold and purple lustres were made to a slight extent, but more extensively later. Under Samuel Wainwright in 1825, as the Leeds Pottery Co., in 1837, under Stephen and John Chappell in 1841, Stephen Chappell in 1849, Warburton and Britton in 1853, Richard Britton in 1861, Richard Britton and Sons in 1872, the works gradually declined and only made the commoner kind of domestic ware, although for short periods a partial revival took place. The works were closed in 1878, but reopened by Taylor Brothers for a few years about 1898, after which they were finally closed.' Each proprietor became bankrupt after the end of the Hartley régime.

Creamware was the staple product of Leeds, for there was a huge demand for it on the Continent, where the craze for china could never be met by costly Oriental porcelains, and where the lightness in weight of Leeds creamware gave it a tax advantage over its English rivals. Leeds creamware, in comparison with Wedgwood of the early period, seems warmer and lighter in tone. Those who have the best claim to know the genuine ware are convinced that the glazes supply the real clue, but it is only by long and engrossing study that one can really know the tone gradations that distinguish the glazes of Leeds, harder, more brilliant, less even and altogether more lively than those of Wedgwood.

[1] *A Catalogue of the Boynton Collection of Yorkshire Pottery:* A. Hurst (1922).

The creamware of Mayer, which it most nearly resembles, is distinctively yellow; Herculaneum is greyer. The Leeds glaze has a tendency to run into a faint green tinge wherever the glaze is full. The best Leeds has a glaze that seems floated on and spread without bubbling; it scratches less easily than most contemporaneous creamware.

Lovely and most celebrated was the plain creamware depending solely on gracious design for its appeal. Most spectacular were the centrepieces planned to give an air of grandeur to the dessert. Here the silversmith set the example with basket-hung epergnes, but he could not offer the warm, light colour of the creamware in which elaborate grouping of figures and cornucopias, dolphins and shells, presented their sweetmeats and suckets.

On the Continent, import duty was charged on ceramics by weight. Leeds, in common with other potteries, made their wares as light as possible, and in this they were more efficient than their competitors. Not satisfied with this, the firm commenced to perforate every possible surface, such as rims of plates and covers, as well as more elaborate pieces such as baskets and shell dishes. This fine and varied decoration was, of course, an adaptation of the famous 'rice grain' porcelain of the Orient, without even the protection of clear glaze over the perforations. But to its English purchasers of the perforated ware the obvious comparison was with the silver that few could then afford, and it was even created by the metal-worker's technique, cut sharply and clearly—diamonds, hearts, circles and so on—shape by shape with a simple hand punch while the unfired clay was 'leather hard'. There the similarity ends, however. Wedgwood copied the idea, using block punches which prevented even the slight unevenness of the hand-cut article.

Other Leeds decorations included printed ornament in red and in black, production being known to cover the period 1780–1822. The George IV coronation jug is in a reddish-brown transfer. A canary-yellow ground colour was used early in the 19th century, the articles being issued either plain or decorated with a fruiting vine in dark red.

The pattern book issued by Hartley, Greens and Co. in 1814 was illustrated with the same copperplates as the 1794 edition. These designs appear to be an assimilation of three styles—rococo, Chinese and classic. The debt to Chinese porcelains is important. At Leeds, for instance, they made the gourd and melon-shaped sugar boxes and sauce-boats from China and also the typical strap handle for teapots and coffee-pots which ended in a cluster of leaves and berries, not unlike those on Chinese Lowestoft. Similar handles had been used early in Staffordshire, but it remains a distinctive attribute and one which the squat low teapots, with their curved spouts and flower finials, seldom do without.

The 1814 pattern book shows the range of articles to be almost limitless and to include: sauce tureens with stands and spoons; pickle leaves and scallop shells; pierced dessert dishes with openwork rims; pierced fish trowels; fruit baskets and stands of basket, twig and openwork; pierced chestnut basket and stand; cockle pot or pot-pourri; caper jar or pot-pourri; confectionery basket and stand; a pot-pourri whose top inverts to form a candlestick; tea or coffee tray with openwork border; milk pots with covers; milk ewers; tea-canisters; covered dessert; pierced covers and bowls; candlesticks; melon tureen and spoon; quintal flower horn; large casters; oil and vinegar stands; inkstands and many other items.

These catalogues were issued with title-pages and indexes in German and French. Their importance is proved by the fact that by 1791 the yearly trade exceeded £50,000 and included Germany, Holland, the Baltic countries and even as far as Rio de Janeiro.

The catalogue title-page refers to enamelled ornament and gilding, specifically naming coats-of-arms, cyphers and landscapes. There is plenty of evidence that decoration was by no means equal. Much enamelled ware for domestic use was decorated with a bold, round rose, characteristic of the factory. The enamel colours over the glaze were in yellow, green, red and blue, all capable of maturing during one firing in the kiln. From 1810 there was a deterioration in enamelled decoration.

From 1805 creamware was made in diminishing quantities. Quality deteriorated and the glaze might be tinged with a brighter green than formerly, and unmarked ware could easily be mistaken for Staffordshire creamware. The whiter pearl ware was preferred, its harder surface being more durable and taking the blue transfer printing more efficiently. The glaze was less easily marked with disfiguring scratches. This early-19th-century ware tells its own tale of increasing struggle against cut-price methods at home and war-ruined markets abroad. It would be foolish to attempt to compare, say, Leeds's somewhat mediocre enamel paintings—Chinese figures, Dutch landscapes, flowers, insects and so on —with the superb grace of the plain creamware with its restrained delight in raised ornament.

Black basaltes ware was made at Leeds in considerable quantity if not quite in Wedgwood quality. Often this has engine-turned decoration particularly suited to its austere air. To the tentative collector it has the merit of frequently bearing the Leeds mark so elusive on other wares. There is Leeds lustre ware, too, in silver, purple and rose colour. Mugs, jugs, tumblers, goblets and other inexpensive ware was made in agate and tortoise-shell, marbled, splashed and mottled. The decoration was applied as slip worked up with comb, feather, brush or sponge.

Leeds productions were seldom marked until the 1790s, and then almost invariably the mark was impressed. The name LEEDS POTTERY was the most usual mark. This might be accompanied by an asterisk, dot or hyphen, either on the right or separating the two words. On blue-printed ware towards the end of the period the name might be impressed twice and crossed. The name HARTLEY GREENS & Co / LEEDS POTTERY dates from 1814; this might also be in the form of a double horse-shoe. Marks were used more frequently in the 19th century than earlier.

The collector of pierced Leeds creamware must examine each acquisition judiciously. In 1888 a potter named Slee established a bussines in Leeds makings creamware ornamented with moulded designs and elaborate perforations, copying the forms and decorations of the earlier period. Both failed to reach the excellence of the Hartley, Greens creamware, and by this they may be recognised. Figures were also issued, greyer and more crazed than the originals. Slee impressed his creamware with the name LEEDS POTTERY, including various arrangements of asterisks, dots and hyphens. These are favourites with imitators and fakers, and with Leeds contemporaneous continental competitors, who paid both Leeds and Wedgwood the compliment of so marking their imitations of the unwelcomely popular English imports.

At least thirty-five other master potters made earthenware in Leeds during the 19th century. Only two of these are known to have marked any of their products. The Hunslet Hall or Petty's Pottery made creamware in the late 18th century and continued until the 1880s. So far as is known their productions resembled those of the Leeds Pottery. The impressed mark RAINFORTH & Co. was used between about 1792 and 1818.

Burmantofts Pottery made excellent earthenware from 1882. Mr Oxley Grabham records that they made 'vases, flower pots, etc., coloured pure Persian blue, orange, yellow, and *sang de boeuf* (blended colours): later they decorated with flowers in coloured slip. Anglo-Persian and lustred ware was made. Manufacture ceased in 1904'. The impressed mark was BURMANTOFTS FAIENCE or a pencilled monogram B F with the B reversed. The Leeds Union Pottery, under several proprietors, from the 1820s copied old Leeds creamware, but production was of lesser quality.

Yorkshire found employment for at least seventy-five master potters in the 19th century in addition to those of Leeds. Few of these produced collectable ware, and apart from Rockingham (Chapter 15) only one, the Don Pottery, appears to have made bone china. The Don Pottery, Swinton, was perhaps the most productive of all the Yorkshire factories with the exception of Leeds, nearly three hundred people being employed for many years. The factory was established in the 1790s and operated by John Green until 1834, when it was bought by Samuel Barker of the Mexborough Pottery, which he closed in 1844. Jewitt possessed a printed list of this firm's manufactures in 1808: 'All the various kinds of Earthenware, viz., Cream-colour, Brown, Blue, and Green Shell, Nankin blue, Printed, Painted and Enamelled, Egyptian Black, China. Also services executed in Borders, Landscapes, Coats of Arms, and ornamented with gold or silver.'

An engraved pattern book was issued similar to that of Leeds, the plates being identical but with the name Don Pottery in a scroll on each, and a few additional plates, some devoted to tea equipages consisting of a large range of teapots, coffee-pots, milk jugs, sugar bowls, cake trays, tea canisters, basins, tea, coffee and chocolate cups and saucers. A series of teapots was shown decorated with relief work with loose metal 'kettle handles'. It would be difficult to name any article of domestic ware not illustrated. The painted decoration at the Don Pottery was of high craftsmanship. Dessert services were made in the style of Swansea opaque china with a different flower painted on each piece and the name in Latin on the back.

Bone china was made only for a few years, probably 1804 to 1812, and examples are extremely rare. It was marked DON POTTERY in very small letters painted in red. On earthenware the marks were DON POTTERY pencilled in red or impressed, or GREEN/ DON POTTERY impressed. The same inscriptions might be printed in blue from the early 1820s around a demi-lion *rampant*; or a demi-lion *rampant* holding aloft a pennon inscribed DON and POTTERY below. Several examples of a hitherto unrecorded mark have been seen recently on jugs: DON POTTERY gilded together with the pattern name 'William of Orange' in gold script. These jugs were orange tinted with borders top and bottom in many colours, and were used by the various Orange Clubs active in the early 19th century until 1835.

Twenty-four potteries operated in Castleford at various times during the 19th century, most of them engaged in the manufacture of black and red earthenware and white stoneware. Outstanding among them was David Dunderdale's Castleford Pottery, established in the early 1790s and continuing to 1820. By 1796 Dunderdale had prepared and issued a pattern book illustrating fifty-seven pages of designs and a seven-page index printed in English, French and Spanish. This was evidently highly profitable, for Dunderdale was soon owner of several heavy ships employed solely in carrying his earthenware to foreign ports.

The main production of the Castleford Pottery was domestic ware in cream-coloured earthenware. When drops of glaze have accumulated in corners and hollows they show a distinctly green tinge. Dunderdale's table baskets and dishes may be distinguished from Leeds by the treatment of their flat centres. This area is filled either by the pattern or by coloured intersecting lines, whereas in Leeds ware it is almost invariably plain. Among other productions, Dunderdale made Egyptian black tea-sets of a deeper, brighter black than Leeds; a vitreous semi-translucent ware rather resembling the 'opaque china' of Swansea; and white stoneware jugs and mugs such as were made in Staffordshire. This stoneware jug design has the neck and upper part of the handle in dark brown, the lower part in cane-pattern moulding and the middle encircled with a hunting, sporting or rural scene in relief. Other potters made similar ware, but unmarked Castleford is distinguished by the presence of a grass border encircling the shoulder. A series of interesting stoneware teapots was made with sliding covers; another design had a hinged cover swinging on a metal pin.

Castleford marks were impressed thus: until 1803, D D CASTLEFORD; then, when Dunderdale was joined by John Plowes in 1803, D D & Co/CASTLEFORD or D · D & Co/CASTLEFORD POTTERY.

Dunderdale died in 1820 and Castleford appears to have discontinued potting in 1822, to be re-opened in 1825 by five workmen. Under ever-changing proprietorship, production of useful wares continued throughout the century.

Of the seven potteries operating at Stockton-on-Tees during the 19th century the most important was the Stafford Pottery, established in 1824 by William Smith as a potter of brown earthenware. Two years later, trading as William Smith and Co., the firm's scope was extended to make cream-coloured earthenware of fine quality, painted and blue printed. Marks show that from the mid-1830s pearl ware was made and from the early 1850s semi-china and opaque china. Collectors search for Stafford Pottery mugs encircled with pictures of early locomotives and carriages in elaborately over-painted transfers. A perpetual injunction was granted in 1848 to Josiah Wedgwood and Sons restraining this firm from marking their productions either WEDGWOOD & Co or WEDGEWOOD. Large quantities of queen's ware bearing such marks had been issued before Wedgwood's attention was drawn to this. The firm's marks, usually impressed and occasionally printed, included WS & Co/QUEEN'S WARE/STOCKTON; WS & Co/STAFFORD POTTERY: SEMI-CHINA in a diamond. From 1873 to 1893 Stafford Pottery was under the proprietorship of Skinner and Walker, marks then containing the initials S & W, such as S & W's/PEARL/WARE.

A pottery was established at Middlesbrough in 1834, producing common earthenware, sometimes excellently painted in colours or blue printed in a brilliant blue with all-over patterns covering the rims, which had no borders. Until 1844 the firm traded as the Middlesbrough Pottery Co., impressed MIDDLESBRO' POTTERY in horseshoe form enclosing an anchor, with the addition of a crown on white-bodied earthenware of best quality. From 1844 until 1852 the pottery was operated by the Middlesbrough Earthenware Co., and from 1852 until its close in 1887 as Isaac Wilson and Co., whose usual mark was I W & Co/MIDDLESBRO impressed. One most interesting mark, printed in green, illustrates a clear view of the pottery with five smoking cones, the pattern name above and MIDDLESBRO/POTTERY below. Another printed mark was the royal arms flanked by flags with ISAAC WILSON & Co. above and MIDDLESBROUGH POTTERY below. Impressed marks include LONDON above an anchor.

The Ferry Bridge pottery operated under about twelve proprietors from its establishment in 1792 by William Tomlinson until Sefton and Brown closed it at the end of the 19th century. The productions were pearl ware, cream-coloured earthenware, cane-coloured, green-glazed, white stoneware, blue and white jasper, black Egyptian. The mark from 1801 until 1834 was TOMLINSON & Co impressed.

17

Pinxton, Torksey, Nantgarw and Swansea

A BIZARRE FIGURE in the world of English porcelain was William Billingsley (1758–1828). Celebrated as a flower painter at the Derby Porcelain Manufactory, he became a master potter, ambitiously determined to produce soft porcelain equalling that of Sèvres. Although never commercially successful, Billingsley was responsible for some of Britain's most exquisite porcelain. His activities in the 19th century may be followed at Pinxton, Mansfield, Brampton-in-Torksey, Worcester, Nantgarw, Swansea and finally Coalport.

Billingsley's mannerisms in flower painting at these factories are almost an equivalent of a signature. He was apprenticed as a decorator to Duesbury of Derby, and when he left in 1795 he was chief decorator. At Derby he introduced a new painting technique, abandoning sharp outlines in favour of colour applied in soft washes. Instead of leaving the white ground unpainted to represent high lights, Billingsley spread colour over the whole motif and produced contrasting light tones by removing surplus colour with a cotton-wool stipple or a clean brush. The effect was more softly delicate than anything previously achieved in flower painting. The roses for which he is celebrated are painted from countless angles. His favourite appears to have been the Maiden's Blush variety. In many instances the calyx is turned right back from the corolla to emphasise the contrast between massy, rounded petals and feathery sepals. Invariably one rose in each group is found bending over, leaving the calyx standing out from a deep cavity at the flower-base; foliage is often attached to the stem. When painting a small posy, Billingsley placed one or more rosebuds bending over the main flower. Foliage is natural and irregular, with carefully painted thorns.

After several years of spare-time experimental work in a kiln built behind his father's home, he evolved a porcelain which he claimed to be equal to Sèvres. Then, in 1796, financed by John Coke and trading as Coke and Billingsley, he established a pottery at Pinxton in Derbyshire, the firm employing about thirty operators and decorators. Here he made a milk-white soft-paste frit porcelain, rather more translucent than that of Derby.

It had a slightly undulating surface and when viewed against the light showed faintly green. The thick, glassy glaze had a cold, greyish tone.

The favourite decorations were landscapes and country mansions, some in a monochrome russet-red colour. The so-called Tournay sprig and the Paris cornflower were used almost to the exclusion of other flowers. Unfortunately distortion occurred so frequently in the kiln that the venture was a financial failure and the partnership was dissolved in April, 1799. The mark found on this soft-paste porcelain consists of the name PINXTON impressed in various upper-case letters.

After Billingsley's departure, John Coke assumed direction of the Pinxton pottery, making bone china. In 1803 John Cutts, formerly a decorator under Billingsley, became partner and later proprietor, continuing until 1813, when he moved to Lane End and established himself as an independent decorator. As might be expected, Pinxton bone china was of poor quality, faintly grey and flawed with black specks, virtually opaque, with a slightly bluish tint to the glaze, and bearing painted ornament following the styles of near-by Derby. Meissen canary-yellow grounds are characteristic of Pinxton.

The mark used on bone china during Coke's period was an open crescent with a star between the horns, adapted from his coat-of-arms. Later a script P was painted overglaze in various colours, usually in red; also various forms of arrows in red. The name 'Pinxton' is found occasionally in gold script.

Meanwhile, Billingsley had established himself at Mansfield as an independent decorator. He bought bone china from Staffordshire—marked examples show that some came from Josiah Spode—and from Rose of Coalport, and hard-paste porcelain from France. No doubt all of this was bought from merchants in London or Birmingham. It is known that Billingsley employed at least two experienced decorators in addition to his two daughters —George Hancock, a flower painter from Derby, and a gilder and painter named Joseph Tatlow. Some fine groups of garden flowers were painted by Billingsley against backgrounds of Meissen canary-yellow enriched with heavy gilding. A marked jug recently came to light with typical Billingsley roses on each side. Few authenticated pieces are known and these are signed 'Billingsley Mansfield' in gold or puce.

In 1803, feeling the urge to make porcelain once again, Billingsley established himself at Brampton-in-Torksey, near Gainsborough in Lincolnshire. With four partners, one of them his son-in-law Samuel Walker, soft-paste porcelain was again produced. Traces of a kiln and fragments of porcelain have been found. Decorations were little different from those of Mansfield. The partners traded as William Sharpe and Co., Brampton China Manufactory. Use of the word 'china' in the title suggests that bone china was made. Examples have been recorded marked BRAMPTON MANUFACTORY; others with the initials SWWBB.

Financial difficulties made it convenient for Billingsley to leave Brampton-in-Torksey during 1807. A few weeks later he was back in Derbyshire, operating again as an indepen-

53 to 56. Staffordshire lustre earthenware: (Above left) 'Peace' on square plinth, in gold and pink lustre over white glaze: by Wood & Caldwell, Burslem. Height 17 inches. (Above right) 'Madonna' bust in copper lustre. (Below left) Pastille burner, in rose-splashed lustre. (Below right) One of a pair of ornamental plates, double resist decoration in yellow and silver, touched with burnt orange lustre. Attributed to Joseph Stubbs, Dale Hall Works, Burslem.

57, 58 and 59. Staffordshire lustre ware in silver resist: (Above) jugs decorated with foliage and scroll work. (Upper right) Three from a garniture of fine urn-shaped vases decorated with sepia transfers adapted from 'Sportive Innocence' by Adam Buck. Buff ground with silver lustre ornament. (Below right) A sporting ale jug encircled with partridge shooting scene in blue transfer printed against a silver resist ground.

dent decorator at Wirksworth, assisted by Walker and his two daughters. Tradition has it that Billingsley was attracted by the presence of a white clay deposit of excellent quality formerly worked by a porcelain maker named Gill during the 1770s. Wasters have been unearthed, but they were of hard porcelain of a later period. No marked Wirksworth porcelain is recorded.

Within a few months Billingsley and Walker were on the move again, and for the next five years they worked for Flight, Barr and Barr at Worcester (see Chapter 14). This was followed by another attempt by Billingsley to make superb porcelain, when he founded the celebrated factory at Nantgarw in the Taff Valley, South Wales. A two-kiln pottery was built on a capital of £250 and by late 1813 they were making a soft-paste porcelain then reported as being 'a combination of the best French porcelain, Whiteness and Transparency with the firmness and closeness of Grain peculiar to the Saxon and Dresden porcelain'. Unfortunately the old troubles of fire cracks and distortions occurred. These seconds, instead of being decorated and sold at a cheap rate, were warehoused in accordance with Billingsley's practice throughout his career. The paste of Nantgarw porcelain was notable for its whiteness and translucency, with a distinct yellow tone when held to the light. Like the porcelains of Pinxton and Torksey, it broke with a granular-looking fracture. The thickly applied glaze devised by Billingsley was soft (too soft for practical use), pure white, with a brilliantly lustrous surface, crazing being rarely found on Nantgarw porcelain. This was made from late in 1813 to October, 1814, and again from 1817 until the spring of 1820.

The early productions consisted chiefly of heavily moulded plates and dishes made by flat pressing the clay into plaster-of-paris moulds. They are wide-rimmed, and low in proportion to their width. The scroll-moulding in relief repeated six times on the rim of a plate so closely resembled early Sèvres that when sent by Mortlock to Robins and Randall for decoration it became difficult to distinguish between the two. So heavily pressed was the clay into the mould that the design was clearly outlined on the underside of the rim, a feature omitted by the fakers. Many plates were smooth-rimmed. Output never exceeded twenty-five dozen perfect plates in a week, and it is doubtful if much hollow-ware was produced during this period.

Independent enamellers fired their muffle furnaces with charcoal, securing depth and brilliance of colour unobtainable when using wood or coal. Their work was not, however, hard-wearing. W. D. John has noted that 'the London-decorated Nantgarw porcelain may be readily identified by the presence of a narrow iridescent halo around the enamel colours, and by the dentil gilding at the outer edge of the border'.

Typical decoration on this flat-ware consisted mainly of conventional flower sprays painted between each border motif in relief, and a central expansive posy. Exact copies of early Sèvres were made and attractive effects were achieved in the fashionable naturalistic manner of individual flower painting. Sets of twelve were popular, each with a different life-size motif, a vogue associated also with bone china of other potters. Yet other plates were ornate cabinet pieces painted with pictures, landscapes, birds and so on covering the entire field, and with grounds and borders in deep green, turquoise and claret.

In September, 1814, Billingsley applied to the Board of Trade for a state subsidy such as was granted to certain continental potters by their governments. Through his local Member of Parliament he claimed that his porcelain equalled the best of soft-paste Sèvres. L. W. Dillwyn, of the Cambrian Pottery Works, Swansea, was authorised to investigate the claim, but aid was refused. Dillwyn, however, was personally convinced of Billingsley's *bona fides* and of the fine quality of the porcelain placed before him. He thereupon invited Billingsley to his better-equipped factory at Swansea.

From October, 1814, to September, 1817, Billingsley and Walker operated specially designed plant at Swansea, but still a surprisingly low proportion of perfect examples emerged from the kilns. Obviously the formula was continually being changed and the resultant porcelains differed slightly in appearance. A more tractable porcelain was evolved after two years of costly experiment. Known to collectors as duck-egg porcelain because of its greenish translucency, this was also a commercial failure, and after six months production ceased. This has been reproduced widely with forged marks.

Soapstone was incorporated in the formula in an effort to strengthen the paste and this porcelain was marketed from the spring of 1817. It lacked the white translucency associated with Billingsley's name and orders were seldom renewed. When held against the light a smoky yellow cloudiness was revealed, and its thin, dull glaze was disfigured with pigskin pitting. A variant of this paste with the soapstone reduced by half was dully white, very hard and glassy of surface.

Swansea porcelain included much small hollow-ware adapted from the French and some outstandingly large pieces. Decorations included landscapes within floral borders, and scattered sprays of flowers, as well as flowers and scrolls in low relief. A dark green enamel of uncommon tint is characteristic.

Dillwyn closed the porcelain kilns in September, 1817, Billingsley and Walker then returning to Nantgarw, where they continued porcelain making until the spring of 1820, employing about twenty workpeople including twelve children. Their product was more translucent than the former Nantgarw ware and the potting more expert. The original glaze was continued. Dessert and tea services were the chief productions, occasionally decorated with well-spaced simple floral groups and single roses. Distortions and fire-cracks continued unabated, however, and when funds came to an end Billingsley and Walker moved to Coalport, where Billingsley was employed in a managerial capacity. The great stocks of biscuit seconds that had accumulated at Swansea were glazed, in a more creamy tone than the glaze made by Billingsley and lacking its high surface brilliance. Because it was thinly applied, the texture of the biscuit is clearly visible and such porcelain is thus easily recognised. Much of this was decorated by Thomas Pardoe, an independent enameller of Bristol. Apart from the glaze his decoration is characterised by the gritty textures on red, green, blue and yellow, all of which were fired at one time to minimise costs. All kinds of patterns came from Pardoe's enamelling shops—lightly-painted sprays of garden flowers, sprigs of foliage, birds, animals, butterflies and other insects, fruit, shells, landscapes and chinoiserie work. His borders were in a bright underglaze blue.

Nantgarw flat-ware of both periods was usually impressed with the name NANT-GARW with or without the hyphen, and with the letters CW (china works) below. A considerable amount of porcelain was issued unmarked. Swansea's porcelain made under Billingsley's management was impressed SWANSEA. Duck-egg porcelain was marked SWANSEA impressed, printed in upper-case letters or written in red or gold script. Soapstone porcelain was impressed SWANSEA together with a single trident or crossed tridents.

The Cambrian Pottery Works was established in the 1760s and from 1790 to 1802 was operated by George Haynes. He made a fine-quality cream-coloured earthenware transfer printed in blue, black or brown, many of the outstanding engravings being the work of R. Rothwell, Strand, London. An excellent series in black transfer printing illustrates Welsh scenes and costumes. In the mid-1790s he evolved a good-quality hard pearl ware which he named 'opaque china'. It was thought by many to be in fact porcelain, for it was faintly translucent and emitted a slight but unmistakable ring when struck. Examples are found backstamped in transfer BEST GOODS and accompanied by a mark resembling a portcullis. The marks of this period were CAMBRIAN POTTERY in capitals forming one or two lines, or in cursive script of one line; the name CAMBRIAN; and the letters GH & Co. These might be impressed or in gold or red.

In 1802 L. W. Dillwyn, already an established naturalist with several books to his credit, acquired the factory and concentrated on finely painted pearl ware or opaque china, adopting a new style of decoration immediately copied by the bone-china potters. At that time Swansea was a fashionable health resort, and those who drank the waters made a point of visiting the Cambrian Pottery Works. Among these was Lord Nelson, who late in 1802 ordered a tea service. His letter of appreciation still exists.

Dillwyn's natural-history work had been illustrated by W. W. Young, who was now instructed in the art of enamel painting. Soon he was producing naturalistic flowers, birds, butterflies and shells, usually life size, with their names in Latin inscribed beneath or inside. These were enamelled on pearl ware with the glaze faintly blue-tinged. Some reserves and panels were set against blue marbled grounds. Bird subjects painted time and again were the kestrel, hen-harrier, merlin and golden eagle; butterflies included peacock, red admiral, painted lady and speckled wood. Semicircular flower-holders might be decorated on their bow fronts with birds and foliage. Landscape painting of unusual skill came from the Swansea studios during this period. In addition to Young, their recorded decorators include Morris for fruit, Colclough, Pardoe and Bevington for flowers, Beddoes for heraldic work and Thomas Baxter for clever figure work. Dillwyn's artists used charcoal-fired muffle furnaces to ensure depth and brilliancy of colour, ordinary domestic ware being kiln fired.

Earthenware figures were made in the style associated with Staffordshire. F. W. Blacker considered that they could be distinguished by the presence of a brown or orange line encircling the square plinth. Biscuit figures were also made late in L. W. Dillwyn's period. Toby jugs impressed SWANSEA beneath the octagonal base were made in earthenware. An example in the Truro Museum resembles the typical Staffordshire toby with facial lines less meticulously defined. It has a black tricorn hat, brown coat, grey hair, white jug, yellow breeches, white stockings and black-and-white handle.

At about the time that Billingsley left Swansea, Dillwyn leased the business to his flower painter Bevington, who took a partner and traded first as Bevington and Roby, then as Bevington, Roby and Co. They added bone china to their earthenware and pearlware productions. Dillwyn again came into possession of the factory in 1824 and installed his son Lewis Llewellyn Dillwyn as manager. For twenty years, it is thought, nothing but purely commercial earthenware was made such as blue and white, agate and sparsely decorated pearl ware.

In about 1845 the firm introduced imitation Etruscan ware such as Battam was already selling in London. Specimens of this work are now collectors' prizes. From a deposit of red clay found on the Penelergare estate, seat of the elder Dillwyn, a richly-coloured, close-textured terra-cotta was made. The designs were copied by Mrs Dillwyn from vases at the British Museum and elsewhere. On the thrown and turned vases, Etruscan figures and borders were printed in black outline. The background was then painted over with fine jet-black enamel in such a manner that the transferred figures stood out in the original red of the terra-cotta. The mark, printed in black on the base, was DILLWYN-S/ETRUS-CAN/WARE in an ornamental label. Production was discontinued in 1849.

Swansea figures and vases in black basaltes date from 1845 to 1852 and are impressed CAMBRIAN POTTERY. To this period, too, belongs the ornamental hollow-ware in unglazed buff terra-cotta with figures in relief. Dillwyn retired in 1852 after half a century of association with the Cambrian Pottery Works. The firm was acquired by the Evans family, who made inexpensive earthenware table services and other domestic ware until 1870, when the pottery was dismantled. From 1860 their ware might be backstamped in blue, red or green D. J. EVANS & Co above a crown, with three plumes and a pattern name below.

There were other potteries at Swansea, the largest being the Glamorgan Pottery Works run by the firm of Baker, Bevan and Irwin. This factory, making useful earthenware closely resembling Dillwyn's, was established in 1815 and continued until 1839, when it was sold to L. L. Dillwyn. Here were made huge quantities of the well-known cow milk jugs, decorated both by painting and by transfer-printing, and figures of milk-maids. The mark, when used, was OPAQUE CHINA/BB & I. The Landore Pottery, established in 1848 by J. K. Calland, produced earthenware dinner, tea, breakfast and toilet services in the white, and blue printed, until 1856. They were marked J. K. CALLAND & Co/ LANDORE POTTERY or CALLAND/SWANSEA.

The South Wales Pottery, established at Llanelly in 1839, continued under many managements until the end of the century. Jewitt listed their early productions as 'white or cream colour, edged, dipt, painted and printed... also coloured bodies, figured, enamelled, and parian ware, were tried and discontinued'. He also added that the copperplates from the Cambrian and Landore Potteries were acquired and taken into use.

18

Spode and Copeland

JOSIAH SPODE II might be surprised today to observe how proudly collectors arrange his table wares in their display cabinets—his colourful 'peacock' dinner service, for instance, or his tea-sets in the rich 'Japanese' harmonies of deep velvety blues, intense reds and spectacular gilding. For it was he, in the early 1800s, who brought colour and grace out of the china cabinet and on to the dining table, who captured the superb whiteness and translucency of fragile, costly 18th-century Meissen porcelain and presented it in a ceramic ware that was both strong and comparatively inexpensive—England's renowned bone china (Chapter 5).

William Copeland, a Staffordshire-born tea-merchant of London, had managed the Spode warehouse at 45, Fore Street, Moorfields, from its establishment in 1785. Under his vigorous guidance business had prospered, so that when the Salopian China Co. vacated its warehouse in Portugal Street, Lincoln's Inn Fields, Josiah Spode bought the spacious property, formerly the Theatre Royal, where Gay's *Beggar's Opera* was first performed in 1728. This was in 1795. At about this time Josiah Spode II and William Copeland were made partners in the firm. Josiah Spode I died in 1797, but sixteen years elapsed before Copeland figured in the business name of the firm. This may have been because he was also operating as a china-seller on his own account. *London Directory* entries dating from 1799 to 1818 show a William Copeland to have had a 'Staffordshire Warehouse' at 1, Devonshire Street, Queen's Square, London.

The Spode firm's entries during the same period show several changes. In 1799 the entry was 'Josiah Spode, Staffordshire Potter, Portugal St, Lincoln's Inn Fields'. By 1806 this had changed to 'William Spode & Co., Porcelain, Earthenware and Glass Manufacturers, Portugal Street'. William Spode was brother to Josiah II. Following the visit of the Prince of Wales to Spode's factory in 1806, a royal warrant was granted, and the *Directory* entry for 1808 reads: 'William Spode & Co., Porcelain Earthenware and Glass Manufacturers to H.R.H. the Prince of Wales'. In 1810 this was changed to 'Wm Spode & Co, Potters and Manufacturers of Stoke Porcelain to His Royal Highness the Prince of Wales, Portugal Street'. Copeland's name first appeared in 1813, and from that year until 1820 the *Directory* entry remained unchanged: 'Spode & Copeland, Potters and Manufacturers of Stoke Porcelain to H.R.H. the Prince Regent, 5, Portugal St., and Stoke Pottery, Staffordshire.' In 1822 'H.R.H. the Prince Regent' was changed to 'His Majesty the King'. In 1824 the partnership became Spode, Copeland and Son—the son being William Taylor Copeland.

Josiah Spode II was an able technician. When he became master of the pottery at Stoke-upon-Trent in 1797 he developed his father's techniques in regard to blue underglaze transfer-printed earthenware (Chapter 4) and bone china (Chapter 5); and he evolved felspar porcelain in 1800 (Chapter 6) and stone china in 1805 (Chapter 6). Under his management progressive improvements were made in every department. During the Spode-Copeland period, 1813—1824, black basaltes were made, one being a bust of the Duke of Wellington—a dignity held from July, 1814—with his name impressed on the plinth and a tablet at the back impressed SPODE & COPELAND FECIT.

William Copeland died in 1826 and Josiah Spode II in the following year. They were succeeded by their sons, Josiah III, who survived for two years, and William Taylor Copeland, who bought the business. In 1833 Thomas Garrett was taken into a partnership that continued until 1847, since when the name of Copeland has stood alone to continue the old Spode traditions. In 1867 William Taylor Copeland took his four sons into partnership and the firm traded as W. T. Copeland and Sons.

As regards the decoration of Spode ceramics, both eastern and western forms of ornament were important to Spode's early-19th-century designers. Among eastern designs the Chinese predominated; blue transfer-printed work constituted the major part. The Spode interpretation of the willow pattern was the version which most widely influenced other Staffordshire potters. Direct Chinese sources were found on imported East Indian porcelain and on the tea-papers found pasted on chests of Chinese tea. Fortunately, Spode blue and white bone china and earthenware, having unflawed surfaces, could escape the crowded design that too often disfigured other and later 'well-covered' Staffordshire ware. This freedom from overcrowding characterised not only the blue transfer-printed decoration but also the polychrome Chinese designs.

The 'Shanghai' pattern, for instance, was of Chinese inspiration. But here Spode demonstrated his sympathy for English tastes by changing the colours and the blossoms in the floral pattern and using those familiar to Englishmen. With this exception the design is faithful to the original and includes insects of special significance in Chinese mythology of three thousand years ago. The butterfly represents the Chinese cupid and the bug the emperor.

The evidence of Spode's priceless old pattern books proves that decoration on bone china in the brocaded *Imari* manner, with its deep velvety blues, bold patches of scarlet and green and its rich gilding, long antedated the flood of Japanese decorations emanating from the Derby factory and commonly known as Crown Derby japan patterns. Spode *Imari* is in general superior to that of Derby. If closely analysed, however, these Spode decorations are found to be more essentially Chinese than Japanese, although their superficial resemblance to the *Imari* has led to their classification as Japanese. Less numerous, but equally adventurous, were decorations of the *Kakiyemon* type.

Spode's western decorations covered a wide range of skilful adaptations from English, French and German sources. Floral subjects, birds, fruits, landscapes and figures were associated with the prolific use of gold, and in conjunction with ground colours as well as on the white. Spode's most frequently used ground colours were dark blue, scale blue apple-green, deep yellow, grey, marbled blue, salmon, rich yellow-green, lavender, canary-yellow and biscuit or cane colour. There were also solid gold grounds, which might be either burnished or matt, dotted or stippled gold grounds and gold-scale-on-blue grounds. Handsome vases were richly decorated in gold, many of them having the gilded handles which were a Spode feature until about 1830 and which were revived by W. T. Copeland about twenty years later.

Spode transfer-printing challenges the attention. The notable advances achieved in transfer-printing affected the whole subsequent course of English china manufacture and decoration. Josiah Spode I had grasped the idea of using outline transfer under the glaze as a basis for colour display. The development of outline transfer combined with painting made possible some of the most pleasant commercial ornament to issue from the Stoke works, and was soon used by other potters. The Spode pattern books trace the development of this process. Tentatively used at first for pieces demanding brilliant colour, it soon produced technical difficulties. The sharp black of the transfer outlines showed through the brush-applied enamel colours. Josiah II soon overcame this problem. The outlines were transfer-printed in colours that harmonised with the chromatic scheme of the enamels to be brush-applied afterwards. The transfer-printed 'scaffolding' was thus concealed and the guide-lines were filled in with colour. In a later phase entire portions of the transfer print were left undecorated, the painters confining their brushwork to outstanding features in the pattern.

The second Josiah Spode was the finest imitator of his day. Coalport, Madeley and Minton made admirable copies of Sèvres, but Spode went further and copied Chelsea, with great success in its simplest forms although, of course, his productions were in bone china and the original Chelsea in soft-paste porcelain. His most ambitious attempt, perhaps, was the claret ground with bird decoration in gold. Although the ground colour is not quite perfect and the paste is entirely different, some examples find their way into Chelsea collections. Spode's copies of Meissen would be difficult to distinguish from the genuine ware, if it were not for the comparative softness of his paste. The same is true of his numerous French imitations. It was, however, in his efforts to copy Dr Wall's Worcester that he was most successful, his *gros bleu* being a perfect copy, although his salmon-scale decoration was livelier than the original.

Under the Copeland-Garrett partnership little change was made apart from technical

60. Rockingham pot-pourri dishes on three scroll feet, with low-domed, pierced covers encrusted with hand-modelled flowers in high relief.

61 and 62. (Above) Colebrookdale globular bowls and covers with green rustic handles and flower sprays in full relief. (Below) Pot-pourri vases and covers by Rockingham.

63 and 64. (Above) Handleless teacups and saucers with coffee pot in New Hall hard-paste porcelain. (Below) Porcelain decorated with enamels, attributed to factories operated by William Billingsley: top plates impressed NANT-GARW C W; lower plates (*left*) impressed SWANSEA and a trident, (*right*) marked SWANSEA in red; the goblet was made at Pinxton and is impressed G.

improvements and changes in shape and decoration. A considerable number of exceptionally life-like animals were modelled, particularly dogs in all sizes (see Chapter 24) and grotesque figures such as the monkey musicians adapted from the Meissen issues. One collector possesses nearly thirty different monkey figures, enamelled in red, blue, orange and green. These and the monkey-figure groups were backstamped in green with the name COPELAND & GARRETT surmounted by a crown.

W. T. Copeland was endlessly experimenting with new bodies, such as parian statuary (Chapter 8) and with colours. His cyclamen ground appeared in 1850, and the *Art Journal*, 1865, referred to Copeland's cerulean blue as of intense brilliance and the richest, fullest blue yet produced. His Sardinian green and fine vermilion were also noticed.

Like Josiah Wedgwood in the 18th century, neither the Spodes nor Copeland encouraged artists to sign their work, but under Copeland several outstanding artists have been recorded. Thomas Battam (1810—1864) was Copeland's art director from 1835 until his death. He was the son of Thomas Battam, the Fleet Street decorator of terra-cotta (see Chapter 2) and bone china. Charles Ferdinand Hurton, recognised as Europe's finest flower painter, entered Copeland's service in 1848 and remained with the firm for forty years. He painted the celebrated 'Copeland Vase' for the International Exhibition, London, 1862. This has an oviform body on a square base and measures twenty-eight inches in height. Its turquoise-blue ground is gilded with exquisite bows and foliage and the radiantly coloured central panel displays a cockatoo, fruit, flowers and foliage, with a subsidiary scene in the distance, in a style reminiscent of 17th-century Dutch artists. Copeland's finest birds were the work of Weaver, while R. E. Abraham painted in the Etty manner with spectacular success.

Copeland pioneered the manufacture in bone china and semi-porcelain of handsome panels for mounting in ornamental furniture, many being painted with large flower groups. Table tops were made without any surface undulations. Several were displayed at the Great Exhibition, outstanding being an example in cyclamen green with gold panels, Watteau vignettes and wreaths and flower groups. Another was bordered with chased and burnished gold enclosing festoons of fashionable convolvulus against a blue ground. Slabs for dressing-table tops measured as much as fifty inches by twenty-eight inches. One example was painted with a scene composed of Flaxman figures enclosed in a blue-and-white Greek border with gold enrichments. The Duchess of Sutherland was the first to commission slabs for insertion into shutters and dados.

The Jury of the Great Exhibition reported on Copeland's display: 'The flower-painting and gilding on plates and other articles of cabinet porcelain are excellent, especially in the centres of the plates. Some large vases of Etruscan shape and style of decoration are handsome. Mr Copeland has also some articles in which the effect of inlaid pearls and other jewels is rendered with considerable success. The value of this novel style may be a

question of taste, but it undoubtedly exhibits much skill in the processes of manufacture.'
This appears to be the first reference to jewelled porcelain made in England.

Later, the Report adds: 'The porcelain both of Messrs. Copeland and Messrs. Rose holds a high place for form and colour; and some of the most successful of the larger efforts at enamel-painting on china in England are exhibited by the artists in the employ of these manufacturers, as well as some excellently-finished statuettes. The application of porcelain to decorate the jambs of fire-grates has produced some well-designed slabs from both Messrs. Copeland and Minton; although perhaps one of the best designed of such works, with certainly some of the best English flesh painting, is to be found in some jambs exhibited by Messrs. Stuart and Smith.'

Under Copeland's four sons the firm produced the celebrated ivory-tinted earthenware body considered to be one of the greatest pottery achievements of its period. This has a delicate, warm ivory hue without any of the harshness associated with cream-coloured earthenware. Table and toilet services had a tremendous appeal, painted in radiant, colourful patterns adapted from Josiah II's pattern books and richly gilded. Patterns in relief also might be heightened with gold.

This firm also made a notable contribution to 19th-century English ceramics by introducing and developing parian ware. This is discussed fully in Chapter 8. No pottery has adopted more various marks by which its products may be identified. Spode specimens were marked with an unmistakable clarity. Although frequently altered they were never cryptic nor resembled in any way the marks of other potters. On the earlier productions the name SPODE is usually impressed, in some instances painted in minute letters in red or blue.

19

Minton, Wedgwood, Davenport and other Staffordshire Potters

MASTER POTTERS working in Staffordshire during the 19th century exceeded two thousand. Only a few of these did more than pot commercially for a world market, turning out ton after ton of useful wares quickly and gaudily decorated, but all precisely alike. Thomas Hughes of Brownhills, for instance, was able to export his entire output to America, and from 1856 to about 1880 found no necessity to add a new form or pattern to his short but ever-in-demand list of ironstone china.

The great potters worked lavishly and earned for themselves princely fortunes. At great cost they entered upon long-term experimental adventures, scrapped kilns and plant as new methods were designed, such as James Edwards, who in 1842 redesigned his factory throughout and increased production sixfold without extending a single workshop. A vast industry was concentrated around Stoke-upon-Trent, but it is little realised that at least fifty potters operated in the Stourbridge-Wednesbury district of South Staffordshire.

The Minton firms has been described by Mr Geoffrey Bemrose as 'a veritable branch of the Sèvres manufactory in matters of taste'. Thomas Minton, founder of this celebrated pottery, began life as an apprentice copperplate engraver to Thomas Turner of Caughley (see p. 33). By 1789 he had established himself as a master engraver of copperplates at Stoke-upon-Trent, supplying stock transfers to minor potters. By 1796 he had built a pottery and residence, and in May began to manufacture blue-printed pearl ware on a small scale. A contemporary record notes that 'to start with there was one "Bisque" and one "Glost" oven with a slip house for preparing the clays, and only such other buildings and appliances as were necessary to make a good working commencement'.

Minton secured the services of Joseph Poulson, a practical potter formerly manager to Josiah Spode, and Samuel Poulson as modeller and mould-maker. They were probably partners in the new pottery. By the end of the century the demand for Minton's excellently potted and skilfully printed blue earthenware was so great that a financing partner was introduced, William Pownall of Liverpool. The firm was then styled Minton, Poulson and Pownall. Pownall's brother Arthur became their London agent, with a warehouse at 104, Swallow Street. In 1800 his sales exceeded £2,000.

Experiments were made with bone china in the early years of the 1800s, but proved unprofitable under the Minton policy of selling none but perfect ware. John Turner, an expert in stone-china production, but whose business had failed in 1803, was then employed by Minton. His unceasing experiments in bodies and glazes were responsible for improvements in Minton's pearl ware and stone china. In 1808 Minton had become sole proprietor following the deaths of his partners, and Turner was appointed manager. About fifty workers were then employed.

Decorations for the next twenty years were simple. The early pattern books illustrate sparsely placed flowers, festoons, shells and seaweed patterns in enamel colours, or in sepia, red or blue monochrome, without gilding. In 1817 Minton took his sons Thomas and Herbert into partnership. Thomas soon left to join the Church, but the undoubted genius of Herbert made the Minton firm the most influential of all early Victorian potters. By 1820 excellent bone china was being marketed. It was white of body, seldom flawed and therefore could be lightly decorated; glaze was lustrous and enamelling brilliant. Some exceptionally beautiful tints were displayed by Minton's ground colours from the early 1830s, based on various combinations of pure gold with salts of ammonia and other chemicals. From these emerged the splendid carmine purple, Sèvres green, turquoise blue, *rose du Barry* and Vincennes blue of the late 1840s and beyond.

After the death of his father in 1831, Herbert was joined in partnership by John Boyle, trading as Minton and Boyle. Ten years later Boyle joined the Wedgwood firm. Herbert Minton, three times married and childless, then took his nephew Michael Hollins into partnership and traded as Minton and Co. When Minton died in 1858 he was employing more than fifteen hundred workers.

The Sèvres factory acquired many outstanding examples of Minton dessert services and vases in bone china immediately they were issued in 1826. They are now in the Sèvres Museum, and alongside are exhibited others bought in 1840. These emphasise the remarkable advance in paste and in technical features of potting, design and decoration. Minton figure painting is also to be seen at Sèvres, one series, dating between 1837 and 1847, showing the work of John Simpson, Minton's principal enameller. The chief designer at this period was Samuel Browne. The influence of pupils taught at schools of design brought about a change from purely English patterns to ornament in the French style. This prompted Herbert Minton to bring French artists to the works. Among the first were the sculptors Hugues-Protat, Carrier-Belleuse and Victor Simeon. There was also Leon Arnoux from Sèvres, already described by a critic as being 'more profoundly versed in the mysteries of ceramic manufacture than any other savant in France'. Emile Lessore, a pupil of Ingres, came to Minton in 1858 from Sèvres, where in 1851 he had introduced a new style of painting on china with the freedom of the artist's brush. Formerly pictorial painting on ceramics, as distinct from commercial enamelling, had been stippled in the same way as a miniature painting on ivory; Lessore worked in subdued, delicate colours.

Although fashionable shapes followed the styles of old Sèvres, a wide variety was made purely English in character. By introducing new plant that speeded production without affecting appearance, Minton so cut costs that he was able to convert what formerly had been expensive table services into ware bought for everyday use. Labour costs on these never exceeded thirty per cent of total production outlay; on ornamental and cabinet ware the proportion was rarely less than sixty per cent.

Herbert Minton and Dr Turner in 1839 were granted a patent for the manufacture of hard porcelain, but little was made except for experimental purposes until 1849, when the formula was perfected. The paste was infusible at very high temperatures and the ingredients were so pure that they were unaffected by chemicals. This resulted in the finest laboratory porcelain in the world. Formerly Germany had been the only source of supply, imports costing £60,000 a year. Minton's porcelain was of better quality and cheaper, with the result that he scooped the entire trade.

Minton became celebrated for his exceptionally handsome ornamental ware—parian statuary (see Chapter 8); *faience d'orion*; Palissy ware; Della Robbia ware; *pâte-sur-pâte* (see Chapter 25); and majolica ware (see Chapter 25). The faience is highly valued, its body being a pure white clay covered with interlacing arabesques whose spaces are filled with vari-coloured pastes giving an effect of intricate inlay. Palissy, majolica and Della Robbia display very distinct characteristics, but all were made from a calcareous clay body covered with opaque white enamel composed of sand, tin and lead. Enamel glazes supplied the colour decoration.

The early mark was MINTON or M impressed, and on stone china this was accompanied by NEW STONE to which was added BB in the case of 'best body'. From 1831 MINTON & DOYLE was impressed and a blue-printed mark was used composed of an elaborate cartouche enclosing the pattern name and the initials M & B. After 1841 MINTON & Co was impressed. During this period, too, a blue-enamelled mark resembling the crossed L's of Sèvres with the initial M was in use on fine porcelain and cabinet ware. The pattern number might be painted below. An example of this mark has been noted on the 'Butterfly Pattern' bearing the registration mark for November 13th, 1868. Another mark dating from 1841 is the filled-in trefoil or ermine spot with three dots, either impressed or painted. The globe with the name MINTON inscribed across the equator in 1868 and in variations was used until the end of the century. Use of the name MINTONS dates from the late 1870s. Date of manufacture symbols were printed or impressed from 1842.

The Wedgwood firm during the first half of the 19th century appears to have relied on the wares and designs evolved under the management of the first Josiah Wedgwood, who died in 1795. These were mainly queen's ware, jasper, terra-cotta and cane ware. Wedgwood entered the bone-china branch of the industry in about 1812. The quality of the paste proved uneven and texture was inclined to be dense, although examples are known in which colour and translucency are equal to those of contemporaneous Spode. Decorations were the stock patterns that had been used on earthenware during the previous forty years. These had little chance of competing successfully with the more brilliant patterns used by other Regency potters. Production of bone china was abandoned in 1822.

By 1850 the Wedgwood firm was in the forefront with their parian statuary, which they named 'carrara ware'; they reintroduced solid jasper in 1856; the manufacture of majolica began in 1860 (see Chapter 25), and at about the same time they introduced malachite ware, an excellent imitation of the beautiful green stone with dark marblings in its texture.

Jewitt in 1878 reported that the firm still used 'the original block moulds; the same principles are acted upon and carried out; the same mixtures of bodies and glazes, with certain modifications are in daily use; the same varieties of goods are manufactured; and consequently many vases, medallions, services and other goods of the 18th century are reproduced at the present time'. He emphasised that, as in the days of the first Josiah, the name 'Wedgwood' still stood far ahead of its competitors. In 1878 the manufacture of bone china was revived.

Marks are few. The name WEDGWOOD in various sizes of upper-case type has been impressed on queen's ware and other earthenware from 1769 to the present day; after about 1800 the name might be printed in colour. From about 1780 the same mark has been impressed on jasper, basaltes, terra-cotta and cane ware. The name ENGLAND was added in 1891. On the bone china made between 1812 and 1822 the name was printed in either red, blue or gold. WEDGWOOD/ETRURIA was used for a short period after 1840, but never on fine-quality goods. The bone-china mark from 1878 was the Portland vase above three stars and WEDGWOOD printed in various colours. Date cyphers have been impressed on Wedgwood ware from 1860.

John Davenport, of Unicorn Bank, Longport, made every kind of earthenware and porcelain until 1882. The pottery was established in 1792 for the manufacture of blue-printed earthenware. Davenport achieved outstanding success with his openwork rimmed dishes and plates. In 1797 he entered the litharge and white-lead trade; in 1801 he established a flint-glass factory; a few years later he was making a good-quality stone china; and by 1820 bone china of a faintly greyish paste was being manufactured. When John Davenport retired in 1831 at the age of 65 he employed fourteen hundred workpeople and had sales branches in London, Liverpool, Hamburg and Lübeck.

Like Josiah Spode II, John Davenport adapted Oriental patterns to the English taste, doing this so skilfully that the casual observer would mistake Davenport stone china for Oriental hard-paste porcelain. Flower and fruit decorations were enamelled in naturalistic colours on best-quality bone china, white and translucent in comparison with the greyish but less costly second-quality china. Gold might be used lavishly, handles, feet, rims and borders being heavily gilded and brilliantly burnished. Borders of encrusted flowers might enclose painted landscapes on ornamental or cabinet ware. Much decoration was copied from the work of other potters, but this was probably the natural result of attracting good decorators from his competitors, particularly Derby.

The earliest mark was D painted in red above three small irregular circles. Towards 1820 Davenport adopted the foul anchor as his trade-mark and this might be impressed or painted, often below the name DAVENPORT lettered to form an arc. At about the same time a red transfer-printed mark was brought into use, the words DAVENPORT/LONG-PORT/STAFFORDSHIRE surmounted by a foul anchor. This might be accompanied by 'stone china' in printed script. After 1831 the anchor was replaced by a royal crown. A circular garter inscribed DAVENPORT & Co surrounding 82 FLEET ST/LONDON dates from the late 1840s. The printed mark from 1850 was DAVENPORT in a semi-circular ribbon enclosing an anchor.

Hollins, Warburton and Co., of the New Hall China Manufactory, Shelton, were successful makers of hard-paste porcelain at the opening of the 19th century. Since 1781 they had worked the formula evolved by William Cookworthy, for which he had been granted a patent in 1768. Richard Champion, after buying the patent in 1773, had been granted an extension until 1796. New Hall hard-paste porcelain, like many another porcelain of the 18th century, possessed a faintly greyish hue, but was free from pinholes, with a thin, transparent glaze, clear and brilliant although tinged faintly blue or green, and never crazed. This continued in production until 1810, almost the entire output being confined to tea ware and dessert services. Cups might be handleless and saucers without wells. The well-known 'silver-shape teapot' associated with New Hall was the most popular of its period. Transferred outlines were first used in about 1800; earlier, hand-drawn outlines in black had been filled with coloured enamels.

It is surprising to find that the firm owning the monopoly in china clay for fifteen years prior to 1796 (see p. 39) should delay in the manufacture of bone china. It has been shown by G. E. Stringer in *New Hall Porcelain*, 1949, that New Hall did not enter this branch of the trade until 1810, when competitors were many. Their bone china was however, whiter and more translucent than their hard-paste porcelain, pure white with a glittering glaze notably increasing the brilliance of the enamel. Gilding was used, also flower and foliage patterns in relief. Production ceased in 1830.

The pattern number is pencilled under the glaze on nearly every piece of New Hall porcelain and china, designs being numbered consecutively as they were added to the list. Mr Stringer, after thorough investigation of this problem, declares that numbers up to 1040 are found on hard-paste and some of them continued on bone china. Pattern numbers

1041 to 1669, marking work more in harmony with Regency and George IV styles, are found only on bone china.

On early 19th-century hard-paste porcelain an incised cursive freehand N might precede the pattern number. Bone china was marked with the name NEW/HALL within two concentric circles printed over the glaze. From 1820 this mark was under the glaze.

Job Meigh established a pottery in 1790 at the Old Hall, Hanley, and was succeeded by his son and grandson, both named Charles, until 1861, when the business was converted into a company, the Old Hall Earthenware Co. During these seventy years the Meighs made almost every kind of ware. Their blue-printed earthenware with a hard, durable body and a clear, faultless glaze was made throughout the period. Meigh's stoneware differed from that of his competitors. From the 1830s it was given a semi-matt finish by smear-glazing, this and its vitrified texture bearing some resemblance to the later parian ware. It was, however, much stronger and became in great demand for dressing-table sets, jugs, mugs and candlesticks. Its marble whiteness prompted Charles Meigh to apply this stoneware to architectural designs and it is not surprising that he selected the highly fashionable Gothic. The 'Minster jug', registered by Meigh in 1842, was probably the most outstanding example of the Gothic influence in Victorian ceramic art. Made in considerable numbers until 1860, this straight-sided jug was crowded with ornamentation in relief, the body being encircled with pointed arches containing figures of the Apostles. A considerable range of goods in Gothic design was displayed at the Great Exhibition, some classical subjects also being issued.

Of the finer table ware Jewitt writes: 'Patterns are of surpassing beauty, the excellence of the painting, the gilding, the jewelling, and the enamelling, being very apparent to all, and the combination of printing and hand painting carried to great perfection.... The colours of transfer printing are clearer and brighter than elsewhere.... The richer and more costly chinas are equal in body, in shape, in pattern and in artistic treatment.... In Egyptian ware, elegant little table tea-kettles, spill cases, vases and other articles are made, and are effectively decorated with dead and burnished gilding. In parian, vases, groups, figures and other ornamental articles are produced.'

The early mark was MEIGH impressed. By 1820, blue-printed and other earthenware bore a blue-printed oval cartouche composed of small flowers and foliage and containing the name of the pattern with JM & S below. Stoneware might be printed in black with the royal arms above CHARLES MEIGH/HANLEY. An imitation Chinese seal is found between 1835 and 1847. After 1861 the mark, printed in red, was a castle with three turrets above OLD HALL with the date 1790 in an oval. After 1870 the initials OHECL were used.

John Ridgway built the Cauldon Place Works at Hanley in 1802, operating it successfully with his two sons John and William under the style of Ridgway and Sons. John

65. A collection of bone china assembled at Kensington Palace by Queen Victoria. The figures on the two top shelves were made at Derby and presented to the Queen. The flower-encrusted basket on the third shelf was made at Belleek, and the bowl of flowers immediately in front by Derby.

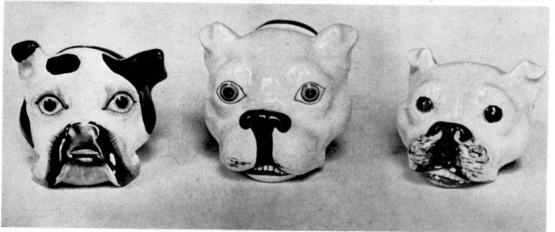

66, 67 and 68. (Above) A group of loving cups dating from 1802: centre of top row is decorated with Oriental scenes in black transfer overpainted in clear reds, orange and green, and inscribed 'A Present from a Friend'. (Below) Earthenware stirrup cups.

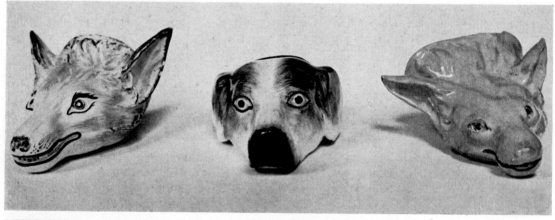

senior died in 1814, and the business was then styled J. and W. Ridgway until the early 1830s, when William established the Bell Bank Pottery and eventually absorbed at least six other firms, including Elijah Mayer and Son; Hickes, Meigh and Johnson; and Palmer and Wilson. He traded as W. Ridgway and Co.

John Ridgway continued the Cauldon Place Works with the aid of partners, the business being styled John Ridgway and Co. He became the Queen's potter in 1842, and in 1851 the Jury of the Great Exhibition rated him as one of the most important potters in the country. In 1855 the firm was sold to T. C. Brown-Westhead, Moore and Co. The goods made at Cauldon Place included almost every description of ware in china and earthenware, from inexpensive to costly table ware and cabinet pieces, although the latter are rare. The firm's most popular production was a translucent cane-coloured ware. A characteristic plate in bone china has a rim decorated with loops of ribbon extending from the beaded edge.

In 1852 John Ridgway patented (No. 14080) a means of lustring ceramics in silver and copper, using the electro-deposit method invented by George Elkington in the 1830s. The specification states that the vessels were first thinly varnished, dried and then immersed in a solution of 'phosphorus reduced by bisulphureted carbon, then in nitrate of silver and set aside to dry'. This produced silver lustre, copper lustre being produced with sulphate of copper.

John Ridgway was one of the earliest potters to protect his designs by registering them at Stationers' Hall; the earliest so far noted was a jug marked 'Published by J. RIDGWAY & Co/CAULDON PLACE/October 1 1835'. Jugs dated in this way may be found for every year until mid-1842, when industrial designs could be registered at the Patent Office (see Chapter 26). From 1840 the name on the mark was JOHN RIDGWAY & Co. A miniature dinner set in bone china registered July 28th, 1855, bears the same name.

Early marks were impressed: I RIDGWAY until 1814, and RIDGWAY & SONS. Printed marks include I RIDGWAY over a potter's kiln until 1814; a shield containing the pattern name and the initials J W R in script until about 1830; JOHN RIDGWAY & Co/CAULDON PLACE/POTTERS TO HER MAJESTY, with the royal arms above and 'By Royal Appointment' below, from 1842.

William Henry Goss established his pottery at Stoke-upon-Trent in 1858, specialising in terra-cotta, parian statuary and ivory porcelain—a fine-quality parian capable of making paper-thin hollow-ware. He soon began the manufacture of jewelled porcelain, such as had long been made at Sèvres and was also being produced by Minton, Worcester and elsewhere. The jewels tended to fall out, however. Goss evolved a new process of jewelling porcelain: he indented the designs for the jewels in the damp clay and in these inserted the jewels, all previously cut. They were thus made secure by contraction of the paste during firing. Goss's process also resulted in more brilliant effects. He decorated cabinet ware, tea and coffee services, pastille and scented ribbon burners and vases, as well as scent flasks, pomade boxes, rice powder jars, to be filled by London and Parisian perfumiers.

Then in 1872 Goss was granted a patent for improvements 'in manufacturing articles of jewellery, dress ornaments, dress fastenings, smoke shades for lamps and gas-burners and the handles of cups ... also brooches, ear-rings, the heads of scarf pins, hair pins, and shawl pins, the trinkets called charms, bracelets, necklaces, stud and ring fittings and many other articles'. The floral brooches became very fashionable, and several other potters produced similar jewellery, notably Minton, Worcester and Belleek. The flowers and foliage were modelled in the round with paper-thin delicacy in pure white, often naturalistically tinted in colours.

Towards the end of the century his son Adolphus W. H. Goss, always keen on heraldry, conceived the idea of issuing ornamental ware in ivory porcelain decorated with town and other coats-of-arms in full colour, and he invented a series of brilliant enamels ideal for the purpose. Goss's heraldic china became a best seller and continued so for a quarter of a century.

The name 'W. H. Goss' was impressed or printed on early ware. Heraldic porcelain was similarly marked, with the addition, on fine pieces, of a rising goshawk ducally gorged.

T. and R. Boote moved from the Kiln Croft Works to the Waterloo Potteries, Burslem, in 1850, and in the following year the *Art Journal* noted that the firm 'has already attained considerable eminence as producers of fine earthenware.... Some is made by their patent mosaic process [see p. 76] the patterns being let in and giving the effect of bas-reliefs without being raised.... Other jugs are in flown-coloured parian with flowers and fruit beautifully modelled in high relief in white'. These are now very rare, as are copies of the Portland vase, measuring about three feet in height and decorated by the patent process. Flower vases were made in the Gothic style with stained glass inserted in perforated niches.

Ornamental ware was discontinued from about 1865, shortly after the firm had been granted a patent (No. 2795 of 1864) for 'improvements in articles made from clay and other like plastic materials'. The Boote firm then concentrated entirely on carefully decorated ironstone china, the entire output of the factory being exported to the United States of America.

The only marks noted until 1865 have been T&RB impressed or printed, or a Staffordshire knot containing the letters B&Co. Thereafter the mark, printed in black or red, was the royal coat-of-arms as shown on the patent grant, above ROYAL PATENT/IRONSTONE /T&R BOOTE.

Wedgwood is a name invariably associated with Josiah Wedgwood of Etruria. There was, however, in mid-Victorian times another powerful potter named Wedgwood. This was Enoch Wedgwood, trading as E. Wedgwood and Co., who in 1862 acquired the Unicorn Pottery, Tunstall, and shortly employed nearly seven hundred workpeople. The firm specialised in stone china of various qualities, particularly ironstone china, which was made in an endless range of shapes and decorations. The Asiatic pheasant was introduced by this firm and became a standard pattern for inexpensive ware throughout the Potteries. Some cabinet ware was produced, and services painted with heraldic devices. Jewelled ivory porcelain was also made. Enoch Wedgwood built up a considerable export trade by designing goods especially to the requirements of foreign countries.

The marks were E WEDGWOOD & Co impressed; STONE CHINA/WEDGWOOD & Co impressed; and IMPERIAL IRON STONE CHINA in a circle enclosing the name WEDGWOOD & Co.

Pinder, Bourne and Hope, Burslem, succeeded Enoch Wood and Sons in 1846. Figures patted by them from the Enoch Wood moulds will be found. They are painted in the style of the third quarter of the 19th century, and are thus not difficult to distinguish even when not impressed BOURNE. The firm's chief productions, however, were terracotta and good-quality earthenware decorated in styles fashionable on bone china. From time to time, table services are found painted with landscapes in monochrome, each piece with one or two different views, deep orange being a favourite colour. These sometimes bear the signature 'E. Gedge'. In 1877 the firm was acquired by Henry Doulton.

John Adams and Co., Hanley, who traded as Adams and Bromley from 1873, were specialists in high-quality jasper ware, some of which is now attributed to much earlier periods, particularly in the case of vases, tea- and coffee-pots, table kettles, tea services, candlesticks, fruit bowls, jugs, cameos and medallions after the 18th-century designs by Josiah Wedgwood. Adams's parian portrait busts were notable for their life-like character and included the rare 'Charles Dickens' and the more frequent 'Gladstone'. Majolica (see p. 165) was skilfully potted and decorated and included garden fountains and seats, vases exceeding four feet in height, figures, bread trays and cheese dishes. The impressed marks were ADAMS & Co; ADAMS & BROMLEY; A & B.

20

Liverpool

THE HERCULANEUM POTTERY was the only Liverpool pottery that continued into the 19th century. Solon writes: 'No special improvements can be traced in connection with it. Its aim was chiefly to reproduce, not unsuccessfully, the work of Davenport and other Staffordshire potters.' It was in 1793 that Richard Abbey established his factory, specialising in the manufacture of finely printed pottery jugs. He was an engraver formerly employed by Sadler and Green, and the designer and engraver of the celebrated series of quasi-heraldic jugs. In 1796, under Worthington, Humble and Holland, the plant was reorganised. A foreman was obtained from Burslem, together with about forty workers experienced in the various branches of the industry. As Wedgwood had called his factory Etruria, the Liverpool venture was named Herculaneum. Thus, at the very beginning the traditional potting methods of Liverpool were abandoned in favour of those of Staffordshire.

The early earthenware, light in weight and with a fine, creamy glaze, was obviously patterned on Wedgwood's queen's ware, but is somewhat greyer in tone, and differs from Leeds in being less yellow. Transfer-printing was the chief decoration, designs being applied to all manner of useful pieces—dinner, tea, coffee and toilet services, punch bowls, jugs, mugs. In some instances the popular pierced basketwork edge was used, and one service, printed in blue, bears views of the principal towns in England.

The other chief resource of the early years was hand-painted ware, and here the Staffordshire decorator excelled. With so fine a base, and so successful a glaze, there was no reason why this type of pottery should not be of superlative quality, providing that the decoration was free and charming. Among the wares decorated by hand are some displaying landscape panels, well painted in colour or in sepia shading.

Another class of ware, made from about 1800, consisted of jugs with bas-relief decoration, rivals of the famous Turner jugs. This type of ware is a late development of the old stoneware decorated in relief, and, though retaining some of its crudeness of expression, is bright and cheerful in design. These jugs are often classed by collectors as 'Pratt ware', even though impressed with the Herculaneum mark. This type of decoration often showed some contemporary event, or concerned itself with simple caricature.

The jugs were decorated with a peculiar olive-green, gaudy orange, brown and dark blue.

This was the period marked by the introduction of bone china, which had created apprehension among the old-established porcelain potters. Herculaneum decided to enter this field, the first oven being fired in 1800. Every kind of table ware was made, transfer decoration being used extensively. Combined tea and coffee services ornamented with bat printing were featured in red, black, green and brown, figures of men and women being adapted from Bartolozzi prints. These might be enriched with thin washes of colour Views of spas, country houses and the like were printed and may often be identified by printed titles beneath the ware. Heraldic services date from 1805. Urn-shaped vases in sets of three were decorated in brilliant colours, the body usually being of a solid tone— red, blue or orange—with a reserve on either side containing flowers, figures or landscape. Handles were in the form of conventionalised birds, dolphins, winged heads and so on. From 1833 Herculaneum bone china was heavy and opaque, although potting and glaze remained of excellent quality.

In addition to bone china and earthenware, other varieties of ceramics were introduced. Caneware, Egyptian black, terra-cotta and a bright green glaze in imitation of Wedgwood's are some of the kinds that may be encountered. Blue printing was carried out on pearl ware of hard, compact body. Figures were modelled closely on Staffordshire lines, including excellent busts in both bone china and earthenware. Biscuit vases are noted occasionally. Like any other lively concern of its day, Herculaneum was anxious to please the public taste and was forced to experiment widely.

The final phase of the factory is less distinguished. It continued under much the same management from 1806 to 1833, when it was reorganised under the control of Thomas Case and John Mort. Manufacturing continued in the cheaper and more commerical wares until 1841, when the factory closed, bringing to an end the notable record of half a century.

Many of the products issuing from the Herculaneum kilns were marked, and from these it is possible to distinguish between the two periods. There seems to have been little consistency about the early work, but after 1800, and continuously to 1822, the name HERCULANEUM was frequently used, printed in an arc, enclosing a crown, or carried on a strap round a crown. In 1822, upon a resolution of the committee of management, it was decided to identify the products more fully by causing the words HERCULANEUM POTTERY to be impressed or printed on all china and earthenware. This later mark, which continued to 1833, is sometimes associated with the liver bird, the heraldic device of the city of Liverpool, either with or without a scroll. For a short time an anchor was used.

At near-by Warrington in 1798 two brothers named Bolton, with Joseph Ellis as the practical partner, established a large pottery which ended in bankruptcy in 1812. The collection in the Warrington Museum includes blue-printed pearl ware, painted cream-coloured ware, Egyptian black and gold and silver lustre. Jewitt refers to the manufacture of bone china here and describes it as of inferior quality, creamy in colour, ornamented with raised borders and groups of figures painted in blue. No mark has been recorded. In 1941 I chanced to be on the site of the pottery immediately after the discovery of an old bricked-in oven. This contained about a hundred and fifty pieces of domestic ware in the biscuit, almost black with dust but otherwise uninjured.

21

Sunderland Pottery

SUNDERLAND, FOR six centuries one of Britain's principal shipbuilding centres, was well known during late Georgian and early Victorian days for its inexpensive decorative earthenware made by a group of enterprising potters. Productions covered a wide range, from common brown earthenware to enamelled creamware and silver lustre, in which practical service and robust ornament were combined. As a general rule, the lighter the weight of a piece of Sunderland pottery the older it may be considered. Now eagerly collected, it has already been reproduced by the fakers.

Much factual information regarding the various makers of this ware, hitherto unpublished, is to be found in *Potteries of Sunderland and District*, edited by James Crawley (Museum and Art Gallery, Sunderland, 1s. 6d.). This booklet enables the collector to place marked pieces within well-defined limits by referring to the chronology of name changes, and I am indebted to its editor for many historical details regarding the makers.

White earthenware was first made at Sunderland in 1740, when furnaces and mills for calcining and crushing flints were established at near-by Newbottle. Early in the 19th century several such mills were in operation, one with a weekly output of twenty tons of powdered flint, an essential ingredient of white earthenware. Ample flints were close at hand, coal was plentiful, white clay was carried to the district as colliers' ballast, and local deposits of clay suitable for common brown ware had been worked for centuries.

The first pottery in the northern counties to produce transfer-decorated earthenware, and celebrated for its pink lustre ware during the first half of the 19th century, was the Hylton Pot Works on the banks of the Wear, three miles west of Sunderland. This pottery was established in 1762 by William Maling and continued in operation until 1867. Maling moved to Newcastle-upon-Tyne in 1815, the premises then being acquired by John Phillips, a former works manager who had left to operate a pottery of his own. He re-named the works the Hylton Pottery.

Among early productions were commemorative mugs in white earthenware, hand painted with floral patterns, for distribution to guests at weddings and other social gatherings. Transfer-decorated and enamelled domestic ware was produced, chimney ornaments, frog mugs, and jugs displaying views of the Wearmouth Bridge, nautical scenes, and masonic emblems. In Sunderland Museum are examples of ware from this pottery impressed with the following marks: MALING; HYLTON POT WORKS; PHILLIPS & MALING; JOHN PHILLIPS HYLTON POTTERY; J PHILLIPS HYLTON POTTERY. This list suggests that earthenware from this factory was unmarked after the death of John Phillips.

The wares produced at Hylton Pottery and the Sunderland Pottery reveal many similarities, and transfers from the same copperplates were used by both establishments. The early history of the Sunderland Pottery, known locally as the Garrison Pottery, because of its proximity to Sunderland Barracks, has not yet been unearthed, but in 1807 the property was leased to John Phillips. It is assumed that he operated the factory until about 1812, when he was joined by Robert Dixon. They remained partners until about 1819, after which no more is heard of Phillips. William Austin became Dixon's partner, the firm being styled Dixon, Austin and Co. until 1826. Alexander Phillips, believed to have been a nephew of the founder, then became a partner, and until 1840 the firm was known as Dixon, Austin, Phillips and Co. No more is known of Austin from that year, and until the pottery closed in 1865 it operated under the name of Dixon, Phillips and Co.

The Sunderland Pottery during its life of sixty years produced a wide variety of sponged, printed and pink lustre ware, well-modelled figures, frog mugs, bridge mugs, Jack Crawford mugs, Easter and birthday eggs, tobacco jars, stands for clocks and watches, models of greyhounds, plaques, carpet bowls and copper and silver lustre.

Marks impressed on examples in the Sunderland Museum are: J PHILLIPS SUNDERLAND POTTERY; PHILLIPS & Co; PHILLIPS & Co SUNDERLAND POTTERY; PHILLIPS & Co SUNDERLAND 1813; DIXON & Co SUNDERLAND 1813; DIXON & Co; DIXON & Co SUNDERLAND POTTERY; DIXON & AUSTIN'S SUNDERLAND POTTERY; DIXON AUSTIN PHILLIPS & Co; DIXON PHILLIPS & Co (enclosing an anchor).

Southwick, or Scott's Pottery, established in 1788, made some good-quality decorative ware during its existence of 109 years. Anthony Scott, with his father Henry Scott and Edward Atkinson, were the founders and until 1800 they operated as Atkinson and Co. The name was then changed to Atkinson, Scott and Co., Atkinson retiring from the firm to become a china and earthenware merchant. Upon Anthony Scott's death in 1829 the firm became Scott and Sons, changed in 1844 to Scott Brothers.

From Scott's Pottery came some of the most clear-cut of Sunderland lions, a streaked pottery resembling Linthorpe ware, olive-grey or brown mosaic made by a process devised by Thomas P. Scott (1801—1864), fire-proof Welsh trays, religious plaques, smokers' companions, pink lustre, enamelled creamware, blue-and-white striped ware, and bridge jugs, mugs and plates, as well as some excellent jasper ware in the Wedgwood style.

Transfer designs on marked pieces of Scott's ware in the Sunderland |Museum collec-

69 to 73. (Above) A lidless Cadogan teapot with relief ornament and rich chocolate coloured glaze: impressed COPELAND & GARRETT, c. 1840. (Top right) Galleried teapot in bone china in colours and gold: Rockingham c. 1840. (Right) Coffee pot of bone china by Josiah Spode II. (Lower right) Stone china teapot by W. T. Copeland with blue ground and white figures applied in relief, c. 1850. (Below) Teapot in bone china with gold ornament by the bat printing process on a blue ground: W. T. Copeland.

74 to 77. (Above left) Teacup and saucer made at New Hall in hard paste porcelain. (Above right) Worcester cup and saucer marked 'Chamberlain's Worcester and 155 New Bond Street'. (Below) Jug in Rockingham stone china with applied decoration in blue, and the mark affixed to the base.

tion include a south-east view of Wearmouth Bridge with the initials E A (Edward Atkinson) in the design; a west view of the bridge; an east view of the bridge with the name 'Edward Barker' in the design; 'Crimea'; 'The Flag that Braved a Thousand Years'; 'Sailor's Return'; jugs with transfer designs of game cocks, and plaques with portraits of John Wesley and Adam Clark. Transfers, mottoes and verses are often the same as those used by Moore of Southwick. Those used by the Scotts, however, were embellished with additional floral transfers in black, and these may be found on interior and exterior rims of jugs and mugs.

Marks found on the Museum examples of Scott pottery are: SCOTT (usually impressed); Ed. ATKINSON; ANTHONY SCOTT & SONS; S & SONS SOUTHWICK; SCOTT BROS (impressed); SCOTT BROTHERS & Co; S B & Co; SCOTT'S SUPERIOR FIREPROOF; SCOTT'S WARRANTED FIREPROOF (impressed).

The Wear Pottery, established by John Brunton in 1789 and closed in 1883, was Scott's adjoining neighbour. In 1803 Samuel Moore and Peter Austin acquired the business from Brunton, and in 1861 the name of the firm became S. Moore and Co. Productions of interest to the collector include decorative flower pots, frog mugs, bridge jugs, chintz pattern jugs, copper, silver and pink lustre, plaques displaying coloured transfer pictures and blue and white domestic ware with key borders enclosing scenic views.

The Wear Pottery apparently did not mark its productions earlier than 1861. The presence of post-1861 marks on jugs and other ware ornamented with views of the old Wearmouth Bridge is interesting to those who have always attributed such ware exclusively to the early years of the 19th century. In addition the Museum possesses marked wares with transfer designs resembling those used by Scott's Pottery. These include plates with a series of eight scenes depicting 'The Bottle', portraying the evils of drink and believed to have been designed by George Cruikshank; sporting and Waverley designs on plaques; an east view of the new Wearmouth Bridge; a frigate in full sail; and designs commemorating Nelson's victory and the Crimean war. The marks used at this factory were: MOORE and Co STONEWARE SOUTHWICK; S MOORE & Co; S M & Co; MOORE and Co (impressed); MOORE & Co SOUTHWICK.

The Low Ford or Dawson's Pottery was founded before 1796 when it came under the ownership of John Dawson (1799—1848). A new works was built in 1836 and up-to-date machinery installed, and output soon became the largest of any Sunderland pottery. After the death of John Dawson business declined and the pottery ceased work in 1864. Collectors' pieces from the Dawson pottery included queen's ware, copper, silver and pink lustre, rectangular tiles in colour and sepia with landscape views, round table tops to fit into cabinet work, canary-yellow mugs with the bridge in black, inkpots shaped like birds' nests, bachelors' supper sets, and tea-sets with coloured transfer designs bordered with pink lustre. 'John Gilpin's Ride' was a popular transfer series at Dawson's Pottery. Marks found on Sunderland Museum examples are: DAWSON (impressed); J DAWSON LOW FORD; FORD; FORD POTTERY SOUTH HYLTON 1800; DAWSON & Co; DAWSON & Co LOW FORD; J DAWSON & Co LOW FORD POTTERY.

Thomas Snowball owned Sheepfold's Warehouse where, from the late 1860s to 1885, he added lustre decoration to ware already printed, finishing it off in an enamelling kiln. He also bought biscuit ware from the near-by St Bede's Pottery and from Staffordshire, his brother Ralph supervising the application of the transfer designs while Thomas himself was responsible for the lustre decoration. Religious plaques were issued in large numbers and glass rolling-pins decorated in oils. The St Bede's Pottery was established in 1874 by Ralph Seddon who, in addition to making common white ware, supplied frog mugs and other articles to Thomas Snowball who, for a short time, probably 1884 and 1885, was proprietor. When Snowball went out of business in 1885 the St Bede's Pottery was closed.

William Ball established the Deptford Pottery in 1857 and after his death in 1884 his two sons continued, trading as Ball Brothers. They made coarse earthenware, and bought from other potters white earthenware which they decorated with pink-lustre transfers and overpainting. The Ball firm's lustre is notable for its distinctively orange tint, very different from Sunderland's characteristic pink lustre. Ball acquired the original moulds for the well-known Sunderland lions; those made by him may be recognised by the even teeth which replaced the vicious-looking fangs of original productions from the Sunderland Pottery. Occasional pieces from this factory are impressed BALL BROTHERS SUNDERLAND.

The foregoing firms comprise the Sunderland group of potters whose work is collected. Many collectors specialise in Sunderland lustre ware, of which a vast quantity was issued between about 1820 and 1860. A considerable proportion of this appears to have been exported to France and Germany; production on a smaller scale continued until the 1880s. The so-called silver and copper lustres of excellent quality were made, marked pieces now finding their way into museums, but Sunderland is better known for its pink lustre.

Lustre ware, its surface metalised rather than lustred, was produced by the action of heat on a metallic-oxide solution, usually gold and platinum for silver lustre. Silver oxide was not used because the resulting lustre quickly blackened by exposure to the air.

Copper lustre was for long believed by collectors to have been produced by copper oxide; such lustre, when used, has discoloured. By using gold oxide the potters avoided this danger. Gold lustre was applied to a red-brown body to reduce the yellow metallic brilliancy of the gold. The pink and purple shades of Sunderland, with their faintly golden sheen, were obtained by a thin application of the metallic solution over a white or cream body, or over a white glaze. In those pieces displaying a deep bronze or copper ground and pink lustre, a reddish brown earthenware was used, the parts to be lustred pink being prepared by covering with a thick white glaze.

Sunderland was renowned for its mottled lustre—speckled, marbled or spotted are alternative terms—and although Staffordshire, Liverpool and Bristol potters manufactured precisely similar effects, the decoration earned for itself the generic name of 'Sunderland'. The pink and white mottled effect was achieved by using the old Chinese methods of spraying by blowing thin oil through a tube, the far end of which was covered with fine muslin. The oil was forced through the gauze in the form of tiny bubbles that burst upon the ware, forming irregular spots, waves and marblings. In some instances reserved panels were left for painted enamel or printed decoration over the glaze.

Sunderland figures in earthenware have a purely decorative quality entirely their own. At their most ambitious they might be copied from the early porcelain figures of Chelsea, such as the 'Four Seasons' in silver lustre made by Phillips and Co., a set of which was sold at Christie's in 1818 for fourteen guineas. Somewhat similar sets decorated in colours and pink lustre, on square plinths, were issued between 1820 and 1826 by Dixon, Austin and Co., whose name was impressed beneath each figure. The same firm made the magnificent bulls in dark-hued copper lustre, remarkable examples of earthenware statuary, as were the well-known Sunderland lions from the same pottery. Among other earthenware figures made by this firm were 'Joan of Arc', the 'Duke of Wellington', 'Napoleon', the 'Child Samuel', pairs of shepherds and shepherdesses, and busts of Nelson, Wesley and Queen Victoria. Watch stands were made in the form of grandfather clocks and church towers. To ensure stability, a couple of moulded figures were mounted on the plinth.

The Sunderland potters were well known for their animal figures, usually issued in pairs. Familiar among their chimney ornaments is the dog somewhat resembling a spaniel and known as a comforter or spaniel's gentle, a cross between the Maltese dog and a King Charles's spaniel. In Sunderland these ornaments were made in five sizes, ranging from about six inches to eighteen inches in height. They were almost invariably white, with their long ears and scattered spots in copper or pink lustre.

Familiar, too, is the cream jug in the form of a cow with the tail looped upward and over the haunches to serve as a handle. On top of the hollow body was fitted a flat lid, which, oddly enough, lacked a handle such as appeared on the silver prototype of the 1760s. The jug was filled through this opening and the milk was poured from the animal's mouth. The obvious difficulty in keeping such a jug clean enough for fresh milk and cream has made collectors suggest that it really served as a pastille burner, but this has yet to be confirmed. The cow stood on a shallow oval plinth and was usually decorated with lustre —the Staffordshire variety were enamelled. A Sunderland example in enamels has been noted, however, bearing a mark consisting of the impressed name of Dixon, Phillips and Co. encircling an anchor, thus dating it between 1840 and 1865.

Sunderland cats, sitting upright on square cushions, were made, but are now extremely rare.

Sunderland transfers were usually printed in black, sometimes with over-painting in red, green, yellow or brown; blue and white ware was issued throughout the great period of its popularity. Transfers in green, yellow and red might be used from 1840, but seldom more than a single colour on one piece of earthenware as each needed individual firing, adding to the cost. The Sunderland pottery from about 1850 appears to have made use of the Collins-Reynolds method of printing designs in red, blue and yellow from a single transfer with one firing. Identification of unmarked pieces by means of transfers is unreliable as transfers could be bought from specialists in this branch of the pottery industry. There appears, too, to have been some interchange of copperplates and transfers between the Sunderland potters.

Sentimental and religious verses applied to pottery in black transfer were a feature of Sunderland ware. Many of these verses were directed to the sailor, such as: 'The Sailor Boy'; 'When first I was a foremast man'; 'Jack on a Cruise'; 'Sailor tost in stormy seas'; and 'England, England, Glorious Name'. More than a hundred of these verses have been collected. Religious plaques, some of them in frames coloured yellow to resemble carved and gilded work, were best sellers in mid-Victorian days; some displayed hand-painted texts such as 'Prepare to meet thy God'. Many of these were decorated by Thomas Snowball.

For almost a century Sunderland pottery was issued decorated with transfer pictures of the Wearmouth Bridge, often wrongly termed Sunderland Bridge, the latter being fourteen miles away at Croxdale. The Wearmouth Bridge, opened in 1796, was a renowned engineering feat of the period, being the longest single-span cast-iron bridge in the world. Some of the pictures are captioned with factual information, describing the bridge as having a span of 236 feet, a height of 100 feet, the amount of cast iron as 214 tons, and wrought iron 46 tons. The bridge was levelled and widened in 1859, and replaced in 1929. Wearmouth Bridge was usually printed in black and might be over-painted by hand; rare examples are to be found in blue underglaze.

The Sunderland Museum exhibits twenty-two different pictures of the bridge, fourteen of which are rarely found. The Museum booklet notes that 'each of these varies in detail such as numbers and types of ships, figures on the river banks and so on. They fall into the following categories: west views, 7; east views, 6; south-east views, 4; and of the bridge after alteration in 1859, 4 east views and 1 west view. The standard of design varies: two of high artistic merit are to be found on queen's ware mugs, one with the initials E A, and the other with the name Edward Barker, included in the transfers. Marked specimens bear the following views: jug, J. Phillips, Hylton Pottery—south-east view;

quart frog mug, Moore & Co—east view; quart mug, Dawson & Co—west view; jug, Dixon & Co—west view; mug, Moore and Co—west view; frog mug, Dixon & Co 1813—west view; bowl, Moore and Co—east view of bridge after alteration'.

A series of mugs was issued by the Sunderland potters to commemorate the exploit of Jack Crawford, the local hero of the Battle of Camperdown, 1797. During the heat of the engagement Crawford nailed the flag to the topmast after it had been shot away by the Dutch. The transfer print is adapted from a lithograph published in 1797.

Frog mugs were a Sunderland speciality intended to provide fun in convivial company. A well-modelled, naturalistically coloured frog with wide-open mouth was fixed inside the mug in such a position that it appeared to follow the liquor into the mouth as the last drops were drained. Such mugs were invariably intended for right-handed drinkers. In some examples the frog was hollow and of a trick variety arranged to spurt a stream of liquid into the face of an unwary drinker. As late as the 1870s such mugs were being made at the St Bede's Pottery.

The Sunderland potters quickly acquired a reputation for inexpensive 'gift china' of a jovial type as well as for special social occasions. Birthdays, christenings and weddings might be commemorated with inscriptions painted to commission and often fired in a local muffle kiln. Much was made merely to be peddled by hawkers or offered as gaudy prizes at fairs.

Ewers and jugs were sold in sets which might consist of as many as a dozen matching pieces. The smallest would then be a cream jug, and the largest of two-and-a-half-gallon capacity with a small extra support beneath the lip for holding it steady while pouring, thus relieving strain upon the handle. Bowls, too, were made in matching sets, and some collectors find interest in re-creating a set in which each bowl is ornamented with a transfer design illustrating the month of the year.

22

Chesterfield Brown Ware and Spirit Flasks

CHESTERFIELD WARE, a salt-glazed stoneware made by the Derbyshire potters, is a ceramic lying half-way between hard porcelain and pearl ware, and considerably harder than either. Wholly opaque, intensely hard and non-porous, it displays a glassy texture when fractured, suggestive of hard porcelain. It was generally made from a single plastic clay with the addition of felspar, and quartz in the form of sand or crushed flint. When fired at a high temperature the clay becomes highly vitrified, ensuring a closeness of texture which makes it as hard as stone. The colours to which good-quality clays usually burn range from a yellowish buff to a dark brown.

Chesterfield ware of the early 19th century was usually glazed by introducing salt into the kiln. This resulted in a durable, inexpensive, non-poisonous glaze which gave the surface an attractive sheen. Variation in tint was obtained by slip-glazing parts of the surface before firing. The heat of the kiln combined with the salt-glaze to colour this a rich brown. It was made throughout the 19th century, but much of it was catalogued as 'antique', and resembled 18th-century patterns, so that much Victorian ware is now wrongly attributed. The 19th-century Chesterfield ware is, however, of higher quality than earlier work owing to technical improvements in manufacture and the discovery of finer clay deposits.

In 1806, when a coaching road was being constructed from Derby to Alfreton, the navvies' picks and shovels revealed stoneware clay of a quality eventually found to be the finest in Europe.

William Bourne, a stoneware potter at near-by Belper, immediately acquired the working rights of the land. Three years later his son Joseph, then twenty-one, began working the new clay beds, founding what became the Denby pottery. He concentrated at first on producing domestic ware and a certain amount of ornamental work. By 1815 he was facing competition from the Lambeth firm of Doulton.

Bourne invented an improved stoneware kiln for which he was granted a patent (No. 4871) on November 22nd, 1823. Known as 'Chesterfield brown ware kilns', these improved quality and greatly reduced costs. They were double the height of the old kilns, and while the lower half was fired by mouths opening into the kiln, the flame passing perpendicularly upward, the upper portion was fed by heat passing from the kiln through flues at the side. A further patent was granted to Bourne in August, 1847 (No. 11831). In this two kilns were stacked one above the other, the 'lower one being heated at two levels, at bottom and half-way up. The heat of the lower kiln passes into the upper. Instead of five flues as formerly there is only one chimney at the top'.

Three qualities of ware were fired in these kilns. At the top was burned ware of Brampton clay. This was incapable of withstanding the full fire, but produced Chesterfield ware of much closer texture than any other and when glazed would resist the action of acids. Fire clay known as Lidd clay was burned in the lower part of the oven. In the middle portion was placed ware made from equal proportions of Lidd and Brampton clays. It is possible for collectors to distinguish these three qualities of Chesterfield ware from that made under the 1823 patent, and this from earlier ware.

The Derbyshire potters of Chesterfield ware made articles that differed little one from the other and are difficult to distinguish except by mark or by comparison with known pieces. Puzzle jugs were made in forms unaltered from those of the 18th century. The most usual form is a baluster or bulbous shape with a long wide neck, an alternative being spherical with a narrow neck about as long as the body, which might be entirely plain or decorated with simply incised patterns, but more frequently was encircled with figures and other designs in relief. Height normally ranges between seven and eight inches, but examples have been noted as short as five and a half inches and as tall as ten inches. Perforations in the neck may be simple or elaborated, such as series of hearts, diamonds, semicircles and circles arranged in formal patterns. Spouts may number three, four or five. For success the drinker would have to hold the jug and close a hole beneath the handle with one hand and with the other, held above the wide mouth, close two diametrically opposing spouts. In this uncomfortable position, slowly syphoning the liquor through the narrow tubes, it is difficult to empty the jug without spilling a drop.

Hunting jug was the trade name for the Chesterfield brown-ware jug encircled with hunting or dead game subjects in high relief. Stag- and fox-hunting scenes were popular from the 1820s until the 1890s. These depicted a scene of huntsmen and hounds chasing their quarry, with other relief subjects of trees, windmills, beehives, men seated smoking or drinking, or in groups walking. The handle was usually in the form of a cleverly modelled greyhound and the beak spout might have a mask below. These jugs were listed as being used for serving hot punch and toddy as they held heat longer than any comparable ware. Cylindrical jugs, catalogued as canettes, and mugs also belong to the hunting series. Some of the larger of these vessels might possess two, three or four greyhound handles. Two-handled posset pots and loving cups were made in Chesterfield brown ware as late as the 1880s, some of them incised with inscriptions, names and dates of the 18th century. The *Art Journal*, 1869, illustrated a contemporaneous example made at Brampton dated 1750.

Other productions which collectors are often inclined to attribute to the 18th century were made between 1850 and 1890, such as candlesticks, following the classical styles evolved by the silversmiths and repeated by Josiah Wedgwood in fine stoneware and by Leeds in cream-coloured earthenware; tea kettles heated by spirit lamps, in styles also adapted from mid-Georgian silversmiths; tobacco jars elaborately encircled with sporting scenes or dead game in relief, and with domed covers supporting candlesocket finials; grotesque and twisted tobacco pipes for wall decoration.

Toby jugs were also in considerable production in patterns copied from the old models. Toby jugs in enamelled earthenware and in Rockingham ware were made during the third quarter of the 19th century, at the Swadlincote Pottery, Derbyshire. The so-called Rockingham toby jugs are often wrongly attributed to the Bramelds of the Rockingham factory at Swinton, Yorkshire. But the term 'Rockingham' applied in this connection indicates a lead glaze heavily stained with oxide of manganese, the result being a rich purple-brown.

Jugs modelled in the form of a bear, sitting upright on its haunches and closely hugging a dog that has been set to bait it, were perpetuated from the 18th century in Chesterfield brown ware and continued to be made until the 1880s and probably later. The surface of the body may be smooth, but in others it is roughened with applied chippings of clay. The detachable head forms a drinking cup. Touches of slip suggest ears, eyes, muzzle, teeth, paws and collar.

At least twenty potters produced Chesterfield brown ware which the London merchants preferred to market under the term 'Nottingham Ware'. Most of this, obviously, was unmarked. Impressed marks found on fine hard ware include: KNOWLES—the Welshpool and Payne Potteries, Brampton; OLDFIELD—John Oldfield and Co., Brampton; BRIDDON—William Briddon, Brampton; BOURNE in several styles—Bourne and Son, Denby; WILLIAM BURTON—Codnor Park until 1833.

Chesterfield ware was put to many other uses and perhaps the most interesting to collectors are the spirit flasks, which had a considerable vogue in the second quarter of the century; specimens have been recorded dating to the 1860s. Although designed for the rough wear of taverns and inns, these were of a quality which has earned a place for them in collections.

The early makers of brown stoneware made huge jars used by manufacturers of spirits, cordials and other liquors to convey supplies to inns and taverns. With the decline of the popularity of punch and punch-houses in the reign of George IV, they sought to extend their spirit trade in the taverns and inns. With this in view they ordered small stoneware spirit and cordial flasks, the shelf display of these attractively modelled flasks carrying clearly incised inscriptions of their contents such as 'Spicer's Cordial' and 'Old Tom'.

78 to 82 (Above) Vases with oviform bodies, in bone china: (*left to right*) painted in 1862 for W. T. Copeland & Sons by C. F. Hurton; painted in 1830 by Edwin Steele at Rockingham, with gilded oak leaves. Height 3 feet $2\frac{1}{2}$ inches; Rockingham, *c.* 1825, painted with fruit and flowers and lavishly gilded. (Below) Two vestibule vases in Mason's ironstone china, painted in the Chinese style; a Colebrookdale vase with a jade-green ground.

83 and 84. (Above) Victorian pottery: (*left to right*) plate painted by Thomas Bott of the Royal Worcester Co. in 1867; wall plate painted by Emile Lessore at Etruria in 1861; covered vase made by Copeland in 1862; vase designed by Alfred Stevens for Minton in 1864. (Below) Pottery designed by William de Morgan: (*left to right*) lustre-painted covered vase, between 1888 and 1898; lustre-painted dish, 1880s; vase painted in 'Persian' colours, 1887 or earlier.

Soon these flasks were given lively and popular imitative shapes ranging from barrels, pocket books and gunpowder flasks to pigs, grandfather clocks and tipstaffs. These containers led to more ambitious work culminating in a large variety of figure subjects. The upper half of the flat-faced oval flask was surmounted by a bust of a celebrity. Later the whole flask might be shaped in the form of a full-length figure. Early spirit-flask figures were highly individualistic portraits, but later they were superseded by jolly sailors and the like.

Considerable skill went into the creation and production of these stoneware flasks. Absorbent plaster-of-paris moulds were cast from the designers' original models and the liquid clay poured into these, so that exact facsimiles of the hollow complicated shapes could be produced in unlimited numbers.

There was intense political excitement associated with parliamentary reform early in the reign of William IV (1830—1837), inns and ale-houses witnessing many a stormy scene. Cordial and spirit merchants realized that where their flasks were displayed customers would generally be on the side of reform. Accordingly they packed their liquors in stoneware flasks favouring Whig propaganda.

The plain surface of the lower part of such a flask might be impressed with the name of the individual represented, accompanied by an appropriate slogan such as 'Reform Cordial', 'The Spirit of Reform', 'The People's Rights', 'Bread for the Millions', or 'Irish Reform Cordial'. In the spirit flask representing Lord John Russell, the sponsor of the first Reform Bill is represented holding a scroll impressed with the legend 'The True Spirit of Reform'. Many thousands of reform spirit flasks were issued when the Great Charter became law in 1832.

Other bust portraits found on stoneware spirit flasks include William IV, Queen Adelaide, the Duke of York, the Duke of Wellington, Earl Grey, Lord Brougham, Sir Francis Burdett, Sir Robert Peel and the Irish patriot Daniel O'Connell.

The figure normally appears on both sides of the flask, but on rare occasions a different bust may be found on each side of a flask, set in a Gothic niche. An early example shows the Princess Victoria on one side, her mother the Duchess of Kent on the reverse.

More ambitious flasks presenting figures in the round were issued at the beginning of the new reign. Joseph Bourne at Denby issued a full-length figure of the queen in her coronation robes inscribed 'Queen Alexandrina Victoria', and on the reverse 'May Peace and Prosperity Reign'. These are also to be found with a handle to the back. A more capacious flask impressed 'Queen Victoria 1st' was issued at this time by Oldfield of Chesterfield. Prince Albert made his first appearance on a spirit flask in 1840. A full-length model of Sir Robert Peel shows him standing on a plinth, impressed beneath with the mark of Joseph Bourne. Later, 'Jenny Lind' and 'John Bull' flasks had a considerable vogue; probably the last of these flasks in the round was 'Jim Crow', issued in about 1860.

Each potter of these flasks issued his own version of a jolly sailor seated on a barrel impressed with the name of the spirit or cordial contained within, such as 'Old Tom' on the Oldfield flask. Doulton modelled tipsy sailors dancing and a man sitting on a barrel, both impressed 'All around my bar good customers I see'. Flasks modelled with figures representing 'Smoking' and 'Snuffing' came from the Vauxhall Pottery of John Wisker in the 1830s. Stephen Green, Lambeth, specialised in marine subjects such as mermaids and fishes, in various sizes up to about thirteen inches. Green also produced a very popular pistol design, as well as flasks in the form of the tipstaffs carried by sheriff's officers. The fifteen-inch examples have the letters v. r in relief on one side, the insignia of the Order of the Garter on the other. Shorter tipstaffs bear the arms of the City of London in relief.

Stoppers for spirit flasks were a problem and seldom are they found complete. In early examples they were modelled in the form of heads and each was ground individually by hand into its flask mouth. In 1833 John Wisker of the Vauxhall Pottery patented (No. 6523) a machine by which it was possible to grind stoppers into the necks of flasks mechanically and so ensure an airtight fit.

23

Belleek

EXQUISITELY DAINTY, feather light and eggshell thin, the hard parian ware of Belleek became renowned because its surface displayed an iridescence suggestive of mother of pearl. The Belleek Pottery was established in Ireland just over a century ago, late in 1857, by Robert William Armstrong, a London architect whose interest in ceramics had been aroused when his professional duties brought him in contact with Kerr and Co., Royal Porcelain Works, Worcester.

John Caldwell Bloomfield, owner of the Castle Caldwell estates in County Fermanagh, below the Donegal highlands, had long been aware that his lands contained vast deposits of felspar and china-clay. The huge success of the great potters at the Exhibition of 1851 prompted him to contact the Worcester establishment. Test consignments of Irish felspar sent to W. H. Kerr for experimental purposes proved to be of higher purity than any known English deposits. Kerr and Armstrong visited Castle Caldwell.

The delicate porcelain known as parian, then much in vogue for statuary, contained a large proportion of felspar. Final results were notably improved by the use of Castle Caldwell felspar, and by the spring of 1853 Kerr and Co. were advertising 'Irish Statuary Porcelain'. For the Dublin Exhibition of that year they produced a magnificent dessert service in statuary parian and glazed bone china with relief and gilded decoration, painted medallions and free-standing figures of characters from Shakespeare's *Midsummer Night's Dream*. This costly service was catalogued as made 'from materials the produce of Ireland'. Rival makers of statuary parian immediately demanded Irish felspar and Bloomfield was soon shipping consignments to the Mersey for despatch by canal to the Staffordshire potteries.

Armstrong, observing the huge demand for parian statuary, determined to establish a parian pottery in County Fermanagh, where ninety per cent of the raw materials and also fuel were immediately available, free of costly transport problems. His dominating idea was to undersell Staffordshire in the American market. Following consultations with possible financiers in London, Armstrong eventually laid his project before David M'Berney of Carlisle Bridge, Dublin, proprietor of a store then advertised as 'the Largest and Most Complete in the Three Kingdoms'. After long investigation M'Berney agreed to find the entire capital.

A factory of two ovens and other necessary kilns was built at Belleek on a small island in the River Erne about six miles from the sea, and navigable by small coastal craft. A 100-horse-power water-wheel made by Fairbairn of Manchester provided power for grinding, mixing and other mechanised processes.

In the autumn of 1857 the partners, trading as M'Berney and Armstrong, later as D. M'Berney and Co., began production, at first manufacturing what they termed 'ordinary useful goods'. Soon they began to make statuary parian, and it is obvious from the quality of early examples that skilled artists and workers in all branches were attracted from England.

Belleek statuary might be almost incredibly large and complicated, such as 'The Prisoner of Love', twenty-five and a quarter inches tall, and the magnificent equestrian group 'Richard Coeur de Lion' from Marochetti's statue facing the House of Lords. Statuary parian is a highly vitrified translucent biscuit porcelain, described in Chapter 8.

Belleek also made hard parian from a simpler formula: 67 parts felspar and 55 parts Cornish stone. Described by Silliman and Goodrich in 1854 as 'true hard porcelain', this ware had its fine granular surface smear-glazed by the Staffordshire potters. Lead glaze was inclined to follow the granulations, causing a faintly undulating surface. The Belleek firm found that by glazing their hard parian with a white lustre then newly invented by a Frenchman, Jules Brianchon, they achieved an absolutely smooth surface impervious to dirt and dust. They thus overcame contemporary criticism that hard parian was easily soiled and difficult to clean. Enamelled decoration and gilding were used successfully to ornament this ware, the most frequent colours being green and pastel pink, fired together in a muffle kiln at a temperature too low to melt the lustrous glaze.

The Castle Caldwell felspar ensured that Belleek parian was pure white. Slip was cast or paste manipulated so that shrinkage during the various processes reduced the ware to eggshell thinness, thus producing the delicate ware for which Belleek became celebrated.

The white lustre associated with Belleek parian ware was invented the same year that the pottery was established at Belleek. This French invention made it possible to glaze ceramics with a nacreous lustre giving the effect of mother of pearl. The manufacturing rights, protected by patent No. 1896 of 1857, were acquired by M'Berney and Armstrong, but the date of transfer is unknown. The patent was granted on January 1st, 1858, to 'Jules Joseph Henri Brianchon of Paris in the Empire of France', whose specification stated that the 'invention had, for its object, to import to ceramic substances the colour of gold, white and coloured mother of pearl, variegated and changing reflections of shells, of all kinds of minerals, and of the optical prism'. When correctly fired in the kiln, this displayed 'a splendour and metallic brilliancy comparable to that of mirrors, and of such solidity that the colours have the appearance of being under glass'.

Brianchon's glaze or lustre was prepared by melting 30 parts of resin and thoroughly stirring into it 10 parts of bismuth nitrate, followed by 45 parts of lavender oil. When cool a further 50 parts of lavender oil was added. Lustres of various tints were made possible by replacing the bismuth with another salt, such as nitrate of gold, for instance, which produced the rich tints of shells.

The Belleek technicians discovered that a film of this glaze, over the pure white of their hard porcelain pressed to eggshell thinness and delicacy, resulted in an effect yet unequalled in British ceramics. The high polish and mother-of-pearl iridescence at once made an immense appeal to Victorians.

The association of thin parian with mother-of-pearl lustre obviously influenced a style which met with immediate response and does not appear to have been reproduced by any other potter. This found expression in ornately modelled forms associated with marine life, sea shells being characteristic, with mermaids, sea-horses, dolphins, corals and marine plants. Jewitt illustrated thirty-six examples of Belleek parian reproduced from the *Art Journal*, 1877, about twenty-five incorporating marine devices in their modelling. Among these sketches is 'a grounds basin of a tea service made for Queen Victoria', composed of a sea-urchin supported by branches of coral.

Following the lead given by Herbert Minton in 1851, when he combined parian statuary with units of enamelled and gilded bone china, Belleek contrasted unglazed statuary parian with lustred hard parian. This effect does not appear to have been copied elsewhere, and could be achieved only by well-directed, highly skilled artist-potters. The results were costly.

This innovation was particularly effective for the stemmed dishes—centres and compotiers—of dessert services. The stem, rising from a substantial plinth, was virtually concealed by the surrounding statuary group composed of such details as a mermaid, a mythological sea-horse, and two amorini with fish tails, separated by three cardium shells as sweetmeat or comfit containers, the whole supporting a shallow shell-shaped dish for fruit.

Belleek became celebrated for parian baskets, already being made in Staffordshire. In 1863 John Smith of Hanley was recorded as a maker of 'parian twig baskets and brooches'. They were perhaps not made at Belleek until much later, for no mention is made of them in the *Art Journal* review of Belleek in 1877. Belleek baskets, almost unbelievably light in weight, are superb examples of the potter's craft, enriched as they are with hand-modelled flowers of gossamer-like fragility and resplendent with pearly lustre. The most frequent flowers and foliage are rose, thistle and shamrock in association, but chrysanthemum, dahlia, honeysuckle, picotee and carnation have been noted, all dependent for their beauty on the subtleties of texture and lustre. Baskets were made with and without covers and usually with D-handles, rarely with tall bail handles, and in sizes ranging up to about eighteen inches in length.

These oval and round baskets were hand constructed by women over plaster forms, originally from flat strips of parian paste, later in hand-rolled strips of round section cut into suitable lengths and kept plastic until required by covering with a damp cloth. Each part of every flower, petal, leaf, stem and the rest was modelled separately by girls on the palms of their hands, a process which impressed the paste with skin markings, sometimes still faintly visible beneath the lustre. The segments were skilfully assembled, finished with the aid of a few small wooden tools, and fixed into position with a touch of slip. No two flowers are precisely similar.

Ornamental productions during the period of financial control by the wealthy M'Berney were in effect subsidised. Profits from purely commercial ware were ploughed back so that well-paid designers and highly skilled operators could be retained. Following the deaths of M'Berney and Armstrong in 1884, their successors sold the business as a going concern to a local group of business men who, of necessity, were concerned mainly with profits. Mother-of-pearl parian continued in production, but in less costly versions than formerly. In addition, the firm made some excellently enamelled table services in felspar porcelain, and domestic ware in white granite, jet, red and cane-coloured earthenwares. Luxury employees were discharged. Some returned to Staffordshire, where at least one, John Harrop, established himself as a parian potter, while others emigrated to America.

Authorities declare that the formula for making the nacreous lustre remained in the possession of Armstrong's two sons, who became the new owners' sole source of supply. This is very improbable, for Brianchon's patent had expired on New Year's Day, 1872, and a copy of the specification containing the formula could then be bought for fourpence. The sons emigrated to the United States, where they were employed by W. S. Lenox at the Trenton Pottery to duplicate Belleek parian. The project was successful, although American Belleek was rather more translucent than the original and the mother-of-pearl lustre less brilliant.

Belleek parian was invariably marked. The early statuary was impressed beneath the base BELLEEK POTTERY and this probably indicates production before 1863.

The mark most frequently used was transfer-printed in black, sepia, red or brown, the design incorporating a tall round tower, an Irish harp to the right, and an Irish wolfhound to the left, with the name BELLEEK below in a ribbon with three shamrock leaves at each end. Less frequent is an Irish harp surmounted by a crown. This might be printed or impressed, the latter sometimes in association with a printed tower mark, apparently denoting an early phase of the M'Berney-Armstrong partnership.

Baskets have no flat surface beneath upon which the trade-mark could be printed. This was overcome by attaching a narrow, flat pad of parian impressed BELLEEK; sometimes an additional pad impressed CO FERMANAGH was placed immediately beneath. A translucent flint-glass glaze was used to fix the pads in position, but sometimes they have fallen away, leaving rough scars. When the name IRELAND is incorporated in the mark it indicates manufacture after 1891 when the McKinley Tariff Act came into operation.

An applied pad impressed a diamond-shaped registration-of-design mark indicates manufacture before 1882, when their use ceased. Dates of registration may be interpreted (see Chapter 26). Thus the design for the painted spider dish was registered on April 15th, 1878, and the dragon teapot (Fig. 42) on March 9th, 1880, giving them three years' protection against piracy.

24

Figures

ENGLAND'S FIRST important collector of Staffordshire earthenware figures and groups was himself a celebrated potter. Enoch Wood (1759—1840) had been apprenticed to Humphrey Neale as a portrait modeller and in 1783 established his own pottery at Fountain Place, Burslem. A year later he modelled the famous bust of John Wesley while the preacher was his guest during a tour of the Potteries. This bust created an enormous impression among potters and among Wesley's followers, indelibly associating the name of Enoch Wood with figure modelling in earthenware. During the next half-century tens of thousands of Wesley busts were issued in enamelled earthenware and black basaltes.

The Wood collection became well known during the Regency period, and by 1820 was housed in England's first recorded works museum. Here designers, technicians, potters and decorators had access to a chronological series of Staffordshire earthenware illustrating a century and a half of progressive improvements, extending from the well-known Burslem butter pots, through slipware, salt-glazed stoneware, lead-glazed earthenware decorated with coloured glazes and fine stonewares, to samples of 19th-century industrial productions.

Wood's collection first became known on July 26th, 1816, when it was displayed to the principal master potters of Staffordshire at a commemorative dinner. Fifty years before, Josiah Wedgwood had cut the first clod for the Trent and Mersey Canal, which provided cheap water transport between the Potteries and the Mersey Estuary in pre-railway days. In 1835 Wood presented 182 of his finest pieces to the King of Saxony and these are now in the Dresden Museum.

Staffordshire earthenware figures were long known as image toys, a term used by Josiah Wedgwood when recording experimental work in 1752—3. By the end of the century they were known merely as toys. Directories of the early 19th century entered such figure-makers as Obadiah Sherratt under the heading of 'Earthenware and China Toy Manufacturers'. From the 1820s, potters usually referred to earthenware figures as chimney ornaments.

Earthenware figures from about 1800 were less pretentious than formerly, the majority bearing no trade-mark, and many being productions of unrecorded potters working in a very small way.

156

85 and 86. (Above) Late Victorian pottery: (*left to right*) vase in parian porcelain decorated in *pâte-sur-pâte* by M. L. Solon for Minton in 1873; lustre-painted dish designed by William de Morgan; tankard in salt-glaze stoneware decorated by George Tinworth for Doultons. (Right) Salt-glazed stoneware designed and made by the Martin Brothers: a jug and vase made at Southall in the early 20th century.

87, 88 and 89. Statuary parian: (Left) 'Boy with the Rabbit' by W. T. Copeland. (Right) Comport with pedestal and plates in bone china enamelled in turquoise and parian cupids by Herbert Minton. (Below) Belleek statuary: 'The Prisoner of Love', height 25 inches, and 'Erin Awakening from her Slumbers', height 18 inches.

The high speed of production and low rates of pay associated with the figure-making branch of the pottery industry were recorded in *The Report on the Employment of Children in Factories* (1842). Here nine-year-old William Cotton, employed by Deakin and Sons, Longton, is shown to have been paid two shillings a week, producing forty-two figures an hour throughout a week of seventy hours. Another nine-year-old, Richard Morton, employed by Hilditch and Hopwood, Longton, stated in evidence: 'I work by the piece and can make 40 dozen small figures in a day: I get one penny for ten dozen, that is about two shillings a week.' This child in a year of fifty-two weeks—holidays were rare—might produce about 145,000 figures, for which he was paid about five guineas. The quantity of figures made must indeed have been vast.

A prolific maker of figures and busts was John Walton, who potted at Hadderage, Burslem, from 1790 to 1839 and, succeeded by his widow Eliza Walton, used a cheap, brittle earthenware capable of being fabricated at high speed for inexpensive markets such as fairs and village shops. Although as a rule coarsely and crudely made, his figures have an enduring charm that endears them to many a collector.

John Walton was one of the first Staffordshire potters to adapt to his needs the mid-18th-century bocage of the porcelain potters. This he did effectively and decoratively, introducing a vogue that spread to other potters and continued until the end of the Georgian era. A tree, rising behind the figure or group, consisted of a short trunk supporting a few branches thickly covered with conventional leaves, carefully arranged by hand, each branch having in its centre a coloured flower.

The well-known Walton figure of a sheep with a lamb is always vigorously modelled and coated with chippings from the turner's lathe to simulate wool. The lamb is placed below the sheep in a rocky recess of the green base. This model was made by other potters, but the wool was produced by mechanically tooling the surface of the green ware. A scrolling motif painted towards the lower edge of the base is a distinguishing feature of one series of Walton figures, some of which are impressed WALTON in a scroll on the back of the base. The title of the subject was often inscribed on the front of the base of each, no matter how obvious the legend, such as 'Lion' or 'Lovers'.

Felix Pratt, Fenton, was a considerable maker of inexpensive figures and busts decorated in underglaze high-temperature colours. The transparent glaze has a faintly bluish tint and the colour range is distinctive—orange-ochre, pale yellow, green, greyish brown, purple-brown. Pratt established his pottery in 1803 and impressed his name on some figures, as a result of which collectors have classed the entire group as Pratt ware. Many other potters produced similar figures in Staffordshire, Newcastle and Scotland between about 1793 and the 1830s. Unless they are marked it is impossible to attribute figures decorated in high-temperature colours to any particular pottery.

Ralph Salt, Hanley, made vast numbers of chimney ornaments from 1812 to 1846, starting as a master potter of ordinary domestic ware at Miles Bank. By 1820 he was making painted figures, particularly bocage pieces, sporting dogs and sheep with hand-raised wool. In 1834 he built a larger pottery in Marsh Street. Salt impressed some of his best productions with his name either above or upon a raised scroll. He was succeeded by his son Charles, a modeller, who operated until 1864, and impressed the name SALT on the back of the plinth. His figures, even when taken from his father's moulds, are less well finished.

Another member of what has become known to collectors as the Walton school of figure-makers was Obadiah Sherratt, of Hot Lane, Burslem. He was at work by 1810 and from the early 1820s a characteristic feature of his square or rectangular plinths was the bracket foot at each corner such as appeared on contemporary chests-of-drawers. The expansive entrance to *Polito's Menagerie* was considered a triumph of casting and firing in the flat. It is painted with an inscription reading: 'The Menagerie of the Wonderfull Birds and Beasts from Most Parts of the World, Lion and Giraffe.' This group is to be found bearing the name 'Wombwell', but otherwise identical, Wombwell having acquired Polito's Menagerie in 1818. Several jugs have been seen displaying similar scenes in relief, some enamelled, and others, later, undecorated but from the same moulds. Small details often enable a figure to be dated closely, such as the well-known Sherratt figure of Paul Pry carrying a hat-box; the play in which Paul Pry was a character was first produced in 1826.

Among the few other early-19th-century potters whose names have been impressed upon early enamelled Staffordshire figures are the following: John and Ralph Hall of Tunstall and Burslem (1805—1821), who were mainly potters of white and enamelled earthenware and issued many attractive figures impressed HALL; Edge and Grocott, Burslem, who early in the 19th century followed the Walton bocage style, their name impressed on a raised tablet at the back of the base[1]; William Walley (*d.* 1842), who potted animals and sporting dogs, which might be impressed J WALLEYS WARE; Turner and Abbott, Lane End, who specialised in very small figures.

The production of models for earthenware figures was a highly skilled and specialist branch of the pottery trade. In 1834 there were three established in Burslem—Joseph Brookes, Waterloo Road; Thomas Holland, Church Street; and William Tunstall, Union Buildings.

Early-19th-century potters preferred the plinth of their figures to be square, shallow, smooth on all surfaces, thus speeding production. The plinth might be encircled by a line of colour or gilding and a title might be painted upon the front. In finer work the plinth was deeper, with in-sloping rims decorated in relief. Groups stood upon rocky bases which themselves might be supported on plinths. Popular in this countless range of chimney ornaments was the inevitable spill-holder—the simplest of deep, narrow vessels given considerable charm by its supporting figure or more ambitious group.

[1] An example described to the author was stated to have lost most of its green enamel.

Figures

Throughout the 19th century until the 1880s many figures were made from local red-burning clays, moulded, coated with a brilliant black lead glaze, enriched with gilding and colours tempered with oil applied overglaze. Jewitt notes this manufacture under the name of 'jet black' by at least thirty Staffordshire and other potters. To collectors the generic term for jet black is 'Jackfield'. Here, and at Benthall in Shropshire, similar black glazed earthenware was made successfully by the Thursfields from the 1750s to 1818.

The present collecting vogue is for the large cast figures made from the 1830s, when this process had become general. This century-old method of shaping was carried out by pouring slip into plaster-of-paris moulds. As the moulds absorbed water from the clay a layer of slip was left, uniform in thickness; surplus slip was poured away and the mould with its contents placed in a dryer. The shaped earthenware could then be easily lifted from the mould. Thin-walled hollow figures of considerable size could be made inexpensively by this method. Until the 1850s these figures were made in the round; with a few rare exceptions the flat back is not to be noted until the 1850s.

Glazing soon became brilliantly white, a technical improvement that led to the fashion for leaving large areas of figures undecorated. A liquid gold, invented by William Cornelius (see pp. 73—4) in 1853, much less costly in its application than any former method of gilding, was used on Staffordshire figures from the following year. These improvements brought more imposing chimney ornaments, many a figure, cast in a single piece, measuring up to eighteen inches in height. The majority of these were coloured with a limited palette of enamels dominated by a brilliant overglaze blue. Other overglaze enamels were less sparkling and chiefly red, green, yellow and black, all possessing a tendency to flake from the glaze when thickly applied. Equestrian figures might have horse and plinth glazed white, the subjects themselves being colourfully enamelled. Names were inscribed on the plinth in gold script.

Enormous numbers of full-length figures of celebrities were issued between the early 1840s and about 1865, although production continued into the present century. Marked examples are very rare. Royal personages, naval and military leaders, preachers, politicians, singers, sportsmen, criminals were all included in the gallery, few of these portraits bearing more than a passing resemblance to their originals.

The range of royal subjects, English and foreign, is almost bewildering. During the late 1840s and early 1850s copies of sculpture by celebrated artists were unmercifully adapted by potters. The series of princes and princesses by Mrs Thorneycroft was widely potted in Staffordshire. Royal groups and pairs date from the late 1850s. An excellent equestrian pair was issued in 1858, at the time of the marriage of the Princess Royal and Prince Frederick William of Prussia.

War heroes form an interesting subject to collect. Apart from figures of Nelson, Wellington, Napoleon and a few others, the demand appears to date from the Crimean war, 1854, when heads of states, such as Napoleon III, the King of Sardinia, the Sultan of

159

Turkey, and various commanders-in-chief were in the public eye. The majority of these appear to have been modelled from contemporary prints and usually display the name in relief on the front of the low oval plinth. More than one hundred equestrian and standing figures associated with Crimean celebrities have been collated, some of them in pairs. The Italian and Franco-Prussian wars brought their crop of figures. Such a series will show a gradual decline in quality from about 1880 and a reduction in the use of colour.

Dogs form an important group among 19th-century figures. Pathetic or dignified, wise or smirking or vapidly expressionless, they have come to be regarded as essential ornaments on the mantelshelf of the real old English cottage, although typical specimens date between 1810 and the 1870s. The Staffordshire potteries turned them out in their thousands each week. Almost every breed then known was modelled and no two dogs are ever identical, for every potter had his own ideas when painting expressions into the animals' faces and decking their backs with gaudy spots. Eyes in particular show endless variation, from unnaturally human to warmly canine in both shape and expression, only the poor examples being mere dots. The whole colouring is sometimes quaint but most generally keeps as close to nature as may be expected in a cheaply-sold article. Symmetry of arrangement on the crowded mantelshelf or ponderous chest of drawers was ensured by the fact that they were nearly always made in pairs.

Characteristically, the dogs portrayed are mostly the sporting dogs popular in those robust and unthinkingly callous days. Greyhound coursing was a national pastime, and among pottery dogs greyhounds and whippets were second only to spaniels in popularity. Prize-winners were known by name and reputation throughout the country and it is not surprising that many a greyhound statuette purports to be an actual portrait of a famous Regency or early Victorian hound. Its name was inscribed in relief on the pedestal front and outlined in gilding or enamel, such as the McGrath and Pretender pair, winner and runner-up in the race for the Waterloo Cup of 1871. Often the hare just killed is displayed in the animal's mouth or laid at its feet.

Many greyhounds are finely modelled, most commonly sitting keenly upright, standing or lying prone with crossed paws. The figure of the fawning greyhound is notable for its anatomical accuracy, grace of action and excellence of modelling. The most usual colour for this animal is a peculiar salmon-orange, against which the features are painted black. The pedestal supporting the standing greyhound was a slender oval with a rough top coloured grass-green. From the centre of this rose a pillar supporting the dog's chest, thus preventing the figure from collapsing during firing. The edge of the pedestal might be plainly white encircled with a gilded line, or touched with green. In some instances the pedestal was enamelled in brilliant Staffordshire blue.

'Jackfield' greyhounds were exquisitely modelled in perfect poses by Staffordshire potters. They were made of red earthenware covered with a lustrous black glaze, usually enriched with markings in gold.

Among other sporting dogs, the pointer standing over the game is an excellent example of figure potting. It appears in several characteristic poses and is invariably modelled by a master. The heavier Spanish pointers are frequently found, usually all black or all white.

The elegant figure of the setter is to be seen in a diversity of colours and poses and showing the thickly curled hair of the old English type. Foxhound models show strong, agile creatures; harriers have an eager, persevering look and are often gripping the hares they have hunted; staghounds and springers display remarkable vigour although their colouring is somewhat strange. Perhaps because they were modelled less frequently, the pointer and setter, like the pug and that most popular Victorian coaching dog the Dalmatian, seem always to have claimed the attention of really skilled modellers.

The Edinburgh Journal of Natural History and of the Physical Sciences, 1857, illustrates sixteen hand-coloured engravings of English sporting dogs. Today, only the pointer and setter bear much resemblance to these portraits of their ancestors; of the other fourteen those that have not become extinct appear to have undergone marked changes.

One engraving depicts a gentle little dog with brown ears and brown spots on its silky coat. Its wide-open eyes and maddeningly meek expression correspond in every detail with that most insipid pottery adornment of the cottage shelf. Bred from the Maltese dog and the King Charles's spaniel, this pathetic creature was called a 'comforter or spaniel's gentle'. Here was the antithesis of all that was required of the sporting dog, and it is possible to feel the good-humoured scorn with which the potter modelled this lady's dog, this lap-warmer, this finicky creature of drawing room and boudoir. That it should have disappeared and left no obvious heirs among our dogs of today is easily understandable from the appearance of these pensive pottery figures.

Pottery comforters were always made in pairs to face each other across the shelf and are found in five standard sizes. Some are as tall as eighteen inches, often serving as door porters; the smallest are about six inches, and the most popular about nine inches high. They are almost invariably white with coloured ears and some half-dozen spots scattered over the body at the whim of the potter. Red was a favourite colour for these markings, and so was gold, but they are found in black, brown, grey, even green as well as copper lustre. The nose is pink and the eyes have almost a human outline. A feature of the comforter is the small gold padlock always hanging from a collar around its neck and the little gold chain falling across the chest and disappearing over the back, which is never decorated. Although invariably modelled in a sitting posture, altogether some two hundred patterns of these quaint little creatures are known to have been devised before they were outmoded by the Victorian pug.

If the earthenware comforter appears a silly specimen of a dog, no better may be said of the even more popular pottery spaniel. It would be impossible to believe that such a poor-spirited dog could have existed with such an inane expression and stony stare were it not for the innumerable replicas showing precisely the same features but obviously the work of several potters. Unquestionably they represent a dog popular at that time but belonging to a breed which has since been immeasurably improved.

Clipped poodles have an air of picturesque unreality that lends itself particularly to the modeller of earthenware figures. They are usually found rather smaller than the nine-inch comforter and less rigidly restricted to the conventional sitting posture. One might imagine that the difficulty of representing the thick curly hair in so stiff a material would have made them costly ornaments. This obstacle was overcome in several ways. On some the hair was made of small granules of earthenware glazed fast in the manner of sandpaper; in better quality it was applied in the form of dry clay to represent a rough, coarse texture, but at the same time produced an effect of depth and, from a distance, real fluffiness. The Rockingham poodles in bone china are of unsurpassed craftsmanship. In these the curly hair on head, neck and forepart of the body is of extremely fine china threads. Although these china poodles were widely reproduced by the Staffordshire potters, the curled hair of these has no more than an effect of matted sheep's wool. Poodles frequently hold little baskets in their mouths—that being a parlour trick taught to their live contemporaries— and are often found in groups of two or three on one base.

The well-modelled miniature mastiff is of special interest. It has peculiarly turned-up toes, tongue out and head turned to the right, and was known early in the 19th century as the mops. When it has a finely painted insect in underglaze on each side of the neck it is intended as a symbol of fidelity and may be associated with the Roman Catholic Society of Mopses. The mops is of German origin, and those made in English bone china were not so well finished or coloured as their hard-porcelain Meissen originals.

The bone-china potters issued some outstandingly lifelike dogs, and in contrast to their earthenware contemporaries many appear to be of mongrel type, their proud four-leg stance and sharply expressive faces comparing favourably with those of the ornately-collared pedigree breeds. In the finer bone-china dogs the pedestals are irregularly shaped, the tops dotted with tiny hand-made flowers painted in natural colours. The Copeland firm devised dogs of numerous breeds, often sitting on their haunches without pedestals, such as pugs with tightly curling tails and St Bernards. Copeland dogs are marked beneath, those impressed COPELAND & GARRETT being made between 1833 and 1846; COPELAND late SPODE, 1847—1867.

Rockingham dogs are always small and belong to the period 1820—1842, those with the griffin mark dating from 1826. Lap dogs and spaniels reclining upon white or richly coloured and tasselled cushions have been noted bearing the griffin mark and the words 'Manufacturer to the King'. These date between 1830 and 1837. Rockingham, too, made white woolly dogs—possibly unclipped poodles since they often carry baskets of colourful roses. Slender greyhounds and shaggy spaniels were made by the firm in earthenware.

Figure groups consisting of a pair of dogs on a single pedestal are not infrequent, usually a pair of dogs sitting on their haunches to the sides of a hollow tree stump for containing tapers or spills. In one series the base was made hollow to form an inkwell. Those noted have been of early Victorian origin. In others a single dog erect on four legs guards the tree trunk. A figure group noted recently, bearing the transferred mark IRIDGWAY in a ribbon with a pottery kiln below, consisted of a cleverly modelled spaniel sitting on his haunches with a cat trying to induce him to play. This was made by John Ridgway, whom the Jury of the Great Exhibition stated to be one of the most important potters in Staffordshire.

Rockingham issued a splendid series of dog and cat pairs in bone china. A pair consisted of two round wicker baskets, one containing a dog with puppies and the other a cat with kittens.

Inevitably earthenware and bone-china dogs have been reproduced. Good originals are copied to perfection in colours just missing correct period tints, but commoner types are poorly modelled and obviously newly decorated in colours little resembling the originals.

25

Art Potteries

THE MOST desirable of 19th-century porcelain in the eyes of many collectors is Minton's *pâte-sur-pâte* bearing the signature of Marc-Louis Solon. *Pâte-sur-pâte* (paste upon paste) is a stained parian paste upon which is painted a translucent white or tinted slip, supplemented by shaping with chasing tools. It is thus both painting and modelling. The reliefs, being highly translucent, allow the darker tones of the background to show through, producing a remarkable effect of perspective and shading. It was covered with transparent glaze.

This technique was invented at Sèvres in about 1860 by Solon. A celadon vase decorated with heavily embossed flowers had attracted his attention in the Sèvres Museum. Attempts to reproduce similar ornament by painting slip on a porcelain biscuit resulted in failure, for the paste peeled off when dry. Solon then conceived the idea of applying the decoration to the damp paste. From this he evolved the process outlined in his biography. He left Sèvres for the Minton firm in 1870 and was shortly producing *pâte-sur-pâte*.

In describing his process he first pointed out that the applied reliefs on jasper ware of Wedgwood were taken from moulds capable of producing an unlimited number of copies. 'A *pâte-sur-pâte* relief, on the contrary, is always an original.... *Pâte-sur-pâte* may be executed upon any semi-vitrifiable body, but the material used for the applied parts must always be of the same nature as the mass of which the piece itself is formed. The hard-porcelain paste is, for density and fineness of substance, superior to any other: it is the one employed in France and Germany. But, as few metallic oxides can stand the high degree of heat to which it has to be submitted, the scale of available colours is very limited. With the body in use at Minton's, on the contrary, a great variety of colours can be obtained. It is a sort of parian, the elements entering into its composition are the same as those used for hard porcelain, but mixed in different proportions. Most complicated forms can be produced in that body: *the biscuit is at first thoroughly fired*, and during this operation the pieces can be properly supported in all their weak points; the glazing is subsequently proceeded with at a much lower temperature; the highest degree of heat has to be reached to bring the glaze into fusion; supports cannot be used, as they would stick to the piece, and therefore only a certain class of shapes can be attempted.' Solon added that bone china is unsatisfactory for this work. *Pâte-sur-pâte* carried out entirely by Solon himself is signed SOLON, MILÈS or MLS in monogram.

This knowledge makes it possible to distinguish between the unsigned work of Solon and that of his immediate followers, and the small school of potters who decorated in this way during the 1920s and 1930s. These potters used semi-china cups and saucers, service plates and other table ware in place of stained parian, apparently no longer in production. Vases and plaques in the Solon manner were also made.

Minton's Victorian competitors seemed to be unable to duplicate the work of Solon, but at least two potters produced outstanding decorations in semblance of *pâte-sur-pâte*. At Worcester until 1890 T. J. Bott painted in white slip on dark blue porcelain, and at Derby M. Leroy painted in white enamel on cobalt grounds.

English majolica was planned as a new ceramic marvel at the Great Exhibition, by Leon Arnoux, art manager for Herbert Minton. Early examples were elaborate and costly ornaments, but imitation majolica continued to be made by a small group of Staffordshire potters until the end of the century. This majolica bears little resemblance to its Italian prototype, which is a colourful opaque glazed pottery of soft, open porous body, usually of inferior clay. Its highly lustrous rainbow iridescences range from bluish purple to ruby red, and from golden yellow to emerald green.

Minton termed his version 'imitation Majolica ware'. This was a coarse, cane-coloured earthenware with relief ornament covered with a white opaque glaze and fired in the usual way. Glazes were applied to this surface, enabling a long range of colours to be used in various tints of green, yellow, blue, purple and red. The word 'imitation' was omitted when other potters entered this branch of the industry during the early 1860s. Minton's entry in the catalogue of the Great Exhibition refers to: 'Vases, etc., in imitation of Majolica Ware.... Wine Coolers of porous ware ornamented with festoons of vine-leaves and grapes and coloured in the majolica style ... a variety of flower pots and stands, coloured in the majolica style.' These were designed and modelled in the style of old majolica.

Baron Marochetti, the sculptor, was commissioned to model a large vase which the Jury of the Great Exhibition commended on account of 'its design and colours and great size'. Tiles for flower boxes were modelled in bold relief with tulips and other flowers richly coloured in naturalistic tints. No competitor ever surpassed Minton in sharpness of detail and the purity of the coloured glazes. An oval dish measuring nineteen and a quarter inches long in the Hanley Museum, made by Minton in 1871, is decorated with majolica glazes of light and dark green, brown, blue, yellow and red. Figures, too, modelled in caneware were ornamented with majolica glazes. The Minton firm continued the manufacture of majolica until the end of the century. Domestic ware in this majolica dates from the early 1860s.

The Wedgwood firm from about 1860 began to manufacture imitation majolica in a white earthenware body. The relief ornament was painted with transparent coloured glazes, providing brilliant effects. The demand for English majolica and for parian was so considerable that in 1863 Daniel Sutherland and Sons, Longton, established a pottery specialising in the manufacture of these wares. Their majolica, impressed S & S, included jugs in a great variety of shapes and sizes; vases, tripods and flower holders; Stilton cheese, butter and sardine stands and boxes; bread, cheese and fruit dishes; water bottles; tea- and coffee-pots; kettles; flower pots; brackets and scent jars, taper stands, candlesticks and numerous other articles.

George Jones, Stoke-upon-Trent, combined majolica and parian into large centre-pieces, such as nude figures in parian on majolica pedestals and supports. A wide range of lidded vases, ornamental bowls and candelabra were among his productions. A beehive skip for honey and a thirty-inch wall plaque have been noted impressed with his mono-gram G J. Jones was awarded gold medals for his majolica at the Exhibitions of Paris 1867, London 1871 and Vienna 1873. Another majolica and parian specialist was Edward Steele, Hanley, whose productions included dessert services with figure centrepieces and comports, vases, teapots and jugs, all carefully modelled on an excellent body. None of these was marked. J. Sneyd, Burslem, made domestic majolica from 1867 impressed SNEYD. Moore Brothers, Longton, issued a small amount of outstanding majolica, including pilgrim bottles, heavily gilded in such a way that the colour glazes appear even more striking. A characteristic production was a vigorously modelled camel forming a teapot, with its spout the animal's neck and head and its handle shaped as an Arab tying on a bale of goods. This firm's majolica is marked MOORE, either impressed or in script incised.

Majolica was also made at Swadlincote, Derbyshire, by James Woodward from about 1860. Large quantities were potted marked with a foul anchor, the cable twisted around the stem to form the monogram J W.

William de Morgan made the finest imitations of the old majolica in his pottery at Merton, established in the early 1870s. Productions were entirely ornamental and included vases, tiles and dishes, displaying hard, distinct colours, particularly a ruby-red glaze over a cream-coloured glaze. He decorated with animals, birds, flowers and fishes in greens and blues, in the style of the later Persian and Turkish faience.

In 1888, in partnership with Halsey Ricardo the architect, de Morgan founded the Sands End Pottery, Fulham. Backgrounds made here formed a haze of beautiful colour glazes. The well-composed designs were all by de Morgan and the decorators included Frederick and Charles Passenger, Joseph Juster and James Hersey. In addition, some painting was carried out in Florence and fired at Fulham. Hispano-Moresque lustre was the inspiration here, de Morgan being first and foremost an experimenter and imitator. Production continued on a large scale until 1908, when de Morgan's health broke down and the pottery closed. The mark used by de Morgan was D M above a tulip with two leaves, sometimes accompanied by the initials of the artist.

The Doulton Pottery under the management of Henry Doulton issued more 'art pottery' than any other firm. Primarily a stoneware pottery, the factory had been established at Vauxhall in 1818 by John Doulton. He was joined soon by John Watts and the business was transferred to Lambeth, where they specialised in commercial and industrial stoneware. In 1858 John Watts died and Doulton took his sons into partnership. It was under the influence of Henry Doulton that the firm entered the domestic ornamental trade which became so successful. A fine-quality salt-glazed stoneware was used for such hollow-ware as tankards, toby jugs, loving cups, hunting jugs, puzzle jugs, bellarmines, flower vases, claret jugs, inkstands and so on. In these the colouring was restricted to the tints of the clays with broad bands of rich brown glaze encircling rim and base.

At the South Kensington Exhibition, 1871, a case of salt-glazed stoneware, decorated and signed by students of the Lambeth School of Art, attracted much attention. This was in ordinary brown stoneware decorated with sgraffito or scratched patterns filled in with colours. Henry Doulton was quick to commercialise this success, which within a few years had developed into an important branch of the trade.

The Journal of the Society of Arts during the last quarter of the 19th century recorded much information concerning the Doultons' art productions made in the following nine groups:

Marqueterie ware: marbled clays in checker-work, obtained by cutting and compressing in various ways, were used for moulding, the pieces afterwards being glazed.

Carrara ware: a stoneware in which the body was modelled while plastic, then covered with a white, slightly translucent crystalline enamel decorated with colours and gilding.

Silicon ware: a vitrified, unglazed stoneware decorated with coloured clays. (Booth, Ltd., Tunstall, made silicon china from about 1900.)

Chiné ware: this might be in salt-glazed stoneware or faience, and decorated with repetitive patterns, the effects being obtained by impressing suitable fabrics on the surface of the soft clay.

Vitreous fresco: a fine stoneware evolved for carved and modelled work.

Impasto: stoneware decorated by engraving the design on the soft clay before drying, colouring this with a neutral tint and then decorating with coloured clays, beaded veins and so on in slight relief. The ware was then salt-glazed. The finished ornament resembles old *gris de Flandres* and is really a revival of this.

Sgraffito: incised outlines cut into the clay immediately the vessel leaves the wheel or while green but soft enough to be worked up easily. To these designs colour is applied with an ordinary pencil brush and burnt in. Bronze, green, brown, blue, chocolate, grey, white and black were evolved to withstand the heat of the salt-glaze kiln.

Lambeth faience: a terra-cotta or earthenware body decorated by paintings fired under the glaze.

Crown Lambeth: an ivory body with underglaze decoration.

Every piece of Doulton art ware bears the name, monogram or mark of the artist, the mark DOULTON LAMBETH and another mark indicating the nature of the product, such as CARRARA. Some of the finer pieces are dated. In art ware no piece or pair of vases was duplicated. In 1887 Henry Doulton joined the established firm of T. S. Pinder, Burslem, in the manufacture of bone china and fine earthenware.

The four brothers Martin of Southall Pottery have been named as England's first studio potters. They were, however, no more than exceptionally capable experimenters and imitators, using salt-glazed stoneware for modelling and colouring in a highly individual style, operating in a studio atmosphere. The creative studio potter did not emerge until the 20th century. The brothers were enthusiasts labouring not so much for gain as for the pleasure of producing fine wares and exploring new methods and techniques. Robert Wallace Martin (1845—1923) was a sculptor's assistant; his brother Charles (1846—1910) had received art training; Edwin (1860—1915) and Walter (1857—1912) were working at the Doulton pottery in the mechanical branch of decorating salt-glazed stoneware, filling in with colour the designs which the artists scratched upon the ware known as sgraffito, when they decided to establish a pottery of their own. In 1873 they began in a very small way at Pomona House, King's Road, Fulham, trading as R. W. and Brothers Martin. Their stoneware was fired at Bailey's Fulham Pottery in the kilns erected late in the 17th century by John Dwight. In 1877 they moved to the Southall Pottery, Southall Green, Middlesex, where they worked until 1915. Three of the brothers by then had died, Robert potting alone until his death in 1923.

At first the Martins produced domestic table ware, including tea-sets, bread platters, cheese and butter dishes and some clock cases. Later in the century they designed and made some elaborately decorated fireplaces, fireplace curbs, tiles and garden fountains, all the work of Robert Wallace Martin. The majority of their productions, however, were purely ornamental, thrown, decorated and glazed vases, bowls, dishes, bottles and hollow-ware grotesques. Colour effects were obtained such as had never before been seen on salt-glazed stoneware; a chronological series of vases will illustrate the progressive improvements of tone. Early blues were strong and crude; later, some attractive low-toned blues were evolved. Greens, browns, yellows and blacks were consistently of fine quality. White in various tints formed excellent grounds for applied ornament. Tortoiseshell and cherry red were frequently used. The palette was limited to colours capable of maturing at a single firing.

Robert Wallace Martin was the modeller, never happier than when creating some fantastic form, or devising some fresh attitude in bird or grotesque. These were entirely imaginative and the birds rarely display any resemblance to nature, many being repulsively ugly. With the exception of the earliest birds the heads were made separately and so designed that they could be turned in any direction. In size they ranged from three to twenty-one inches, but were usually between six and twelve inches. Some were modelled in groups of two or three on a single plinth. Double-face jugs were a popular line, usually with a different face on each side, such as Joseph Chamberlain and Balfour, or John Bull and Brother Jonathan. These are in various shades of brown.

Walter was the principal thrower and the chemist of the partnership. His vases are distinguished by their perfect symmetry and might be square, hexagonal or octagonal on plan, usually ribbed and panelled. These might be decorated with incising and impressed ornament.

Edwin, the designer, introduced into his ornament some unexploited grouping of flowers and foliage or a theme drawn from a sea-shell, gourd or other naturalistic form. Edwin was the expert in inlay work such as honeycomb patterns, and delighted in ornamenting his pieces with such marine life as fish, crabs, jellyfish and floating sea anemones, as well as dragons, flying birds, lizards and insects. He evolved a crackle-finish which appears not to have been used previously on salt-glazed stoneware.

It was Charles Martin who acted, so far as a Martin was capable, as the business man of the partnership, assessing the merit of the pieces, pricing them and eventually arranging for their disposal. The Martin brothers were avid collectors of their own work and appropriated for themselves the pick of each firing, often refusing to part with examples sold before firing. Following the death of the last of the brothers in 1923, their executors were puzzled regarding the whereabouts of this collection, containing as it did many of their finest productions. Eventually it was discovered hidden beneath the floorboards of their tiny shop, 16, Brownlow Street, High Holborn. Why it was so hoarded remains unknown, but many of the finest pieces thus housed were acquired for the London Museum. Charles, in charge of the shop, was able to carry out modelling while awaiting customers. He was also in charge of the illustrated books and the shells and other naturalistic objects required for adapting to their designs. Many examples of Martinware are signed, while others are dated.

At Linthorpe, near Middlesbrough, an art pottery flourished for ten years from 1879. The proprietor of this former brickworks engaged Henry Tooth as manager, and within two years more than a hundred workers were employed. In a letter to J. F. Blacker, Tooth placed on record that 'the wares of Linthorpe present us with all the variety and mingled richness of hue which we perceive in old Chinese wares and which we value in agate, in onyx, and other beautiful stones; and while no attempt has been made in reproducing the effects of Chinese wares, new beauties have been achieved by similar means. Low-toned reds, mottled olives, browns, and yellows of great variety of tone, and rich mingled "juicy" effects of colour are found in the wares of Linthorpe.

'But, besides the glaze effects, Linthorpe made a speciality of incised and perforated wares. Plaques, both large and small, for the decoration of sideboards; card-trays, tazzas, spill vases (up to two feet six inches in height) and many other objects of a decorated character were made, all of which are enriched with carefully executed and tenderly drawn sgraffito ornament.

'As to the shapes of the decorative objects produced at Linthorpe, they were legion in number. Some of the forms have been designed with a view to the production of what was in a high degree graceful and beautiful, while others have been created to give quaintness of effect; and, while many vessels were of original shapes, some few were derived from Egyptian, Greek, Roman, Moorish, Indian, Chinese, Japanese, Peruvian, Mexican and Celtic examples, while some were in the Medieval and others in the Queen Anne spirit.'

Linthorpe became celebrated for the brilliance of its rich flown and speckled colour glazes and, later, also for its flowers in coloured slips.

Early examples of Linthorpe pottery were designed by Dr Christopher Dresser, the architect, who became art director of the works. These were impressed LINTHORPE/ Chv Dresser (in script); this was followed by the name LINTHORPE across an outline urn, with or without Dr Dresser's name, and generally bearing in addition to the pattern number the initials of Henry Tooth.

Linthorpe Pottery closed after the proprietor's death in 1889, but Henry Tooth thereupon established the Bretby Art Pottery, Woodville, Derbyshire. Here, in addition to making umbrella stands, jardinières, vases, hanging pots and similar ware, he made earthenware to resemble hammered copper, bronze and steel. 'Carved bamboo' ware was made in combination with bronze.

Other 'art potteries' were at work in the late 19th century, their general style characterised by modelled decoration with thick coloured glazes. Harold Rathbone established the Della Robbia Pottery at Birkenhead in 1894 and produced painted sgraffito wares such as vases, bottles, jars, bowls and jugs, some in grotesque shapes.

26

Registration Marks

DIAMOND-SHAPED marks are frequently found printed or impressed upon specimens of Victorian ceramics. This mark rightly interpreted contributes interesting information regarding the piece. With its central 'R^d' (registered), its four corner compartments and its surmounting circle enclosing a Roman numeral, it indicates a date of manufacture between 1842 and 1883. Reference to the accompanying key chart (facing page 172) will reveal the exact date on which the design of any specimen so marked was registered at the Patent Office.

Until 1842 manufacturers and artists alike deplored their lack of protection against piracy of original creations. Manufacturers did not consider it economical to employ their own industrial artists, knowing only too well that their designs would immediately be appropriated by copyists. Many manufacturers, therefore, had long abandoned any thought of originality of design for their merchandise. Whereas in France it was customary for a manufacturer to employ several artists, in England one artist might supply designs to eight or ten different firms.

Until 1839, the only English law protecting industrial design was an Act of 1794 giving three months' copyright to designs on linens and calicoes. No other species of commercial art, not even woven patterns, enjoyed such protection. In 1839 two further measures became law. One extended the former Act to cover printed silks and woollens; the second gave protection to numerous other branches of manufacture—three years to designs in metals and twelve months to the remainder.

Even this failed to satisfy industrial designers, and in 1840 a committee of M.P.s was instructed to consider further legislation. This committee, in a 600-page report, proved that more comprehensive copyright of industrial design could be made practicable. The report stressed that the designer who worked on cotton and silk could count upon protection for no longer than three months, whereas the painter who engraved one of his own drawings was secure from piracy for twenty-eight years. The artist who chased his own design upon metal was allowed but three years' protection, in contrast to the fourteen years enjoyed by the sculptor. It was emphasised that our manufacturers were fast becoming mere copyists of designs originated by French and German artists, whose enterprise and original talent were fully protected in their own countries. Recommendations were put forward to the effect that manufacturers of ceramics and glassware seriously needed an extension of their twelve months' protection.

The result was that an Act of Parliament in 1841 extended copyright on ceramics and glass to three years. An amendment in 1842 extended protection to designs not specifically ornamental in character, as, for instance, the shape of a cup.

Manufactures were divided into thirteen classes: class I, articles wholly or chiefly of metal; class II, those of wood, and including papier-mâché; class III, glass; class IV, pottery and porcelain. The number of the class was indicated in a circle surmounting the diamond in the registration mark. The law required the marking of all protected articles with the letters 'Rd' (registered), together with code letters and numerals corresponding with the date of registration. Provision was made for preventing piracy of such registered designs.

The exact date upon which a design was registered may be decoded from the left-hand columns of the accompanying keys. Until 1867 the year was shown by the letter in the top compartment of the diamond, the three other compartments indicating: left, the month of issue, from the third and fourth columns of the keys; right, the day of issue; bottom compartment, the parcel number at the Patent Office which enabled officials to identify the manufacturer. By 1868 the years had utilised every letter of the alphabet, necessitating a re-shuffle in the position of the key letters. The top compartment now represented the day of issue; left, the parcel number; right, the year; bottom compartment, the month.

Those who use the charts should observe the footnotes recording errors in the allotment of marks from time to time: from 1st to 19th September, 1857, possibly during the whole of December, 1860; and between 1st and 6th March, 1878.

Beneath certain stoneware jugs displaying all-over ornament in high relief is sometimes to be found an inscription such as 'Published by W. Ridgway and Co., Hanley, October 1st, 1835'. This showed that the pattern had been registered at Stationers' Hall, thus securing fourteen years' protection against piracy, under the Act of June 21st, 1798. This Copyright Act protected only sculptured work, its original purpose being to drive out of business the many pirates who were copying sculptured work by making moulds from plaster models sold by the sculptor and casting them without acknowledgment or fee. Protection was given to 'any bust or any part of the human figure, or the head of any animal or any part of any animal, and to *any work* either in alto- or basso-relievo in which a representation of the human figure or animals was introduced'. Casting in metal or any other material from any part of an original model became illegal without the owner's signed and witnessed consent.

Any person offering a copyright model for sale and wishing to protect the design was required to sign the work and add the date of first publication. Damages and costs could be claimed for infringement.

INDEX TO THE LETTERS FOR EACH MONTH AND YEAR FROM 1842 TO 1883

1842	X	1863	G	January	C	*From 1842 to 1867*
1843	H	1864	N	February	G	
1844	C	1865	W	March	W	
1845	A	1866	Q	April	H	
1846	I	1867	T	May	E	a class
1847	F	1868	X	June	M	b year
1848	U	1869	H	July	I	c month
1849	S	1870	C	August	R	d day
1850	V	1871	A	September	D	e bundle
1851	P	1872	I	October	B	*From 1868 to 1883*
1852	D	1873	F	November	K	
1853	Y	1874	U	December	A	

For Sept., 1857, from 1st to 19th Sept., the symbol ?R was used.

For Dec. 1860, ?K was used.

From 1st to 6th March, 1878, the following registration mark was issued:

instead of:

Collectors frequently find diamond-shaped marks printed or impressed in some inconspicuous place upon specimens of Victorian industrial art. With their central "Rd," their four corner compartments, and surmounting circle enclosing a Roman numeral, such marks indicate a date of manufacture between 1842 and 1863. Reference to the accompanying Key Chart will reveal the exact date on which any design so marked was registered at the Patent Office, London.

1842—1867. The symbols may be interpreted as follows. The Roman numeral enclosed within the circle at the top of the diamond refers to the class of manufactured article: I, Metal; II, Wood; III, Glass; IV, Ceramics, and so on. The letter in the upper compartment indicates the year of registration, and may be interpreted from the date columns on the left of the chart. The letter in the left compartment indicates the month of issue and is explained in the third column. The numerals in the compartment on the right give the day of the month. The lower compartment contains the number of the parcel at the Patent Office from which the manufacturer may be identified.

1868—1883. The relative positions of the key letters were rearranged as shown on the chart. Various amendments made from time to time were recorded as marginal notes.

Bibliography

Balston, T.: *Staffordshire Portrait Figures of the Victorian Age.* 1958.

Barrett, F. A.: *Caughley and Coalport Porcelain.* 1958.

Bemrose, Geoffrey: *Nineteenth-Century English Pottery and Porcelain.* 1952.

Binns, R. W.: *A Century of Pottery in the City of Worcester.*

Blacker, J. F.: *Nineteenth-Century English Ceramic Art.* c. 1910.

Burton, W.: *A History and Description of English Porcelain.* 1902.

Cannon, T. G.: *Old Spode,*

Church, A. H.: *English Pottery.* 1885.

Downman and Gunn. *English Pottery and Porcelain.* 1910.

Fisher, Stanley W.: *The Decoration of English Porcelain, 1750—1850.* 1954.

Gillespie, F. B.: *Crown Derby Porcelain.* 1951.

Haslem, J.: *The Old Derby China Factory.* 1876.

Hayden, Arthur: *Spode and His Successors.* 1925.

Honey, W. B.: *Old English Porcelain.* 1931.

Hughes, G. Bernard: *The Story of Spode.* 1950.

Hughes, Bernard and Therle: *After the Regency, 1820—1860.* 1952.
    English Porcelain and Bone China, 1743—1850. 1956.
    Encyclopaedia of English Ceramics. 1956.

Hurlbutt, F.: *Old Derby Porcelain and its Artist-Workmen.* 1925.

Jewitt, L.: *Ceramic Art in Great Britain.* 1878.

John, W. D.: *Nantgarw Porcelain.* 1948.
    Swansea Porcelain. 1958.

John, W. D. and Warren Baker: *Old English Lustre Pottery.* 1951.

Mankowitz, W.: *Wedgwood.* 1953.

Nance, G. M.: *The Pottery and Porcelain of Swansea and Nantgarw.* 1943.

Silliman and Goodrich: *The Industry of All Nations.* 1853.

Solon, M.—L.: *A Brief History of Old English Porcelain and its Manufactories.* 1903.

Stringer, G. E.: *New Hall Porcelain.* 1949.

Williams, S. B.: *Antique Blue and White Spode.* 1943.

Index

Figures in italics indicate illustration numbers

174

Pearl pottery, 25
Pearl ware, 23—26, 67, 79; *20, 36*
  figures, 25
  Leeds, 24, 111
  Swansea, 119
  Wedgwood, 24—25
Peel, Sir R., spirit flasks, 149
Peover, F., bone china, 41
Pepper kilns, 40
Perforated ware, Leeds, 110, 112; *39*
Petty's Pottery, Leeds, 112
Philadelphia Exhibition, 1876, 20
Phillips, J., Sunderland, 139, 140, 143, 144
Pilgrim bottles, 105, 166
Pinder, Bourne and Co., terra-cotta, 20
Pinder, Bourne and Hope, 135
Pinder, T. S., bone china, 168
Pinxton, 115—116; *64*
Plaques, Derby, *51*
  Linthorpe, 170
  Sunderland, 140, 141, 142, 144; *27*
Plumier, C., *L'Art de Tourner*, 12
Poodles, Staffordshire, 162
Porcelain, classification of, 39
  hard paste, 131
    Minton, 129
    New Hall, 63; *74*
    Sèvres, 107
  import restrictions, 39
  soft paste, 99, 115—116
    Grainger, Lee and Co., 96
    Madeley, 106—107
    Nantgarw, 117
    Sèvres, 107
  and see Reproductions
Portland vase, copies, Boote, 134
Pot-lids, 84—88; *10, 11*
  series, 87
Poulson, J. and S., working for Minton, 127
Pownall, W., 127
Pratt, F. and R., colour picture prints, 84—88
  terra-cotta, 19
Pratt, F., figures, 157
Prattware, 157
  Liverpool jugs, 136
'Prisoner of Love', Belleek, *89*
'Purple of cassius', 78
Puzzle jugs, Chesterfield, 147
  Doulton, 167

Queen Caroline, Doulton figure, *47*
Queen Victoria, Doulton figure, *47*
  spirit flask, 149
  terra-cotta figure, *7*

Queen Victoria's bone china collection, *65*
Queen's ware, 23, 24

Rainforth and Co., Leeds, 112
Randall, T. M., Madeley, 46, 106—108
'Raphaelesque' porcelain, 96
Rathbone, H., sgraffito ware, 170
Rathbone, W. S. and T., bone china, 40
'Red Barn at Polestead', crime piece, *28*
Regent china, 94
Registration marks, 155, 171—172
Registration of designs, 133
Registration of Designs Act, 28, 59; *42*
Report on the Employment of Children in Factories, The, 157
Reproductions, dogs, 163
  duck-egg porcelain, 118
  pot-lids, 88
  Sèvres, Chelsea, Meissen, 43, 46—47, 105, 106, 107—108, 117, 124
  Staffordshire blue, 37—38
Resist lustre, 79; *56—59*
'Rice grain' porcelain, 110
Ridgway, J. and W., Bell Bank and Cauldon Place, 87, 132—133
  dogs, 163
  lustre, 80
  pot-lids, 88
  registration of patterns, 133, 172
  Staffordshire blue, 34
  stone china, 48—49
Riley, J. and R., banded ware, 68
  bone china, 41
Robertson and Leadbeater, standard parian, 65
Robinson and Chetham, Egyptian black, 14
Rockingham, Swinton, 101—102, 103; *25, 50, 60, 62, 70, 76, 77*
  blue-printed, 37
  bone china, 41
  dogs, 162, 163
  London, 102—103
'Rockingham' toby jugs, Derbyshire, 148
Rockingham ware, Derbyshire, 148
Rogers, J. and J., Staffordshire blue, 33
Rose, J., *see* Coalport
Rose-du Barry, 104, 128
Rosso antico, 13
Royal Porcelain Works, Worcester, *see* Worcester
Royal Worcester Porcelain Co., *see* Worcester
Russell, Lord John, spirit flasks, 149
Ryland, W. W., bat printing, 74

St Bede's Pottery, Sunderland, 142, 145
St Porchaire style of inlay, 75

OSBORNE SWAN.
T R & Co.